Letters to Lauretta
1849-1863

FROM
DARLINGTON, SOUTH CAROLINA
AND A CONFEDERATE SOLDIER'S CAMP,

WITH

ANNOTATIONS AND GENEALOGY CHARTS

Pettigrew, Gulledge, McBride, Blackwell, Burch,
Wingate, Dargan, Commander, Lane, Harrell,
Nettles, and Allied Families

Edited by
W. Joseph Bray, Jr., M.D.
and
Jerome J. Hale

HERITAGE BOOKS
2008

HERITAGE BOOKS
AN IMPRINT OF HERITAGE BOOKS, INC.

Books, CDs, and more—Worldwide

For our listing of thousands of titles see our website at
www.HeritageBooks.com

Published 2008 by
HERITAGE BOOKS, INC.
Publishing Division
100 Railroad Ave. #104
Westminster, Maryland 21157

Copyright © 1993 W. Joseph Bray, Jr., M.D.
and Jerome J. Hale

All rights reserved. No part of this book may be reproduced or transmitted in any form or by any means, electronic or mechanical, including photocopying, recording or by any information storage and retrieval system without written permission from the author, except for the inclusion of brief quotations in a review.

International Standard Book Numbers
Paperbound: 978-1-55613-894-2
Clothbound: 978-0-7884-7269-5

TABLE OF CONTENTS

INTRODUCTION	v
LETTERS FROM DARLINGTON	1
LETTERS FROM BLACKWELL	155
BIBLIOGRAPHY	207
APPENDIX (FAMILY GROUP SHEETS)	211
INDEX	321
ILLUSTRATIONS	
ELIZABETH BLACKWELL PETTIGREW	2
SAMUEL BLACKWELL GULLEDGE	156

INTRODUCTION

Historians are the traditional analysts of the past. They are the chroniclers of those events which shaped and formed the area where we live. Likewise, civil and church records, such as deeds and wills, birth, marriage and death certificates provide us with dates and places, the when and where of genealogical information. However it is contemporary letters written by those living at the time history was being made that give us the true sense and feeling of what life was really like in those days.

So it is with the Letters to Lauretta which include both a contemporary account of the lives of some of the residents of Darlington County, SC in the period prior to and during the Civil War and an insight into life of a young Confederate soldier during that period.

Most of the letters are addressed to Eleanor Lauretta (McBride) Gulledge who was the daughter of Dr. William McBride of Darlington and Chesterfield Co., SC and Mary Jane (Blackwell) McBride. Lauretta, as she was called, married David Gulledge in 1839 and moved first to Mississippi in 1845, then to Texas in 1866.

The letters from Darlington were written by Elizabeth (Blackwell) Pettigrew, Lauretta's aunt, her mother's sister. Lauretta's mother died, and her father had remarried in 1831 and relocated to Chesterfield Co., SC sometime afterwards. Perhaps Elizabeth's letters to her niece were a way of keeping Lauretta in touch with current events occurring in South Carolina. Elizabeth writes of family and friends living in what was at that time Darlington Co. Deaths and marriages, births and a pre-occupation with health are all included as well as much information about the activities of Ebenezer Baptist Church, which numbered the Pettigrew family among its early members.

Samuel Blackwell Gulledge, called Blackwell by his family, authored the Civil War letters to his mother, Lauretta while a soldier in the Confederate forces from 1861 until his death in action in 1863. These letters are perhaps the most poignant of all as one senses the young man's love and concern for home and family and at the same time his desire to serve his country.

There are a few letters written to other family members or by other family members and are so identified. Most however were written by Lauretta's aunt Elizabeth or her son Blackwell.

The letters include such family names as Gulledge, Blackwell, Pettigrew, Harrell, Burch, Commander, Nettles, McBride, Dargan, Wingate and others.

The letters were first typed from the original hand written letters in 1987 by Marie Gulledge Wiggins, historian for the Gulledge Families Association. The originals were lent to Ms. Wiggins by a great grandson of David and Lauretta Gulledge who found them while settling an estate. After making a typed copy Ms. Wiggins returned the originals. Their current location is unknown.

The letters used for this publication are based upon those typed by Marie Gulledge Wiggins. Annotations regarding the identities of the persons mentioned in the letters were made by the current editors. The annotations are as accurate as the sources from which they were obtained. Some punctuation has been added for clarity, otherwise the letters are presented as received by the editors. Family Group sheets for many of the individuals mentioned are provided in the Appendix.

The editors welcome any comments, additions and/or corrections since it is our desire to dissiminate this information to as broad an audience as possible. Changes will be incorporated into subsequent printings and should be addressed to:

Jerome J. Hale
5536 Atlantic View
St. Augustine, FL 32084-7036

PART ONE

LETTERS FROM DARLINGTON

Elizabeth (Blackwell) Pettigrew, author of most of the Letters from Darlington and Mary Jane (Blackwell) McBride, Lauretta's Mother were sisters. They were daughters of Samuel Blackwell, II. and his first wife, a Miss Commander, a daughter of James Commander, I. Elizabeth was born in 1802 and Mary Jane, her older sister, in 1798. Their mother died shortly after Elizabeth's birth. Their father married a second time, on 30 June 1803, Mary Ann Hamlin, daughter of John and Joanna (White) Hamlin. Sometime after this second marriage the Blackwell family moved to a part of Darlington Co. now in Florence Co., SC and settled along Jeffries Creek.

Mary Jane Blackwell married Dr. William McBride in June, 1818 and Elizabeth married James Alexander Pettigrew, son of the late William Pettigrew and Susannah (Dargan) Pettigrew, in January, 1821. In addition to Lauretta, Dr. William and Mary Jane (Blackwell) McBride had 2 other daughters and 1 son. After her mother's death about 1830, Lauretta's father remarried and moved to Chesterfield Co., SC.

Eleanor Lauretta McBride married David Gulledge 12 March 1839 and moved to Jasper Co., Mississippi in 1845. Elizabeth's letters to this eldest daughter of her late sister were a way of maintaining the family bonds.

ELIZABETH BLACKWELL PETTIGREW

(9/7/1802--12/9/1861)

LETTERS FROM DARLINGTON

Elizabeth Blackwell Pettigrew
         to Lauretta McBride Gulledge

April the 13, 1849

My Dear Lauretta,[1]

    I received your welcome letter and one from Louisa[2] at the same time and was truly glad to hear that you were all well and well satisfied. My family is all well except myself. I am very bad off this week with the rheumatism. I think it has commenced to draw my limbs. I am that stiff after sitting awhile that I make almost as bad an out at walking as I did when I first got about after the first hard spell. I have just finished a letter to Caroline[3] that will go to the office with this. She has wrote me one letter. Joseph's[4] family and Sarah's[5] are all well when I heard from them. James Hepburn[6] had the measles there week before last but he was in the shop. I expect they did not let any go about him that had not had the measles. It is in Ma's[7] and sister Isabella's[8] family. Sister Isabella was down with them the first of this week; Joseph Wingate[9] also and Hannah Burch[10]. Hannah boards at Ma's. Your brother[11] was here Sunday before last. He stayed all night with us. How different he is to what he used to be. You know that when he would come, if I was in the room sick, he would not come in unless he was asked and not stay long then; but now he will go about in the house if he does not see me until he finds me. What a pleasure it is to me to see that he wants to be in my company and that he will make free enough in my house to find out where I am. He was well. He lives with Robert Cannon. He hunts runaway negroes with Cannon's dogs and Cannon boards him and gives him half that he's made. Samuel has made about 70 or 75$ to his part already.

    I supposed that you have heard that Hardy Sellers and Mary Sinklah is married. Cousin James Lane[12] is married to a Miss Gouse[13] of Bennettsville. Angelina says that she is a fine woman but not handsome. It is said that Thomas Lane[14] is to be married to Mr. George Jameses daughter. Mrs Issac Cole[15] had one of her breast(s) taken off yesterday. She had a cancer on it. She suffered a great deal with it before she had it taken off trying to cure it.[16] Mrs. Evans is in bad health. Mary Ann Evans has another son. She has named it George Washington. Harriet[17] has a son. Cousin Betsies[18] family are well. She has lost two negroes this year, Washington and Ginny.[19] Ginnys child is living. It can walk now but it could not when she died. Aunt Dargan[20] and Mr. Sims[21] are both dead. Mr. Sims died in November and Aunt Dargan in January. I do not remember whether I have wrote to you since Cousin Mary Smiths[22] death or not. She died the 20th of November. Aunt Dargan died with the dropsy. She requested her friends to bury her on her side. She and Cousin Mary died in a full hope of future happiness. Aunt Dargan told Cousin John[23] that she dreaded the pangs of death but that her hope was brighter. Miss Withy[24] is still teaching Day school for us. She boards at Mr. Jameses.[25] The schoolhouse is near Ivy Burruses.

    We had two negroes badly hurt with the screw. They were fixing the bagging while they were running up the screw and the needle that fastens the follower broke and the follower fell on their hands. Two of Jacob's[26] fingers were mashed so bad that the bones were sticking out of the flesh. Jerry's[27] fingers were not mashed. He was mashed across the back of both of his hands. He had no use of either of his hands but the skin was only grained. Neither of them was able to work in five or six weeks. Two of Jacob's fingers had to be cut off. As soon as brother John[28] got here and saw his hand he said that he was fearful that he would have to take off three. He took off the forefinger to the hand and next to the little finger between the first and second joint and with great care and attention. The middle finger got well but the two that was cut off the place healed first. Nelly[29] has another daughter. It is named Clarinda. Darcas[30] is in a thriving way nearly 4 months. Brother Samuel's[31] property is divided. Sarah[32] got Bill, Lizzy and Alfred.[33] She has sold Alfred to Mr. Bell[34]. Her children[35] got Mose, George and Ginny.[36] The other children[37] got Susan, Isaac, Hager and Tom.[38] Brother Burch[39] sold the oldest children's negroes[40] and the money is to be put out on interest. He bought their negroes all except Susan.[41]

The railroad will be three quarters of a mile from us back of our house.[42] It crosses the road between Mr. Jameses[43] and Mr. Burrases, crosses the road again just below Ebenezer Meeting House.[44] They are working on the road as hard as they can. Mr. Thornell oversees for Will McCall[45]. Mr. Pettigrew[46] had a good crop last year. He made little the vise (sic) of 100 bales of cotton. I hope he may make a good crop this year. George McCowns married to a Miss Mary Margaret Brown[47] an orphan girl that was going to school to Rosanna[48]. He got 11 negroes by her. They live where Sam Muldrow[49] lived; and Sam lives where his mother used to live. He has bought that place at the price of $500.

Mary[50] says that she has a heap of Calico scraps for you to make a quilt if you will get Cousin Davy[51] to stop over after them you may have them. Oh, she says that she missed you so much she has got nobody to run on and help her with her fun. She says that she don't get as many scolds about her nonsense now. She says that you don't miss her half as much as she misses you. She sends her love to every one of you. All of the children, all of them sends their love to all of you. The girls[52] will write to you as soon as they can. They have very little time to spare from their studies, but it won't be long before they will be through. Aneky[53] says that she sends her love to all of you and that she hopes it won't be long before she will hear that you are baptised. May the Lord in mercy grant that it may be so that he may fit you for the reception of that Holy ordinance is my prayer for the Redeemer's sake. Give my love to Cousin Davy[54] and all of the children. Tell Blackwell[55] and Mary[56] that they must study their books and learn fast and you must write me word if they learn fast. Give my love to Louisa[57] and Cousin Thomas[58]. Excuse bad writing for the most of it was wrote at night. Cousin Nancy[59] sends her love to you. I must come to a close by subscribing myself your affectionate aunt. Answer this as soon as you can.

                              Elizabeth B. Pettigrew

FOOTNOTES

[1] Lauretta (McBride) Gulledge (b. 1/1/1820 Darlington, SC), the daughter of Dr. William McBride (b.1/27/1784 near Morven/McFarland, Anson Co., NC; d. 8/2/1861 Chesterfield Co., SC) and Mary Jane Blackwell (b. circa 1798, prob. Georgetown, SC; d. bef. 1831). Married 3/12/1839 David Gulledge (b. 9/4/1813 Gulledge Township, Anson Co., NC; d. 9/14/1895 Edom, Van Zandt Co., TX). Moved to Jasper Co., MS in 1845 from Chesterfield Co., SC.

[2] Elizabeth Louisa (McBride) Woodward

(b. 4/22/1823 Darlington, SC), a sister of Lauretta Gulledge. Married Thomas Woodward of Sumter Co., SC. Moved to Jasper Co. MS & later Jackson Parish, LA.

3   Mary Caroline (McBride) Baker (b. circa 1827; d. circa 1/1/1859), another sister of Lauretta Gulledge. Married 10/17/1850, William P. Baker (b. Dec. 1827, NC).

4   Joseph Harrell (11/14/1818--11/14/1877), Elizabeth's son-in-law. Married on 11/4/1840, her daughter Mary Ann Eleanor Pettigrew (11/8/1823--8/25/1903).

5   Sarah Amanda Perkins (Harrell) Blackwell (2/11/1822--11/5/1863, Darlington Co., SC) was the widow of Samuel Blackwell, III., Elizabeth Blackwell Pettigrew's half-brother. Sarah married Samuel Blackwell, III. as his second wife on 1/7/1840. Samuel died 7/6/1847, leaving 6 surviving children; 3 from his first marriage to Caroline Hunter, and 3 from his marriage to Sarah Harrell.

6   James Hepburn, son of Robert and Elizabeth Hepburn.

7   Mary Ann (Hamlin) Blackwell (10/8/1786--11/20/1869) was Elizabeth (Blackwell) Pettigrew's step-mother, the second wife of Samuel Blackwell, II. Elizabeth was born in 1802. Her mother died probably at her birth or shortly thereafter for her father married Mary Ann Hamlin 6/30/1803. At the time Elizabeth was not even a year old and her sister Mary Jane was only 4 or 5. Evidently they considered Mary Ann as their mother.

8   Isabella Ann (Blackwell) Wingate (b. 9/21/1805) was the half sister of Elizabeth, being the daughter of Samuel Blackwell, II. and Mary Ann Hamlin. She married William Wingate on 9/24/1823 and at one time lived on

Pearl St. in Darlington, SC.

9 Joseph Wingate (1830--1888), Elizabeth's nephew & Lauretta's cousin. Son of William Wingate and Isabella (Blackwell) Wingate, he was later to marry on 11/26/1856 Elizabeth's daughter, (his first cousin), Anna Eugenia Pettigrew.

10 Hannah Burch was Elizabeth's niece, the daughter of her half-sister Joanna White Blackwell (5/15/1804)--5/19/1884) and Edward Sebrey Burch (12/30/1806--9/6/1864).

11 Samuel Blackwell McBride (b. circa 1821; d. 12/1877). He was Lauretta's full brother, son of Dr. William McBride and Mary Jane Blackwell, Elizabeth's sister.

12 James Henning Lane (b. 6/12/1819) was the grandson of Rachel (Blackwell) Lane, Elizabeth's aunt, and James Lane, Sr. Rachel Blackwell was the sister of Samuel Blackwell, II., Elizabeth's father. James Henning Lane was the son of Rachel and James Lane, Sr.'s son, James Lane, Jr. and his wife Martha Eleanor Adair.

13 Maria T. B. Gause of Clio, SC was the daughter of Emily Gause who was born in NC in 1790.

14 Thomas Mitchell Lane was the brother of James Henning Lane and likewise the son of James Lane, Jr & Martha Eleanor Adair.
He and his brother were Elizabeth Blackwell Pettigrew's first cousins once removed.

15 Elizabeth Cole (b. circa 1797) and husband Issac (b. circa 1785) and family were neighbors of Edward S. Burch family.

16 It is interesting that this type of surgery was occurring in 1849.

17 Harriet (Bryan) McBride was Lauretta's step-mother; the second wife of her father Dr. William McBride. They were married August 10, 1831 and were currently living in Chesterfield Co., SC. The new son was Edward H. McBride, Lauretta's half-brother who became a doctor and practiced in Chesterfield Co., Jackson, TN, and Springfield, MO.

18 Elizabeth S. Hepburn (c. 1799--8/22/1859), widow of Robert Hepburn and a member of Ebenezer Church.

19 Slaves.

20 Lydia (Keith) Dargan (7/26/1782--1/19/1849). Daughter of Col. James Keith and Margaret Perkins. Widow of Timothy Dargan, III. (1771-1839), deacon of Ebenezer Baptist Church and member of SC State General Assembly.

21 Alexander Dromgoole Sims (b. 6/2/1803, Brunswick, VA; d. 11/22/1848, Williamsburg Co, SC). Educator, lawyer, legislator. Came to SC c. 1826. Married Margaret A. P. Dargan, daughter of Timothy Dargan, III. and Lydia (Keith) Dargan.

22 Mary Smith was the daughter of Abigail Commander and John Smith. Elizabeth was Mary's first cousin, twice removed. Mary's mother Abigail Commander (b. 1717) and Elizabeth's great grandfather, Samuel Commander, II (b. 1705/6) were siblings.

23 John Orr Beasley (JOB) Dargan (c.1813-1882) son of Timothy Dargan, III. and Lydia (Keith) Dargan. Baptist Minister. Attended Furman Theological Institute, and was pastor of Black Creek Baptist Church for 43 years.

24 Miss Witherspoon.

25 John T. James.

26 Slave.

27 Slave.

28 John Hamlin Blackwell, MD (1815-1891) was Elizabeth's half- brother, the son of Samuel Blackwell, II and Mary Hamlin Blackwell. He was a prominent citizen of Darlington and Florence Co., SC and practiced medicine there for 40 years.

29 Slave.

30 Slave.

31 Samuel Blackwell, III. (3/17/1807--7/26/1847), Elizabeth's half-brother had died without a will.

32 Sarah Amanda Perkins (Harrell) Blackwell (2/11/1822--11/5/1863) was Samuel Blackwell, III.'s second wife and widow.

33 Slaves.

34 Refers perhaps to James Bell who lived in Darlington on the Timmonsville road near the Old Mill. James Bell, was an Irish immigrant who arrived in the area in 1838 and married Miss Isabella Jannett Hunter on 11/5/1845. (Ervin & Rudisill, *Darlingtoniana*, p. 355).

35 Children of Samuel Blackwell, III. and Sarah (Harrell) Blackwell were: Mary Annah (1841-1877); Elizabeth Isabella (1842-1923); James Harrell (1844-1928). An infant son, Joseph Sebrey died 6/30/1846 aged 10 months.

36 Slaves.

37 Children of Samuel Blackwell, III. and his first wife Caroline Matilda Hunter, were:

Martha Aurelia (1831-1913); Samuel Issac (1834-1898); John Caroline (1837-1910). An infant daughter born 1/15/1833 died the same day.

38 Slaves.

39 Edward Sebrey Burch (12/30/1806-9/6/1864). Elizabeth's brother-in-law, husband of her half-sister Joanna White Blackwell.

40 Martha Aurelia Blackwell, Samuel Issac Blackwell, John Caroline Blackwell, aged 18, 15, and 12 respectively.

41 Slaves.

42 The Wilmington & Manchester Railroad was being constructed to connect the port in Wilmington, NC with the town of Manchester (near current Shaw AFB) in Sumter District. The town of Florence was formed as a connecting point for this railroad and two others, the Cheraw & Darlington from Cheraw in the North and the North Eastern from Charleston in the South. (King, *Rise Up So Early A History of Florence County South Carolina*).

43 John T. James who lived 2 miles from Ebenezer Church.

44 The Ebenezer Baptist Church on Ebenezer Road, Florence, SC was organized in January 1778 by Rev. Evan Pugh and Richard Furman. Elizabeth and her family and many of the people mentioned in her letters were members of this church.

45 Will McCall (b. 1795) with wife Elizabeth (b. 1810) and family.

46 James Alexander Pettigrew (11/4/1800--10/14/1879), Elizabeth's husband. James Pettigrew was a planter, the son of William

Pettigrew and Susannah Dargan. In her letters she always refers to him as "Mr. Pettigrew".

[47] George McCown (b. 1827) and wife Mary Margaret Brown (b. 1831) had a son James McCown born April 1850.

[48] Rosanna E. Woods, daughter of Joseph Woods and Hepzibah (Dargan) Woods (1781-1855). Rosanna operated a boarding school in the Donneraile section of Darlington.
(Ervin & Rudisill, Darlingtoniana p. 12).

[49] Samuel Muldrow (b.1822) with wife Ursula (b. 1826) and their children were neighbors of the Edward S. Burch family.

[50] Mary Brown, lived with the Pettigrews.

[51] David Gulledge (9/4/1813--9/14/1895), Lauretta's husband. The family was living in Mississippi at this time. This comment by Mary Brown would indicate that he must have made occasional trips back to SC.

[52] The Pettigrew girls living at home at that time were Olivia (7/23/1833--8/4/1852) and Eugenia (9/1835--4/1892).

[53] Slave.

[54] David Gulledge.

[55] Samuel Blackwell Gulledge (2/6/1840--7/5/1863), eldest son of Lauretta and David Gulledge. Called "Blackwell".

[56] Mary Eleanor Gulledge (1841-1873), daughter of Lauretta and David Gulledge. Married William Pendergrass in January, 1872.

[57] Louisa McBride Woodward, Elizabeth's niece and Lauretta's sister.

58 Thomas Woodward, Louisa's husband. The Woodward and Gulledge families were both living in Jasper Co., MS at this time.

59 Nancy Orr, daughter of John Orr and Mary (Dargan) Orr, sister of Susannah (Dargan) Pettigrew, James A. Pettigrew's mother.

Elizabeth Blackwell Pettigrew
       to Lauretta McBride Gulledge

               Sunday 15th   2 o'clock[1]

Lauretta the snow is falling as thick as if it was in the dead of winter. All of the family is gone to Ebenezer[2] to hear Cousin John[3] preach; none at home but me and Mary Harrell[4] and the boys[5] dressed in their summer clothes. You may be sure that I am uneasy about them, the ground will soon be covered. Mr. Pettigrew[6] has been lamenting that he was so late agetting his cotton planted. He just commenced planting cotton Wednesday. I expect he will be glad now for he sees that it is best. It looks strange to see vegetation so forward and the snow falling so fast. Mr. Pettigrew had just turned his cows in the woods to shift for themselves. I did not have the most distant thought that it would snow. They have all got home now and dined. They came when the snow was falling very fast and thick. It is still snowing. The trees and bushes are hanging with snow. The girls[7] heard that Betty Burch[8] has the measles and that it has fell on her lungs. Her mother[9] can't go to see her for she had not had the measles herself and it would be very apt to fall on her bowels if she was to take it, for her bowels are very easy to be affected since she had that severe spell of sickness. I must come to a close again or I cannot send the letter to the office in a week. Betty[10] is at Ma's.[11]

FOOTNOTES

[1] A continuation of the previous letter dated 13 April 1849.

[2] Ebenezer Baptist Church.

[3] John Orr Beasley Dargan, pastor of Black Creek Baptist Church preached at Ebenezer two Sundays a month at this time. His great grandfather Timothy Dargan was the first Pastor of Ebenezer Church; his Mother, Lydia (Keith) Dargan prior to her death in Jan, 1849 had been a long-standing member of Ebenezer. JOB Dargan, as he was called, was a first cousin of Elizabeth's husband, James A. Pettigrew. James mother, Susannah, was the sister of JOB's father, Timothy Dargan, III.

[4] Mary Eugenia Harrell, Elizabeth's granddaughter, daughter of Mary Ann Eleanor (Pettigrew) and Joseph Louis Harrell.

[5] Referring to Elizabeth & James sons: Thomas Jefferson (7/1/1837--3/17/1855), George W. (9/29/1838--5/21/1910), and Joseph Edward (9/7/1841--5/28/1909).

[6] James Alexander Pettigrew, Elizabeth's husband.

[7] Olivia Albertina (7/23/1833---8/4/1852) and Anna Eugenia (9/1835--4/1892), daughters of James and Elizabeth Pettigrew.

[8] Elizabeth T. (Betty) Burch (1836-1850) was the daughter of Edward Sebrey Burch and Joanna White (Blackwell) Burch, Elizabeth's half-sister.

[9] Joanna White (Blackwell) Burch (5/15/1804--5/19/1884) daughter of Samuel Blackwell, II. and Mary Ann Hamlin.

[10] Betty Burch.

[11] Mary Ann Hamlin Blackwell, Elizabeth's step-mother.

Elizabeth Blackwell Pettigrew
            to Lauretta McBride Gulledge

                              June the 20   1849

My Dear Lauretta,

    I now seat my self for the purpose of writing to let you know how we are. The measles is in our family. There has been but two cases yet, Eugenia[1] and Dice.[2] Eugenia had them four weeks ago. Dice is not well now but it is better than a week since she broke out with them. I don't know how soon there may be more that may take them but if my children that has not had them does not take them from Dice I shall not let go about any of the negroes that may have them for it is so late in the season that it will be very apt to go harder with them. The measles were at Josephs[3] before we knew that they were anywhere nearer than the Village.[4] James Hepburn[5] was at the Village[6] Court week, and three weeks after, he broke out with them. Brother Johns[7] negro boy took them next and James Harrell.[8] Little John[9] had the whooping cough very bad at that time. Joseph[10] came over and requested that we would let one of the girls[11] go over to help their sister[12] nurse the children and we could not refuse. Eugenia went. All of Sarahs[13] children has had them and are well of them but they have the whooping cough. All of Eleanors[14] children has had them but O Lauretta, it proved fatal there. It was more than dear Little Sarah[15] could stand. They fell on her lungs and bowels both an I think that she had the whooping cough too. What the dear little creature suffered is more than can be told. It is five weeks since she took the measles. I think she took the whooping cough about the same time but Brother John[16] does not think that she had any cough but the measles cough. Her liver was affected too. Eugenia returned...to assist her sister in nursing the children for I was unable to go at that time and Olivia[17] was expecting to take the measles, but she has not taken them yet. A few days after Eugenia went over Joseph sent word that Sarah would not live to see night. Mr. Pettigrew[18] and myself went over. We found Sarah and John[19] both very sick and Mary[20] with the measles out thick on her. John's head and lungs and bowels were affected but he got better in about a week, but little Sarah continued no better when her lungs would be a little relieved her bowels would get worse and when her bowels would get better her lungs would get worse. It continued so until on the 17 a little after 12 o'clock she was taken with spasms one after another until after 2 o'clock and she took one that lasted until she bid farewell to this world of sin and sorrow. She was in her senses almost to the last; knew everyone; would call her Ma even after she was spasmed. She always called her mother, Ma. I forgot to tell you the hour she died it lacked 15 minutes of 5. She was buried at my father's[21] head, a little towards the swamp side.[22] John was worse off when I left. He had taken the bowel affection again. We know not how it may end with him. I never saw a better child to take medicine than Sarah was, even Castor Oil, the Rheubarb (sic); in fact she never refused to take a dose of medicine even if it made her gag. I expect you would like to know how the parents takes this affliction. You are a parent yourself. You may judge that the separation was severe when Eleanor[23] came to look at her after the breath left her for she could not stand by to the last for she died so hard. She prayed that their separation might not be forever but that they might meet in that world wher parting would be no more and that the affliction might be sanctified to both mother and father and that both might live nearer to the Lord that they had. Both of them takes the bereavement very much to heart but not more than would be expected. She was the most interesting child to her age they had and she was so affectionate. She would sit by her mother when she was at work and beg her Ma to take her. If Eleanor refused to take her she would say that she was sleepy or sick. I never saw a little creature love their father and mother more than she did. Afflicitions though they seem severe, in mercy oft are sent. May the Lord grant that this afflicition may be to the salvation of Joseph's[24] soul is my sincere desire. The Lord tries his blessings. If that won't bring us to him, he sends them in love and mercy for he willeth not the death of a sinner but that all should turn and live. My dear Lauretta I entreat of you to seek the Lord for he says those that seek me shall find me for what will it profit us if we gain the whole world and lose our soul for we have to live it all when we are summoned to appear at the bar of God. Brother Burch[25] has lost two little negroes with whooping cough. I have not seen your brother[26] in some time. The last I heard from him he was gone to Georgia after some more dogs. Cannon sold the dogs that he had and got Samuel to go to Georgia after more. I received a letter from Caroline[27] a few week ago. Your father's family were well. She wrote that May Buccannon was murdered a few yards from his own gate. It was supposed that he was knocked out of his buggy, for there was a pine pole near him broke in three pieces and his soul broke.

They had not found out the one that committed the murder then but Sarah[28] has received a letter from Mary Sellers since which states that his first son by his second wife and a negro was suspected. The negro was taken. He was found in possession of $200 and confessed that he and Buccannon were the murderers. They then searched and found things in young Buccannons possession that his father had purchased that day. He is now in gaol. Mary Whitworth and Godard are married. Mrs. Issac Cole had a cancer on her breast. Brother John[29] cut her breast off about two months ago. The place healed up very fast but she was taken with inflamation of the stomach. It is doubtful if she will recover. James Burch[30] lives at Ma's[31] place and attends to her crop. Mary Jane[32] is in a family way. I have heard that Eleanor[33] is on the way again. She did not tell me so but I suspect it is so. I expect that is you(r) situation.[34] You must let me know in your next letter and how Louisa[35] comes on, if she has got another prospect of one. You must excuse all mistakes and bad writing for I wrote this in a great deal of pain for I am very bad off at this time. I expect I took some cold sitting up with the children at Josephs which had increased the rheumatism. I am fearful that I will be a cripple for it draws me so that it is with difficulty that I walk and it is so severe in my shoulders and arms that I can scarcly sew. There is (sic) times that I cannot, when the pain wages, that is, in the mornings.

Olivia[36] wrote a letter to you last week but it was not sent to the office when I came from Josephs[37] and I thought it was best to write another and not send that for there was no room to write the particulars respecting the health of Josephs family. She will write to you when she comes home. She is at Josephs with her sister.[38] I could not bear the thought of Eleanors being left in her distress without me or one of the girls staying with her. All of your Aunt Wingates[39] family has had the measles. She lost one negro with the measles, Liddy, Rachels[40] daughter. She was a young woman just grown. Manly[41] is a preacher. He is still at the Wake Forest institution. He will finish his education. That is, he will graduate this month. The Physician has advised him not to return home until the sickly season is over. I wish you could see Manly. I was in his company in January. I was perfectly delighted with him. He is so affectionate. I never saw a son appear more devoted to their mother.[42] In fact he showed nothing but affection to all about him. Joseph Wingate[43] is the same Joseph, yet wild and rattling but very kind. Ma's[44] family has all had the measles but herself. Hannah and Elizabeth Burch[45] boards with her. Mary Ann[46] went up and nursed the girls when they had the measles and the boys and Caroline[47] too, and when she took them, the girls attended to her and by that Ma did not take them. The measles has been in brother Josephs[48] family but I have not heard how many of his family has had them. Cousin Betsy Hepburns[49] health is bad. she is a good deal like I have been. She says it makes her think of what I have suffered.

Tell Blackwell[50] and Mary[51] they must study or Cousin Edward[52] will beat them. Tell them that I want them to be very smart. Their cousin Edward is counted very smart by the Sunday School teachers. Tell Black that Edward says that he wants to see them very much. All of the boys want to see him. Olivia and Eugenia[53] has wrote to Caroline[54] and sent her some of their hair and mine and she had sent us some of hers. They say there is a young man that has taken a great fancy to Caroline. Perhaps you know him, a Mr. Williams.[55] I have heard that he is a very fine fellow. I wish she would get married if she gets a clever fellow as soon as she can for I know that I will not see her until she marries and I am very anxious to see her. Mary Brown[56] says do write soon for she wants to hear from all of you. Do write to Louisa[57] and let her know how we are for I do not expect that you see her often. Do you and her both write to dear Eleanor[58] for she is in a good deal of distress. Louisa can truly sympathize with her for she has passed through the same and you are a mother yourself. You can feel for her. Give my love to Cousin Davy[59] and all of the children, Louisa, Cousin Tommy[60] and their children and except of the same yourself. Mary[61] and Cousin Nancy[62] sends their love to all of you. Mr. Pettigrew[63] says tell Cousin Davy that he has a good crop. He must let him know how his crop is. Give my best respects to your friend Mrs. Evans. You wrote me word that there was Commanders[64] near to you that thought that they were relations to us. Give my love to them. You see I have wrote you a long letter. You must answer this as soon as you can. I would write oftener if I coud get better of the rheumatism. Tell Louisa to write as soon as she can, as often as she can for I am always glad to hear from you. Tell the children[65] that Aunty has not forgotten them altho we are far apart, that I still love them as good as ever and want them all to be smart and obey their father and mother and love to read the Bible when they can read and strive to serve the Lord that we may meet in heaven where we will never part. Adieu my dear Lauretta for this time.

       Elizabeth B. Pettigrew

This is June 22. I have been three days writing this. Tell Louisa that I will write to her soon. Ursula's[66] baby has the whooping cough and bowel affection. Have you received a letter from Mary Ann Lide?[67] She wrote me word that she had wrote to you and sent some edging for one of the children that you wrote to her mother[6,8] and she was not able to answer the letter and she answered it. Mary Ann writes to me very regular. I have put some edging in here for one of the girls you can give it to which one you please.

FOOTNOTES

[1] Anna Eugenia Pettigrew, daughter of Elizabeth and James Pettigrew.

[2] Dice was evidently a house servant.

[3] Joseph Louis Harrell (11/14/1818--11/14/1877), Elizabeth's son-in-law, husband of Mary Ann Eleanor (Pettigrew) Harrell (11/8/1823--8/25/1903).

[4] The Village referred to the current town of Darlington, SC.

[5] James W. Hepburn, born c. 1824, son of Robert and Elizabeth Hepburn.

[6] Darlington Village.

[7] John Hamlin Blackwell, MD (12/12/1815--1/15/1891), Elizabeth's half-brother, son of Samuel Blackwell, II. and Mary Ann (Hamlin) Blackwell.

[8] James Alexander Harrell (b. 1845), Elizabeth's grandson, son of Joseph Louis Harrell and Mary Ann Eleanor (Pettigrew) Harrell.

[9] John Edward Harrell (b. 1848), another son of Joseph Louis Harrell and Mary Ann Eleanor (Pettigrew) Harrell.

[10] Joseph Louis Harrell.

11   Olivia and Eugenia Pettigrew, Elizabeth's daughters and sisters of Mary Ann Eleanor Pettigrew Harrell, Joseph's wife.

12   Mary Ann Eleanor (Pettigrew) Harrell.

13   Sarah Amanda Perkins (Harrell) Blackwell, widow of Elizabeth's brother Samuel Blackwell, III. (3/17/1807--7/26/1847).

14   Mary Ann Eleanor (Pettigrew) Harrell.

15   Sarah Ann Harrell (1/1846--6/1/1849), Elizabeth's granddaughter.

16   John Hamlin Blackwell, MD.

17   Olivia, Elizabeth's other daughter living at home, evidently had not had the measles.

18   James Alexander Pettigrew, Elizabeth's husband.

19   John Edward Harrell.

20   Mary Eugenia Harrell, Sarah and John's sister.

21   Samuel Blackwell, II. (8/22/1774--2/14/1823), son of Samuel Blackwell, I. and Elizabeth Dozier, was Elizabeth's father.

22   Sarah Ann Harrell and her great grandfather, Samuel Blackwell, II., along with other family members are buried in a small family plantation plot at Burches Crossroads, 3 miles from Florence, SC. In October, 1992, the area was overgrown and untended.

23   Mary Ann Eleanor (Pettigrew) Harrell, Sarah's mother.

24   Joseph Louis Harrell.

25   Edward Sebrey Burch (12/30/1806--9/6/1864), husband of Joanna White Blackwell (5/15/1804--5/19/1884), Elizabeth's half-sister and Lauretta's aunt.

26   Samuel Blackwell McBride (1821-1877).

27   Mary Caroline McBride, Lauretta's sister who evidently was living with their father, Dr. William McBride and his second wife and family in Chesterfield Co., SC at this time.

28   Sarah Amanda Perkins (Harrell) Blackwell, widow of Samuel Blackwell, III., Elizabeth's half-brother.

29   John Hamlin Blackwell, MD.

30   James E. Burch (2/11/1826--4/11/1882), son of Edward Sebrey Burch and Joanna White (Blackwell) Burch.

31   Ma was Mary Ann (Hamlin) Blackwell, Elizabeth Pettigrew's step-mother and James E. Burch's grandmother.

32   Mary Jane (Sinclair) Burch (9/22/1829--8/29/1854), wife of James E. Burch.

33   Mary Ann Eleanor (Pettigrew) Harrell.

34   Lauretta was pregnant with Elizabeth Louisa Gulledge who was born 11/19/1849.

35   Eliza Louisa (McBride) Woodward (b. 5/22/1823, m. Thomas Woodward) was Lauretta's sister and lived in Jasper Co., MS also.

36   Olivia Albertina Pettigrew.

37   Joseph Louis Harrell.

38   Mary Ann Eleanor (Pettigrew) Harrell.

[39] Isabella Ann (Blackwell) Wingate (born 9/21/1805), Elizabeth's half sister. She married William W. Wingate, 9/24/1823.

[40] Slaves.

[41] Washington Manley Wingate, (7/28/1828--2/27/1879) was Elizabeth's nephew, the son of William W. Wingate and Isabella Ann (Blackwell) Wingate, Elizabeth's half-sister. A Baptist Ministerial student at Wake Forest College at the time of this letter, Manley Wingate later became president of this Institution.

[42] Isabella Ann (Blackwell) Wingate (b. 9/21/1805), daughter of Samuel Blackwell, II. and Mary Ann (Hamlin) Blackwell.

[43] Joseph Edward Wingate (1830-1888), Manley's brother and Elizabeth's nephew, another son of William W. and Isabella Ann (Blackwell) Wingate. Joseph was eventually to marry Elizabeth's daughter Anna Eugenia Pettigrew on 10/26/1856.

[44] Mary Ann (Hamlin) Blackwell

[45] Hannah M. Burch (b. 1836) and Elizabeth T. Burch (b. 1835), granddaughters of Mary Ann (Hamlin) Blackwell, were daughters of Joanna White (Blackwell) Burch and Edward Sebrey Burch.

[46] Mary Ann Burch, daughter of Edward Sebrey and Joanna White (Blackwell) Burch.

[47] Probably Caroline Aletha Blackwell, daughter of John Hamlin Blackwell and Aletha Windom.

[48] General Joseph Burch Nettles (9/4/1804--3/5/1886), second husband of Hana Mara Blackwell (10/10/1807--9/15/1889), Elizabeth's half-sister.

⁴⁹ Elizabeth S. Hepburn (c. 1799--8/22/1859) wife of Robert Hepburn.

⁵⁰ Samuel Blackwell Gulledge (2/6/1840--7/5/1863) oldest son of Lauretta and her husband David Gulledge.

⁵¹ Mary Eleanor Gulledge (12/17/1841--1873), daughter of Lauretta and David Gulledge.

⁵² Joseph Edward Pettigrew (9/7/1841--5/28/1909), Elizabeth's and James Pettigrew's son who was approximately the same age as Blackwell and Mary Gulledge.

⁵³ Olivia and Eugenia Pettigrew, Elizabeth's daughters.

54 Mary Caroline McBride, Lauretta's sister.

⁵⁵ Actually William P. Baker of North Carolina.

⁵⁶ Mary Brown lived with the James Pettigrew family.

⁵⁷ Louise McBride Woodward, Lauretta's sister, who also lived in Jasper Co. MS at that time.

58 Mary Ann Eleanor (Pettigrew) Harrell, Elizabeth's daughter.

⁵⁹ David Gulledge, Lauretta's husband, was the son of Joel Gulledge, a Baptist Minister from Anson Co., NC and his wife Zilpha Huntley. David was the youngest of 5 boys and 4 girls.

⁶⁰ Thomas Woodward, Louisa's husband.

⁶¹ Mary Brown who lived with Elizabeth and her family.

⁶² Nancy Orr, daughter of John Orr and Mary Dargan who was the sister of James Pettigrew's

Mother, Susannah Dargan. Nancy was James' first cousin.

63 James Alexander Pettigrew, son of William Pettigrew (1/29/1779--3/19/1803) and Susannah Dargan (2/11/1779--9/13/1946) was 3 years old when his father died. His mother married William Connell on 11/20/1804 who died sometime before 1816 for on 3/6/1816, she married the Rev. John Good, a Baptist Minister who was the pastor of Ebenezer Baptist Church from about 1817 to 1829.

64 Elizabeth's mother was a Commander, the daughter of James Commander. The Commander family living near Lauretta and her family in Jasper Co., MS were James Perry Commander, Jr., a Methodist Minister, the grandson of Jesse Commander who was the half brother of James Commander, Elizabeth's grandfather.

65 David and Lauretta Gulledge's children living at this time were Samuel Blackwell, Mary Eleanor, Zilpha Ann, Sarah Lauretta, and Thomas Huntley.

66 Ursula Muldrow (b. 1826), wife of Samuel Muldrow. The baby was Alitha Muldrow (b. 1848).

67 Mary Ann Lide (11/10/1831--6/25/1879) was the daughter of Eli Hugh Lide and Martha Johnson (Blackwell) Lide, Elizabeth's half sister. The Lide family moved from Darlington Co., SC to Dallas Co., AL in 1835.

68 Martha Johnson (Blackwell) Lide (6/13/1811--12/16/1880), daughter of Samuel Blackwell, II. and Mary Ann (Hamlin) Blackwell.

Elizabeth Blackwell Pettigrew
                Lauretta McBride Gulledge

Sept 4 1849

Dear Lauretta,

I will after so long a time since I received your letter endeavor to answer it. I would of answered it before this but I have been so unwell and the weather so warm that I could not; but as it is cool and cloudy today I will try to write as much as I can so that I may have it ready by the first opportunity I have to send it to the Post Office. You must not think hard of me for not writing to you before for it is not at all times that I am able to write. I am still suffering with rheumatism but I have not had the cholick (sic) in a year. I have been taking Dr. Jones Altevative for better than a month and am still taking it and Jones Sanitive pills. I think it has been of service to me for I only lack one and a half pound of weighing as much as I weighed. I think if I continue taking it for 4 or 5 months it may cure me. Jones medicine are thought more of than any of the patent medicine. He is a regular physician. Mr. Pettigrew[1] has a very good opinion of his medicine. I have taken 11 bottles and Mr. Pettigrew got 6 more for me yesterday. I have been without any for two weeks and I have been worse off. Well the rest of the family are well except some of the negroes. Aneky[2] has been sicker than she ever has been in her life with inflamation of the stomach. She has not been able to work for 6 or 7 weeks though she is able to go about the yard now but not able to work. Darcas[3] has a fine daughter. It was born the 3 of last month. She took cold and was very bad off. We have had a good deal of sickness amongst the negroes. George[4] got a fall from a horse three or four weeks ago. His father allowed him and Thomas[5] to go with the Negro boys to bring up the cattle every evening and the mare got frightened and run with him and threw him. Charles[6] says that he was breathless with his mouth and eyes open when he got to him that he had to rub him for sometime before he drew breath. He then took him up in his arms and brought him to the back of the garden and George said that he could come to the house. Lany[7] was in the yard and said that something was the matter with him. She helped him in my room door and put him on the bed and asked him what was the matter with him. He said nothing. She then went to Mary[8] and Miss Withy.[9] They went to him but they could not get him to tell what was the matter with him. He would beg them to let him alone for he was so sleepy. He was as cold as if he was dead and in a profuse sweat. They thought that he would be dead before the could get word to Joseph,[10] to me and Mr. Pettigrew and for Brother John[11] but they rubbed him and bathed his feet and got the blood in circulation before we got home but he knew nothing from the time that the mare threw him until the next morning but he has got entirely well but it was seven days before he could open his left eye and his face was very much bruised. Josephs[12] family are all well at this time. I suppose you got the last letter that I wrote to you stating how sick Josephs children has been with the whooping cough and measles and about dear little Sarahs[13] death. I thought that little John[14] would die with the bowel affection for the cough went so hard with him and before he got well of that he took the measles and was very ill with them and had just go better when he was taken with his bowels but he is now better than he has been since he took the cough. Sarah Blackwell[15] is in bad health. Brother Burches[16] family are all well but sister Joannas[17] bowels has not entirely recovered from that hard spell that she had before you left here. The least thing that she eats more than she ought, makes her sick. She says that she is oblidged to allowance herself. Sister Isabella[18] was here about a fortnight ago. Her family was well. Louisa Nettles[19] was here with sister Isabella. Her fathers[20] family were well. One of Joseph Wingates[21] negro women was killed with the well sweep a few days before sister Isabella came down. She was drawing water and just as she sunk the bucket the string that tied the hand pole to the sweep broke and the sweep went up with such force that it broke off altho (sic) it was perfect sound it struck her in the forehead and broke the skull and struck her in the breast. It knocked her dead on the spot. The physicians went to her as soon as they could but they could do nothing. The negro had hired herself and lived near Mrs Terrell in the house on the other side of the road. Mrs Terrell heard the crash and went to the door and heard the negroes child scream out that its mother was killed. She went over and found it so. Its not known whether you know the negro or not. It is a yellow woman that Mr. Wingate bought. Her name was Judy. She left three children, one a sucking babe. Joseph Harrells Rose[22] lost her youngest child three weeks after Sarah[23] died. Roses child died with affection of the head and bowels. James Burch[24] and Sam Muldrows[25] family are well. Cousin E Hepburns[26] family are all well but herself. She looks bad. She is passing through what I have. She and Mrs. Evans, they both say it makes them think of what I have suffered. Mrs Evans has to quit the coling and the women that used to depend on her has to get who they can but she says that she will go to Eleanor[27] and her negroes if she is able. Mas[28] family are well. Olivia Wingate[29] says that the flower seeds you sent her that she put them away and when she went to plant them she could not find them. I planted all that you sent me but the rose moss and that got misplaced. None of mine or Eleanors[30] came but two kinds. The one of mine that came up had small blossoms. Eleanors had a blossom like a poppy blossom but it was white. The bush was like the poppy. It was such wet weather that I got one seed from mine. Do Lauretta get the bols from the black rose and open them and get the seed and put them in a letter and send them to me. I dont know that they will come up but I want it so bad that I am willing to try if they will. You have not wrote me word when you expected to be confined.[31] Do write and let me know and tell cousin Davy[32] that he must not wait for you to get well enough to write to me after but that he must write by the first mail and let me know how you are and what for a time you have. You know if it is a girl that I want it named Elizabeth Pettigrew and do you or Louisa[33] name a son James Commander[34]. Tell Sarah[35] that Aunty has not forgot her and that Aunty will send her ribbon in this letter and she must be a good girl and must mind what father and mother tells her and that all of them must read their Bible and try to meet Aunty in a better world that this.

O Lauretta, our being separated makes me feel more anxious if possible for you to seek an interest in the death and sufferings of Chirst. My dear lauretta, it is but a short time that we have to remain on earth even suppose we should live to three score and ten and now is the time that our Creator has given us to prepare for eternity. Now is the accepted time. Now is the day of salvation. Consider how good the Lord has been to you that although you are far from you(r) relations and those that you used to associate with you have met with find friends in a strange land amongst strangers. Do Lauretta consider the shortness of time, the certainity of death and the awfullness (sic) of eternity if unprepared. Lauretta I believe that your mother endeavored to give all of her children into the hands of the Lord and he has taken care of all of you and is now willing to receive you can claim you as one of his children if you are willing. Your lot has not been cast in a heathen land but it has been and is now in a Christian land where you can sit and hear the gospel preached. Do Lauretta let me entreat of you if you are halting between two opinions halt not longer for death is abroad in the land and we know not how soon our time may come to bid adieu to this vain world. You must not think hard of me for entreating of you to seek the one thing needful, for I never expect to see that face in time that I so dearly love, not to grasp that hand in mine that I have so often held and that has done offices of kindness for me when on the bed of affliction. Tell cousin Davy to read this that my desire for him is the same as for you and may the Lord grant that we may all meet in heaven is my sincere prayer for Christs sake. I have not seen Samuel[36] in some time but I have heard from him he was well. Cannon[37] has got more dogs and they are hunting negroes. You wished a receipt for making pickles. For a pot as large as the one of mine that you had, put in one pound of sugar one teaspoon of saltpeter, and make the pickle strong enough to bear up an egg and boil it 20 minutes. Strain it. Let it get perfectly cool. Cut up the beef. Let that get perfectly cool and then put it in and it will be fit for use in a few hours. Put no salt on the beef. The same pickle will do again by adding salt sufficient to make it of the same strength and put in a little more sugar and saltpeter. Boil it. Skim the stuff that rises while boiling. Strain the pickle as before and let is get cool.

Give my sincerest love to Louisa[38] and tell her that if we meet on earth no more I hope we may meet in heaven where parting will be no more. The girls[39] and Mary[40] send their love to all of you. The boys[41] send theirs. Mr. Pettigrew[42] is not at home. Nelly, Lindy,

Aneky and old Sinder[43] send their love and all of your family and cousin Thomases[44] family may except of the same from me. Excuse bad writing and mistakes. I will subscribe myself your affectionate aunt.

E B Pettigrew
Sept the 8

FOOTNOTES

[1] James Alexander Pettigrew.

[2] House servant.

[3] Slave.

[4] George W. Pettigrew (9/28/1838--5/21/1910), son of Elizabeth and James Pettigrew. George was almost 11 years old at this time.

[5] Thomas Jefferson Pettigrew (7/1/1837--3/17/1855), son of Elizabeth and James Pettigrew, who was 1 year older than his brother George.

[6] Charles was a slave.

[7] A slave.

[8] Mary Brown, who lived with the Pettigrew family.

[9] Miss Witherspoon.

[10] Joseph Louis Harrell, Elizabeth's son-in-law, husband of Mary Ann Eleanor Pettigrew.

[11] Dr. John Hamlin Blackwell (12/12/1815--1/15/1891), Elizabeth's brother.

[12] Joseph Louis Harrell.

13 Sarah Ann Harrell, Elizabeth's granddaughter, daughter of Joseph and Eleanor (Pettigrew) Harrell, died 6/9/1849.

14 John Edward Harrell, Elizabeth's grandson and Sarah's younger brother.

15 Sarah (Harrell) Blackwell, widow of Elizabeth's brother, Samuel Blackwell, III.

16 Edward Sebrey Burch, Elizabeth's brother-in-law, husband of Joanna (Blackwell) Burch.

17 Joanna White (Blackwell) Burch, Elizabeth's sister.

18 Isabella Ann (Blackwell) Wingate, Elizabeth's sister married William W. Wingate 24 September 1823.

19 Louisa H. Nettles (b. 1833), Elizabeth's niece, was the daughter of Hannah Mara (Blackwell) and Joseph Burch Nettles.

20 General Joseph Burch Nettles (9/4/1804--3/5/1886) was the second husband of Hannah Blackwell, widow of Edmund Gee. Together they had 10 children.

21 Joseph Edward Wingate (1830--1880) son of William and Isabella (Blackwell) Wingate.

22 Rose was a slave.

23 Sarah Ann Harrell, Elizabeth's granddaughter.

24 James E. Burch (2/11/1826--4/11/1882), Elizabeth's nephew, son of Joanna (Blackwell) Burch and Edward Sebrey Burch, married Mary J. Sinclair. He worked as the overseer for his grandmother Mary Ann (Hamlin) Blackwell on his late grandfather's plantation on Jeffries Creek.

25 Samuel Muldrow (b. 1822) with wife Ursula (b. 1826) and family were neighbors of the Edward S. Burch family.

26 Elizabeth S. Hepburn (c. 1799--8/22/1859), wife of Robert Hepburn.

27 Mary Ann Eleanor (Pettigrew) Harrell, Elizabeth's daughter.

28 Mary Ann Hamlin Blackwell, Elizabeth's step-mother, widow of Samuel Blackwell, II.

29 Isabella Olivia Wingate, daughter of William W. and Isabella Ann (Blackwell) Wingate, Elizabeth's sister, was born 22 March 1825 and was unmarried and living at home in June of 1854.

30 Mary Ann Eleanor Pettigrew Harrell, Elizabeth's daughter.

31 Evidently the expression for period immediately preceding and following the birth of a child. Lauretta was pregnant with daughter Elizabeth Louisa Gulledge who was born 19 November 1849.

32 David Gulledge, Lauretta's husband.

33 Eliza Louisa McBride Woodward, Lauretta's sister who was also pregnant at the time.

34 James Commander (born about 1727) was Elizabeth's grandfather.

35 Sarah Lauretta Gulledge (12/11/1845--3/21/1878), daughter of Lauretta and David Gulledge and Elizabeth Pettigrew's great niece.

36 Samuel Blackwell McBride, son of William M. and Mary Jane McBride, was a brother of Lauretta.

37   Robert Cannon was Samuel McBride's employer.

38   Louisa (McBride) Woodward, sister of Lauretta.

39   The Pettigrew girls were Olivia and Eugenia.

40   Mary Brown lived with the Pettigrews.

41   The Pettigrew boys were Thomas Jefferson, George W. and Joseph Edward.

42   James Alexander Pettigrew.

43   Slaves.

44   Thomas Woodward, Louisa McBride's husband.

Elizabeth Blackwell Pettigrew
             to Lauretta McBride Gulledge

                              Dec the 5   1849

Dear Lauretta

   After waiting so long in expectation of receiving a letter from you or Louisa[1] I have come to the conclusion that there must certainly be a great deal of sickness in one or both of your families. You may be assured that I am very anxious to get a letter from one or both of you for the last that has been received from any of you was the letter that Eleanor[2] received from you in September and you wrote her word that the cholera was in twenty miles of you. I have wrote to you and Louisa (torn). I do not know whether either of you have received the letter. My family are tolerable well. I am better than when you left here but still troubled very much with the rheumatism. Joseph's[3] family are well or was on Monday for Eleanor and the children left here Monday morning. I came from the Village[4] last week. Sister Isabellas[5] and sister Hannahs[6] family were well. Mas[7] family was not well. John[8] had the fever and Ma was bad off with the rheumatism and she is in a fair way to be as bad off (with) the colick as I have seen. Brother Burches[9] family are all well but Sebra.[10] He has the fever. Sarah[11] is up the country.[12] She was at your sister Carolines[13] wedding. Your brother[14] is well. He started to Charlestown with Brother Burches[15] waggon day before yesterday. Samuel was at Carolines[16] wedding. He says that she and her husband will be here the 22 of this month. I suppose that you have heard that Manly Wingate[17] is a preacher. I have heard him preach once and exhort 3 times. He does extremely well, as well as the most of the old preachers. This is not only my opinion but the opinion of a good many. Mr. Pettigrew[18] says that he is hard to beat. How I do wish you and Louisa could be in his company and hear him preach. I know that both of you would be well pleased. He left here yesterday. Before he returned home to Wake Forest[19] he preached to a congregation of three thousand and saw seventy-nine immersed in one hour. He has got through with his collegiate education. He is now going off to study for the ministry. He is as yet undetermined whether to return to Wake Forest or go to the Furman Institution. He is indeed a patron of piety. He feels very much for the welfare of the souls of all of his relations. Louisa Burch[20] is converted. She told Manly that last week was the happiest week that she ever spent in her life. I suppose it was then she obtained a hope she has been seriously empressed (sic) for some time. She will be baptised the fifth Sunday in this month. Elizabeth and Hannah Burch[21] and Betty Hepburn[22] are seriously impressed. How glad would we be if they obtain a hope and be baptised with Louisa. Manly intends to have a three days meeting at that time if Cousin John[23] will come with him. I have been to the Village[24] twice last month. I went to see Cousin Betsy Hool[25] and Cousin Eufrazer[26] came to Sister Isabellas[27] to see me and spent the evening with me. I enjoyed myself very much at Cousin Betseys. She and cousin Eufrazer were so glad to see me. They inquired about all of your mothers[28] children.[29] They had heard that you and Louisa[30] had gone to Mississippi. They asked me how you and Louisa liked the country. I told them very well indeed that you was well pleased with the Country and the people. Eufrazer[31] told me that she and her brother Axalla[32] would try to be at my house on Christmas as I expect Caroline[33] at that time. How glad would I be if it was so that you and Louisa and your families could be here at that time. That I could see all of my dear sisters children together once more but that is not for me to see again in this world but may the Lord grant we may all meet in a far better world that this where parting will be no more. Lauretta you do not know how glad I would be to hear that you and Cousin Davy[34] were both converted. When I see your relations, those that are younger than you joining the church and giving every satisfaction that they are changed it makes my thoughts go to you and Cousin Davy and hope that the same work is begun in your hearts. Do recollect that life is short and that none of us knows how soon death may summon us to appear before the bar of God. O how it makes me feel while I am writing this letter knowing that you were expecting to be confined in a few months when you wrote the last letter and it has been so long since, that I fear you have been very bad off or is at this time. Do you or Cousin Davy answer this as soon as you can. The men have formed a society at the village. They call it the Sons of Temperance. There has a great many joined it. They number near a hundred and fifty. They meet every week and at every meeting there is several added to their number. Your brother[35] is one of the number. He joined them some time ago. I wish you could be at one of their celebrations. They look beautiful, everyone with their white collars on. They march to the church with the drums beating and the brass band of music and there an ovation is delivered. Julius Dargan[36] delivered the last ovation. I was there. I was well pleased. Even the little boys have formed a cold water army. They marched behind the sons with their flags and drums. They have a celebration every three months. I almost forgot to tell you that Evander Hutchenson has joined the Baptist Church. He is a son of Temperance. John Muldrow[37] would of joined Ebenezer[38] if his mother had not of opposed him so strenuously. He was awakened under cousin Johns[39] preaching and delivered under Morgan Timmonses[40] prayer. He went to Brother Morris[41] at the Meeting House and told him he wanted to join that church. He told him to go to his parents first and if they were willing he would baptise him with pleasure. His father was willing but his mother was not and he joined the (torn)...

...come from the negro house with the papers and no letter. When will I get a letter from you and Louisa? As they have all gone to bed and it is Saturday night and near midnight I will have to stop for tonight. Cousin Ann Backhouse,[42] cousin Nancy[43] and Olivia[44] told me to give their love to you. They have been sitting up with me while I have been writing but they have just gone to bed.

       Sunday Evening

The girls have just got home from singing. They heard that Elizabeth Burch[45] is down very bad with the rhuematism. Elizabeth Hepburn[46] came home with the girls. She says that her mother[47] starts to where Mr. Stewart used to live. The old man is dead and cousin Betsy[48] is agoing for her part of the property. She would of got it before but Bateman held the division off thinking that he could sue and get a part but he cannot. Mary Brown[49] says that you must not let Zilphy[50] forget her. Mary Ann McCowan and Robert McPherson will be married the third of January. Give my love to Louisa and cousin Tommy,[51] Cousin Davy[52] and all of the children and accept of the same yourself. Tell the children that they must not forget me and that they must be good children and love their books. All of them that can read and those that can't read now when they can they must love their books. Mr. Pettigrew keeps the same overseer next year that he has this. Betty Hepburn[53] sends her love to all of you and says that you must write to her and she will to you. The girls[54] send their love to all of you. The boys[55] send theirs, particularly to Blackwell.[56] Do write as soon as you can. Olivia[57] has been expecting a letter from you for a long time. Tell Louisa do write soon for I do not know if you and L gets our letters if they are not answered. Give my love to your friend Mrs Evans. No more at present but remain your affectionate Aunt

                      Elizabeth B Pettigrew

Dec the 9 1849

    Excuse bad writing for the rheumatism stiffens my hands so that after writing a little I can scarcely write atol. I will be sure to expect a letter every mail after this has time to get to you. I have sent Mary[58] and Zilphy[59] a piece of the girls dresses. Both of them have a dress of each piece. I send it to amuse them. Tell Sarah[60] I will send a piece of mine the next letter. Mr Backhouse[61] is still in the asylum. Cousin Anns[62] little boy[63] grows finely. Josephs[64] roan horse is dead, the one that cousin Davy got from Mr. Backhouse for him. Mary[65] sends her love to all of you.

FOOTNOTES

[1] Louisa McBride Woodward, Elizabeth's niece and Lauretta's sister.

[2] Mary Ann Eleanor Pettigrew Harrell, Elizabeth's oldest daughter.

[3] Joseph Louis Harrell, husband of Elizabeth's daughter Eleanor.

[4] The town of Darlington, SC was called a village then.

[5] Isabella Ann Blackwell (b. 9/21/1805) married William W. Wingate 9/24/1823, and was widowed on 6/7/1845. At this time, her daughter Isabella Olivia, and son Joseph Edward were living with her in Darlington, probably at the corner of Pearl St. and Edwards Ave.

[6] Hannah Mara Blackwell (10/10/1807--9/15/1889) married first, Edmund Gee (1795-1831) an attorney and after his death, Gen. Joseph B. Nettles in 1832. The Nettles family lived in Darlington.

[7] Mary Ann (Hamlin) Blackwell, step-mother of Elizabeth and widow of Samuel Blackwell, II.

[8] Dr. John Hamlin Blackwell, son of Mary Ann (Hamlin) Blackwell and Samuel Blackwell, II.

[9] Edward Sebrey Burch, husband of Joanna White Blackwell, Elizabeth's half-sister.

[10] Sebrey Burch (b. 1839), son of Edward S.

and Joanna (Blackwell) Burch, was Elizabeth's nephew and Lauretta's cousin.

11 Sarah Perkins (Harrell) Blackwell, widow of Elizabeth's brother Samuel Blackwell, III. was visiting in Chesterfield Co, SC home of her mother, Mary Hollingsworth (Burch) Harrell.

12 Probably referring to Chesterfield Co., SC, the home of Lauretta's father, Dr. William McBride.

13 Mary Caroline McBride married William P. Baker in November/December 1849.

14 Samuel Blackwell McBride (c. 1821-1877), son of Dr. William McBride and Mary Jane Blackwell.

15 Edward Sebrey Burch, was Samuel Blackwell McBride's uncle by marriage.

16 Samuel Blackwell McBride, Caroline (McBride) Baker, and Lauretta (McBride) Gulledge were all siblings.

17 Washington Manley Wingate (7/28/1828--2/27/1879), son of Isabella Ann Blackwell and the late William W. Wingate was a nephew of Elizabeth and a Baptist ministerial student. He and Lauretta were first cousins.

18 James Alexander Pettigrew, Elizabeth's husband.

19 Manley Wingate was a student at Wake Forest College.

20 Joanna Louisa Burch (3/9/1832--11/3/1902), daughter of Joanna White Blackwell and Edward Sebrey Burch.

21 Elizabeth T. Burch (1836-1850) and Hannah M. Burch were daughters of Joanna White

Blackwell and Edward Sebrey Burch.

[22] Elizabeth S. Hepburn (2/17/1832--11/17/1894), daughter of Elizabeth "Cousin Betsy" and Robert Hepburn.

[23] John Orr Beasley Dargan (c. 1813--1882), son of Timothy Dargan III and Lydia Keith, was a well known Baptist Minister at that time and also a first cousin of James Alexander Pettigrew.

[24] Darlington Village.

[25] Elizabeth Stanley Houle was the wife of James Commander Houle. James Commander Houle was the son of Joseph and Elizabeth (Commander) Houle. Elizabeth Commander was the sister of the mother of Elizabeth Blackwell Pettigrew, making Elizabeth Houle and Elizabeth Pettigrew, first cousins by marriage.

[26] Eufrazer Houle (born c. 1827) was the daughter of James Commander Houle and Elizabeth (Stanley) Houle.

[27] Isabella Ann Blackwell Wingate, widow of William W. Wingate lived in Darlington Village.

[28] Mary Jane Blackwell McBride (1798-1831)

[29] The children of Mary Jane Blackwell and Dr. William McBride had all reached maturity at this time and were: Eleanor Lauretta Gulledge, Samuel Blackwell, Mary Caroline Baker, and Eliza Louisa Woodward.

[30] Eliza Louisa (McBride) Woodward.

[31] Eufrazer Houle.

[32] Axalla Houle (born c. 1850), son of James Commander Houle and Elizabeth Stanley Houle.

33   Caroline McBride, Lauretta's sister who had recently married William Baker.

34   David Gulledge, Lauretta's husband.

35   Samuel Blackwell McBride.

36   Julius Alfred Dargan (c. 1816-1861), son of Timothy Dargan, III. and Lydia Keith was a brother of Rev. J. O. B. Dargan. He married Martha J. Woods.

37   John Muldrow was the son of Hugh Muldrow.

38   Ebenezer Baptist Church was organized in January, 1778.

39   J. O. B. Dargan.

40   John Morgan Timmons, Baptist Minister of Florence for whom the community of Timmonsville was named.

41   Rev. James Morris was pastor of Ebenezer Church for about ten years. Many revivals occurred during his pastorate.

42   Edith Ann (Woods) Backhouse "Bacheas" (born c. 1808) was the daughter of Joseph Woods and Hepzibah Dargan (sister of Susannah Dargan Pettigrew Connell Good, the mother of James A. Pettigrew).

43   Nancy Orr, daughter of John Orr and Mary Dargan (daughter of Timothy Dargan, II.) was a first cousin of James Alexander Pettigrew, Elizabeth's husband.

44   Olivia Albertina Pettigrew.

45   Elizabeth T. Burch (born 1836), Elizabeth's niece, daughter of Edward Sebrey Burch and Joanna White Blackwell.

⁴⁶ Elizabeth S. Hepburn, (2/17/1832--11/17/1894), daughter of Robert and Elizabeth Hepburn.

⁴⁷ Elizabeth Hepburn, "Cousin Betsy", wife of Robert.

⁴⁸ Elizabeth Hepburn.

⁴⁹ Mary Brown lived with Elizabeth and her family.

⁵⁰ Zelpha Ann Gulledge (9/12/1844--12/1/1881), daughter of Lauretta and David Gulledge.

⁵¹ Louisa McBride Woodward and Thomas Woodward.

⁵² David Gulledge, Lauretta's husband.

⁵³ Elizabeth Hepburn, daughter of Robert and Elizabeth Hepburn.

⁵⁴ Olivia and Eugenia Pettigrew, Elizbeth's daughters.

⁵⁵ Thomas, George, and Joseph Edward Pettigrew, Elizabeth's sons.

⁵⁶ Samuel Blackwell Gulledge.

⁵⁷ Olivia Pettigrew.

⁵⁸ Mary Eleanor Gulledge (1841-1873), daughter of David and Lauretta McBride Gulledge.

⁵⁹ Zilpha Ann Gulledge

⁶⁰ Sarah Lauretta Gulledge (12/11/1845--3/21/1878), daughter of David and Lauretta Gulledge.

⁶¹ John A. Backhouse

⁶² Edith Ann (Woods) Backhouse "Bacheas", daughter of Joseph Woods and Hepzibah Dargan was a first cousin of James A. Pettigrew.

⁶³ John Backhouse, born about 1846

⁶⁴ Joseph Louis Harrell.

⁶⁵ Mary Brown.

Elizabeth Blackwell Pettigrew
             to Louisa McBride Woodward

January the 3   1850

Dear Louisa,

    I have seated myself for the purpose of writing to you hoping these lines may find you and your family in the enjoyment of good health. My family are all well except myself. I am still suffering with the rheumatism at this moment. I am in so much pain that I can scarcely write but as I have parted with Caroline and her husband[1] this morning. I thought I would commence a letter immediately as it takes me several days to write one for I cannot write long at a time. Caroline is well, all except a cold that she took after she got here but she was much better when she left. Your fathers family[2] were all well when they left. They came from there[3] down here. They came to Mas[4] on the 20 of Dec, from there here the next day. I am very pleased with Cousin William.[5] Indeed I think Caroline has married a very clever gentleman. The longer I was with him the better I like him for from the first evening that they got here, he took us all as his own relations and appeared as much at his ease as if he was at home with his fathers family. You know that pleased me. The girls,[6] Miss Withy,[7] and myself went up with them as far as Mas and saw them start from there for home this morning and we returned home this evening. Your brother[8] went up home with them. He is well. Cousin William will settle near his father.[9] The old man has given him a tract of land but there is no buildings on it. He has rented a house near there that they will live in until he builds in the fall. I was a cousin Betty Hools[10] a few weeks before Christmas and I told them that Caroline would be here Christmas and Cousin Eufrazer[11] said that she would be a my house at that time, she and her brother;[12] but their brother-in-law[13] came over from Sumter and brought their sisters daughter[14] and would not leave her unless cousin Axalla[15] would carry her her back the day before Christmas. He expected his present wife's brother at his house on Christmas Day and he wished to see the child. Therefore cousin Axalla did not come here but cousin Eufrazer wrote to me that she had no way of coming as her brother could not come with her and I sent for her. You may be assured that I enjoyed this Christmas better than I have enjoyed a Christmas in several years as I had Caroline and her husband and Samuel[16] with me that day and knowing that all of sisters daughters[17] are married. Cousin Eufrazer was delighted at being with us for it was the first time that she ever saw as many of her fathers[18] relations. She is a very fine girl. She is very pious I understand. Joseph's[19] family are all well but Eleanor[20] is expecting to be confined before the last of next week. Brother Burches[21] are all well but Betty.[22] She has the rheumatism nearly as bad as I have it. Sister Isabelles[23] family are well. Joseph Nettles[24] family are well. Sarah Blackwells[25] family are well. Ma[26] is very bad off with the rheumatism. The rest of her family are well.

Louisa Burch[27] came forward to the church today and related her experience and was received. She will be baptised tomorrow. Manly Wingate[28] is a preacher. I have heard him preach. It is thought that he will make as good a preacher as John Dargan.[29] In fact he can preach an excellent sermon now. Brother Morris[30] is still the pastor of our church but Brother Culpepper[31] is to preach for us once a month. I must write you word of who Caroline[32] married. Perhaps you and Lauretta[33] has not got the other letters that I wrote for this is the second that I have wrote to you and I have wrote two to Lauretta since I have got a letter from either of you. I enquired (sic) of Samuel[34] and Caroline hoping they had got a letter from you or Lauretta but they say the last they received was in September. I have not receiver a letter from either of you since August. I am very anxious to hear from all of you.

Dec the 6[35]

Lauretta's letter came just as I was writing the word anxious and it excited me so much for I expected to hear bad news that I just finished that sentence and stopped writing until this morning but I will try to finish writing before I stop this time. I am very sorry to hear that Lauretta suffered so much but glad to hear that she is better. I think that her weaving was very bad for her for it is as bad a work as a woman can do that is in her situation. She ought to be very careful for I doubt if she ever gets entirely over the hurt that she got before she left here. Tell her that I say remember that she hasn't aunty with her to caution her now that I use to do it for her good for what would her children do if she was not able to do for them. Louisa do both of you be careful as you can of yourselves when you are in a family way for it takes very little sometimes to injure a woman. Lauretta wrote me word that you have a daughter[36] and that you are as well as could be expected. I am truly glad to hear it. I would like to hear where you expect to live this year so when you write let me know and let me know every letter that you get from me for I have been fearfull (sic) that neither of you have got all of my letters. Tell cousin Davy[37] that I have a crow to pick with him for not writing to me as soon as he could after L[38] had her baby. He could of wrote enough to let me know how all of you was for when Saturday night would come I would set up until 11 or 12 o'clock waiting to see if there would be a letter but to our disappointment no letter. I was sure he would as I wrote word for him not to wait for L to get well enough to write. Well I will tell you now who Caroline married. It is a Mr. Baker[39] from North Carolina, son of a brother to the Baker that married Turner Briants daughter. His mother was a Russian (Rushing), no relation to the Russians that was in Chesterfield. Tell Lauretta that Mary[40] says that she has not seen two people that she has taken such a fancy to in some time as she has to Cousin William and Caroline, that Caroline reminds her so much of Lauretta and that now she has two strings to her bow. She used to tell Lauretta if she died that she would have Cousin Davy and now if she or Caroline dies there will be a chance for her. This is just some of Marys fun, the latter part of what she says for she likes to be ajoking with Lauretta, but we are all well pleased with Caroline and cousin William. We enjoyed their company very much. All that we have to regret is that they did not stay long enough. Mary says tell Lauretta that she wants to see her very bad. Tell Lauretta that Nancy[41] has another son born yesterday evening. Mary Ann McCown and Robert McPherson is to be married the 10 of this month. Sidney Gee Zimmerman is out here. I was in his company two days. His daughter Henrietta is married to a Mr. Muldrow. Melvina is to be married as soon as he returns. The girls,[42] cousin Nancy,[43] Mary[44] and myself sends love to all of you. I will now have to come to a close by subscribing myself your affectionate Aunt.

Elizabeth B. Pettigrew

Manly[45] is engaged to be married to a girl at Wake Forest. Her name is Mary Elizabeth Webb. I don't know when they will be married as Manly has to study for the ministry. I have seen her likeness. If it is a true likeness she is handsome. Tell Blackwell[46] howdy for the boys[47]. They are not here. They are at Church but I know if they were here they would send howdy or rather give their love to him for them. I have wrote the latter part of this letter in such a hurry that I am afraid you can scarcely read it. Mr. Zimmerman has seen Josiah Harrel, the man that married his wife's sister and went off and left her. He has been married twice since he left his wife and is now a widower.

FOOTNOTES

[1] Mary Caroline McBride, Louisa's sister, had married William P. Baker the past month.

[2] Dr William McBride's family living at home included his daughter, Ellen and his second wife Harriet Bryan McBride; and their children: Calhoun; Henrietta; J. William, Thomas J.; Franklin; Ed H.; and possibly one other child.

[3] The McBrides lived in Chesterfield Co., SC.

[4] Mary Ann (Hamlin) Blackwell, widow of Samuel Blackwell, II. lived in the Doneraile section of Darlington.

5   William P. Baker.

6   Olivia and Eugenia Pettigrew, Elizabeth's daughters.

7   Miss Witherspoon.

8   Samuel Blackwell McBride.

9   William and Caroline Baker were living in Union Co., NC in 1850 Census.

10   Elizabeth Stanley Houle, widow of James Commander Houle who was Elizabeth Blackwell Pettigrew's first cousin. James Commander Houle's mother was the sister of Elizabeth Pettigrew's mother.

11   Eufrazer Houle was the daughter of Elizabeth Stanley and James Commander Houle.

12   No doubt referring to her brother, Axalla Houle of Darlington.

13   John Ervin Brown (1808-1898), was the widower of Eufrazer and Axalla Houle's sister, Eveline Gertrude Houle, who died in 1844.

14   E. G. Brown, daughter of the late Eveline Gertrude Houle and John Ervin Brown was born about 1840.

15   Axalla Houle would later become a Colonel in the 8th Regiment CSA and die during the Civil War.

16   Samuel Blackwell McBride.

17   Elizabeth's late sister, Mary Jane Blackwell McBride, wife of Dr. William McBride. Her married daughters now included: Lauretta Gulledge, Louisa Woodward, and Caroline Baker.

18   James Commander Houle, Eufrazer's father,

was Elizabeth Blackwell Pettigrew's first cousin.

19 Joseph Louis Harrell.

20 Eleanor Pettigrew Harrell, Elizabeth's, daughter, was pregnant and due to deliver soon.

21 Edward Sebrey Burch, husband of Joanna White Blackwell, Elizabeth's half-sister.

22 Elizabeth T. Burch, daughter of Edward and Joanna Burch was born 1836.

23 Isabella Ann Blackwell Wingate.

24 Joseph Burch Nettles, husband of Hannah Blackwell, Elizabeth's sister.

25 Sarah Amanda Perkins Harrell Blackwell, widow of Elizabeth's brother, Samuel Blackwell, III.

26 Mary Ann (Hamlin) Blackwell.

27 Joanna Louisa Burch (1832-1902), daughter of Edward Sebrey Burch and Joanna White Blackwell.

28 Washington Manley Wingate (7/28/1828--2/27/1879), Elizabeth's nephew, son of William W. Wingate and Isabella Ann Blackwell Wingate.

29 J. O. B. Dargan, Baptist minister, son of Timothy Dargan, III. and first cousin to James A. Pettigrew.

30 Rev. James Morris was ordained at Ebenezer Baptist Church in 1837 and served as pastor from 1841 to the early 1850's.

31 Rev. John Culpepper was associated with the Rev. James Morris at Ebenezer Baptist Church in 1850-1852.

32 Caroline McBride, Louisa's sister married William P. Baker in Nov-Dec 1849.

33 Lauretta McBride Gulledge, Louisa's sister.

34 Samuel Blackwell McBride, brother of Louisa Woodward, Lauretta Gulledge, and Caroline Baker.

35 This date was probably Jan 6 as the previous portion of the letter is dated Jan 3, 1850.

36 Louisa's daughter was Eleanor Lauretta Woodward.

37 David Gulledge, husband of Lauretta McBride Gulledge.

38 Lauretta McBride Gulledge.

39 William P. Baker.

40 Mary Brown lived with the Pettigrew family.

41 A slave.

42 Olivia and Eugenia Pettigrew.

43 Nancy Orr.

44 Mary Brown.

45 Washington Manley Wingate, son of William and Isabella (Blackwell) Wingate, Elizabeth Pettigrew's nephew.

46 Samuel Blackwell Gulledge, Louisa's nephew, son of her sister Lauretta and David Gulledge.

47 The Pettigrew boys were Thomas Jefferson, George W., and Joseph Edward.

Elizabeth Blackwell Pettigrew
            to Lauretta McBride Gulledge

                              March the 28   1850

Dear Lauretta

    I expect you are almost out of patience waiting for an answer to your letter but I will let you know the reason I have not answered it before this. In the first place I was waiting for an answer to the one that I wrote to Louisa[1] for I did not know where to direct letters to as you wrote me word that you was agoing to move and I did not know whether you would be in the same county but Eleanor[2] received a letter from you a few weeks back and I got information from (her) where to direct a letter to you but since then I have not felt well enough to undertake to write. I was sorry to hear that you and your family has been so very sick but I feel thankful to the Lord that he has spared your lives for it would of been just as easy for him to of removed you from time to eternity but in mercy has he spared you to your family and to give you more time for repentance, perhaps to see if you will turn to him that your soul may live. Lauretta my dear child that spell of sickness ought to be a great lesson to you to seek the salvation of your soul. Delay no longer but form a resolution that if you perish that you will perish apraying. Can't you see the goodness of the Lord in sparing you to your dear children and husband and in giving you more time to seek an interest in the death and suffering of his son. You know not but what the next attack may sever soul and body and how awful will it be if you are not prepared for that great change. Yes, great will it be whether prepared or unprepared. If prepared it will be to enter into eternal joys. If unprepared in to everlasting misery. Let one that dearly loves

you beseach (sic) of you to delay no longer but
fly to the arms of that Saviour who died to
redeem you. He will not spurn you from his
presence. Has he not said he that cometh unto
me I will in no wise cast out? My hearts
desire and prayer to God is that your soul may
be saved. Do Lauretta don't just read this and
put it down and think no more about it or think
that it is just the impulse of a moment with
aunty for you may be well assured that you are
often thought of by me. I will now endeavor to
let you know how we all are. My family are all
well but myself and I am a great deal better
off than I was when you left here though very
much afflicted by rheumatism. Joseph's[3]
family were well last Sunday. Sarah's[4] family
were all well on Tuesday. She and her children
were went (sic) from here. Brother Burches[5]
family were all well last week. Samuel[6] is
overseeing for brother Burch. He was here last
week. He was well. He says that he would of
went to Mississippi with cousin Tommy[7] if he
had of come to Darlington. If Samuel had known
that he would not of come, he would of went to
Sumpter (sic) to of seen him but Sam was up the
country[8] and cousin Tommy was in Sumpter (sic)
some time before he knew that he was here.
James Burch and Mary Jane[9] was well the last I
heard from them. They have had no child.
Nancy[10] came very near killing her baby a
fortnight ago today with laudanum[11] or
paragoric. She says that it was paragoric.
The child is only three months old and she said
tha she gave it a teaspoonful. It was in hard
spasms when it was brought in the house to us
while we were at supper. It spasmed the whole
night until day. Mary[12] and Olivia[13] had to
set up all night and do everything that they
though would help it. If we had not of found
it out as soon as we did it would of died. I
must now close for we are expecting cousin
Axella Hool[14] every minute and I expect that I
won't have any chance to write any more
tonight. I would rather write after night when

the children are abed for you may be well assured that I have a bad chance to write when the children are in the house in bed, rather for it is impossible to keep them still. Mary and Elizabeth Harrell[15] are both here. Elizabeth is going to school. She sends her love to all of you. Do excuse all mistakes for I am in a great hurry. I can say no more at this time but remain your affectionat (sic) Aunt until death. Write as soon as yo can and let me know if you get this for I always like to know if my letters go safe and when you receive them.

                        Elizabeth B. Pettigrew

I have put a small piece of cousin William Bakers[16] hair in this letter; some that Olivia got when they were here. We have his and Carolines.[17]

N B There is something that I almost forgot to tell you. Edgar Charleses[18] son[19] went out to the west[20] last December was a year ago and coveted Mary Ann Lide[21] and they were engaged to be married this last December. About a month before they were to be married he told Mary Ann that he had received a letter from his father that he wished him to return home before he was married. He came home and has not returned nor does he intend to marry her. Brother Lide[22] I understand went to Mobile and spent right smart of money in preparing for the wedding and nothing to the contrary of their marrying until the day before they were to commence cooking for the wedding Mary Ann[23] received a letter from young Charles stating that it was not his intention to return. Don't you think it was shabby treatment and they relations[24] too.

Tell cousin Thomas[25] if I had of went as near his home as he was to mine I would of went to see them. I received a note from Eleanor[26] this morning. She says that her baby is unwell and that Sarah[27] and Martha[28] Blackwell is at her house that all of Sarah's children are sick and that Martha is very bad off with a nervous headache. Eleanors baby is named Samuel Joseph.

FOOTNOTES

[1] Louisa McBride Woodward, Lauretta's sister.

[2] Mary Ann Eleanor (Pettigrew) Harrell, Elizbeth's daughter.

[3] Joseph Louis Harrell, husband of Mary Ann Eleanor Pettigrew.

[4] Sarah Amanda Harrell Blackwell, widow of Samuel Blackwell, III., Elizabeth's brother.

[5] Edward Sebrey Burch, husband of Joanna White Blackwell, Elizabeth's sister.

[6] Samuel Blackwell McBride, Lauretta's brother, was living with the Edward S. Burch family in the 1850 Darlington Co, SC census.

[7] Thomas Woodward, husband of Louisa McBride Woodward, Lauretta and Samuel's sister. Thomas and Louisa were living in Jackson Co. MS at the time, as were Lauretta and David Gulledge. Evidently Thomas was visiting in Sumter, SC his former home.

[8] Up the country--Chesterfield Co., SC where Samuel's father, Dr. William McBride lived.

[9] James E. Burch (2/11/1826--4/11/1882), son of Edward Sebrey Burch and Joanna White Blackwell was married to Mary Jane Sinclair (9/22/1829--8/29/1854).

10   A slave.

11   Laudanum was an opium based drug frequently used for treatment of pain in those days.

12   Mary Brown lived with the Pettigrew family.

13   Olivia Pettigrew, daughter of James A. and Elizabeth Pettigrew.

14   Axalla Houle, son of James Commander Houle and Elizabeth Stanley. He was a Col. in the 8th Regiment CSA and died during the Civil War.

15   Mary Eugenia Harrell (b. 1844) and Elizabeth Harrell (b. 1842), were Elizabeth's granddaughters, daughters of Mary Ann Eleanor (Pettigrew) and Joseph Louis Harrell were aged 6 and 8 respectively.

16   William P. Baker of North Carolina married Lauretta's sister, Caroline McBride in Nov-Dec, 1849.

17   Caroline McBride Baker.

18   Col. Edgar Welles Charles (2/6/1801--1/10/1876) born in Charleston, moved to Darlington in 1820 and married 2/14/1826 Sarah Kolb Lide, daughter of Hugh Lide and Elizabeth Pugh, the daughter of Rev. Evan Pugh.

19   Referring to either Hugh Lide Charles (3/18/1830--6/20/1911) who later married Caroline A. Bacot or Andrew Blackwood Charles (7/10/1827--2/15/1891) who later married Mary Ann Williamson.

20   Out West in this case was Dallas Co., AL.

21   Mary Ann Lide (11/10/1831--6/25/1879), daughter of Eli Hugh Lide and Martha Johnson Blackwell, sister of Elizabeth Blackwell Pettigrew.

[22] Eli Hugh Lide (4/15/1796--5/18/1854), son of James Lide and Jane Holloway.

[23] Mary Ann Lide later married on 4/2/1856 William Rumph Etheridge in Carlowville, Dallas Co., AL.

[24] Col. Edgar Charles wife, Sarah Kolb Lide was the daughter of Hugh Lide the brother of James Lide. Eli Hugh Lide and Sarah Kolb (Lide) Charles were first cousins. Their children were second cousins.

[25] Thomas Woodward, husband of Lauretta's sister Louisa.

[26] Eleanor Pettigrew Harrell, Elizabeth's daughter.

[27] Sarah Harrell Blackwell, widow of Samuel Blackwell, III., Elizabeth's brother.

[28] Martha Aurelia Blackwell (4/17/1831--6/5/1913), daughter of Caroline Hunter and Samuel Blackwell, III.

Elizabeth Blackwell Pettigrew
             to Lauretta McBride Gulledge

                                    Aug the 24th 1850

Dear Lauretta

After waiting so long for an answer to my last letter I have come to the conclusion that I will write another in hopes that I will get an answer to this. I would of wrote to you before this but I have been bad off with the rheumatism and am bad off now but I heard a few minutes ago that Samuel[1] received a letter from cousin David[2] and it made me feel that I must commence one to you immediately.

August the 30

I commenced this letter Saturday evening and there was storm acoming up and it was so late in the evening that I could write no more at that time and I have not been able to write any more since. I am writing this lying in bed. I am worse off with the rheumatism than I have been for some time. We had harder wind here Saturday night than has ever been since 1822. The rest of the family are all well but Mary Brown.[3] She has the sick head-ache. Joseph[4] and his family left here this morning. They are all well. Eleanor's[5] fatter than she was in her life. She is a fat as you ever saw. Sarah[6] and her children[7] are up the country. Brother Burches[8] family were all well week before last (when) I was there, but Emma.[9] She had the fever and your aunt Annah,[10] she was in her confinement. She had a fine daughter born the 23 July. She was very bad off when she had the child. There was a difficulty after the child was born in getting what was to come after and she flowing. If brother John[11] had not of been in the house she must of died before they could of got him. Her recovery is slow. Ma[12] has the rheumatism right bad. Cousin Betsy Hepburn[13] is bad off with flowing so that she is confined to bed. The rest of the relations is well as far as I know. Cousin Samuel Lane[14] is married to Laura Pierce. Angelina and Edmund[15] was baptised the third Sunday in this month.

Sept the 1

I am in hopes that my letter will be no less acceptible by being wrote by piecemeals. Elizabeth Morrison and Patty Woods and their children came when I was writing and stayed until yesterday evening. Elizabeth has two fine looking boys. The family are all at church but Miss Withy[16] and myself.

Joseph[17] has received cousin Davids[18] letter. Mr. Pettigrew[19] sent Calvin[20] to Joseph in January but it seems that the villian has taken it in his head that he will not be ruled by him. He run away the first or second day after they commenced hoeing cotton and Joseph did not get him until the middle of June and he has been in the woods again a fortnight today and there is no telling when he will get him again. He had the impudence to come by brother Johns[21] shop door and brother John lying in the shop piazza. I suppose brother John would of caught him if he had of had his clothes on but he was in his underclothing but he run him nearly to the second branch up the road. We heard this morning that Silas Cooper caught him las night but he got away from him. Tell Louisa[22] that I would be glad to get a letter from her. I have received but one letter from Caroline[23] this year. Louisa Burch[24] received a letter from cousin William[25] a few weeks back. They were well then. Mr. Pettigrew has a very good crop but the storm has destroyed not less than 20 bales of cotton, he says and some of his corn. There is a great many trees blown down in the fields. Give my love to Louisa[26] and her family and you and all of your family accept of the same. You must excuse bad writing and mistakes for I am in a good deal of pain and in a hurry. I would write a longer letter if I was not so unwell. Sarah Streater, Mr Joseph Burches daughter died the last of June. She has left two children.

Her mother has the baby and Streaters sister the oldest. I must close by subscribing myself your affectionate aunt.

      Elizabeth Blackwell Pettigrew

There is a great many mistakes in spelling but you must excuse all of them. Do Lauretta write as often as you can. I know that your chance is bad with a house full of small children but when you can't write a long letter write a short one. I think Olivia[27] wrote one letter to you and she thinks right hard when her letters is not answered. She has wrote to some of her other relations and she has never received a letter from not one and Eugenia[28] has. Olivia says that it is useless for her to write for she gets no answers but her letters may not of been received. I received you letter of August the 6 on 25 of August.

FOOTNOTES

[1] Samuel Blackwell McBride, Lauretta's brother, the son of Dr. William McBride and Mary Jane Blackwell.

[2] David Gulledge, Lauretta's husband.

[3] Mary Brown lived with Elizabeth and James Pettigrew family.

[4] Joseph Louis Harrell (11/14/1818--11/14/1877), husband of Elizabeth's daughter, Mary Ann Eleanor Pettigrew.

[5] Mary Ann Eleanor Pettigrew (11/8/1823--8/25/1903) married Joseph Harrell 4 November 1840.

⁶ Sarah Amanda Perkins (Harrell) Blackwell, widow of Elizabeth's brother Samuel Blackwell, III., was visiting in Chesterfield Co., SC, her mother's home.

⁷ Sarah Blackwell and the late Samuel Blackwell, III.'s children living at home at that time were: Mary Annah (5/29/1841--6/25/1877), Elizabeth Isabella (11/11/1842--1923), and James Harrell (1/8/1844--5/13/1928).

⁸ Edward Sebrey Burch (12/30/1806--9/6/1864) married Elizabeth's half-sister, Joanna White Blackwell (5/14/1804--5/19/1884) on 15 October 1823.

⁹ Emma S. Burch (10/30/1842--9/24/1904) daughter of Edward S. and Joanna Blackwell Burch.

¹⁰ Joanna White (Blackwell) Burch had recently delivered a daughter, Ada Burch, born 6/23/1850.

¹¹ John Hamlin Blackwell, MD, brother of Joanna and Elizabeth.

¹² Mary Ann Hamlin Blackwell, widow of Elizabeth's father, Samuel Blackwell, II.

¹³ Elizabeth Hepburn, "Betsy", wife of Robert Hepburn.

¹⁴ Samuel Adair Lane, born 23 July 1823, son of James Lane, Jr. and Martha Eleanor Adair, was the grandson of Elizabeth's Aunt Rachel (Blackwell) Lane. Rachel Blackwell was the sister of Elizabeth's father, Samuel Blackwell, II.

¹⁵ Possibly Angelina & Edmond Lane, children of James and Martha Eleanor Adair Lane.

¹⁶ Miss Witherspoon, a school teacher.

17   Joseph Louis Harrell, Elizabeth's son-in-law, husband of Mary Ann Eleanor Pettigrew.

18   David Gulledge, Lauretta's husband.

19   James Alexander Pettigrew.

20   Calvin was a slave.

21   John Hamlin Blackwell, MD.

22   Louisa (McBride) Woodward, Lauretta's sister, who with her husband Thomas and family also lived in Jasper Co., MS at this time.

23   Caroline (McBride) Baker, Lauretta's sister who had married William Baker the previous year.

24   Joanna Louisa Burch (3/9/1832--11/3/1902), daughter of Elizabeth's sister, Joanna White Blackwell and Edward Sebrey Burch.

25   William P. Baker, husband of Lauretta's sister Mary Caroline McBride.

26   Louisa (McBride) Woodward, Sarah's sister.

27   Olivia Pettigrew, Elizabeth's daughter.

28   Eugenia Pettigrew, Elizabeth's daughter.

Elizabeth Blackwell Pettigrew
           to Lauretta McBride Gulledge

Sept the 30th 1850

Dear Lauretta

With my heart filled with joy and thankfulness I take up my pen to address a few lines to you to let you know what a delightful meeting we have had and how the Lord has blessed us in the conversion of our friends and dear relations. I don't think I ever was at such a meeting in my life. It lasted 13 days. It commenced on the 13 of this month and continued until the 25.[1] There was preaching at night as well as in the day. Every night there has been 50 conversions during the meeting. I believe the spirit of the Lord was with the ministers and people from the beginning of the meeting to the close. I never in my life seen people all of them pay stricter attention to the preaching. There were 35 immersed Sunday week and 7 the day that the meeting closed. I suppose you would like to know who our ministers were, also who some to the persons were that were immersed. I think Lauretta that you will rejoice with us when you hear who they are. Well I will tell you some of them for I can't recollect all of them at this time but I will tell you all of the relations and some of the others: James Burch and his wife,[2] Hannah Burch[3] and Betty Burch,[4] brother John,[5] James Hepburn,[6] Olivia Wingate,[7] Eugenia[8] and Sarah Pettigrew,[9] Reden Gee,[10] Ben Burras, Betha Burras,[11] Mr Booth,[12] Betty Smoot.[13] Joseph[14] went up as a mourner and continued as one to the last. He conversed freely with the ministers and with cousin Edwin.[15] Brother Culpepper[16] considers him a converted man but Joseph is afraid that he may be deceived, therefore he has not joined the church yet but it is thought by all that it will not be long before he will be enabled to follow his Lord and Master in all of his ordinances for I do assure you that all shame or fear of man has left him. I went home with him one night during the meeting. He conversed with me the next morning on our way to the church freely. It was very melting and the feeling to see him up to shake the parting hand at the close of the meeting! The invitaion was extend to all that wished to come while the hymn that commences Blessed be the tie that binds was singing. Joseph came up with streaming eyes and he had to seat himself for he was so overcome that he could not stand.

Now, Lauretta I will tell you of another that will I hope if you have not as yet been thinking seriously of your future state that will bring you to serious reflections. I saw your brother[17] come up and relate his experience to the church. Did I say I saw it? I heard him for I went and took a seat near him. He was received and was baptised with the rest of the relations last Sunday week. He was not the last of the relations that came forward. I think James Burch and his wife were among the first persons that came forward at the meeting. Brother John next and the next was Hannah Burch, and your brother. They came together. Samuel[18] said that he has been under deep conviction for three months and that he got relief the week before the meeting began. There is a protracted meeting going on at Elem.[19] It commenced the Friday before our meeting broke. Joseph[20] is attending that. He stayed at home but one day after our meeting broke and he has been going to Elem regular every day since. There has been 25 immersed there. Joseph Wingate[21] was sick during our meeting so that he could not attend untill the last sabbath of the meeting. Sister Isabella[22] left the meeting not expecting to return but Joseph[23] was so anxious to return that she and Olivia[24] came back with him on Monday evening and they stayed until the meeting broke. Mr.

Pettigrew[25] was at Sister Isabella's day before yesterday. She told him that Joseph has been converted since the meeting broke. I will now let you know who were our ministers. Cousin John,[26] Brother Culpepper,[27] Cousin Napare,[28] and Brother Morris.[29] Cousin N stayed with us but 2 days. Some of his family was sick and he was oblidged (sic) to go home. Cousin John stayed from one sabath morning until the next sabath evening and he was oblidged (sic) to leave to go to a protracted meeting at Swift Creek.[30] He left with streaming eyes. There has been a protracted meeting at Mispah.[31] Angelina[32] and Edmund[33] were baptised during that meeting. There will be about 14 more baptised at our church[34] the first sabath in October. 7 is already received for baptism and 7 more expected. I must let you know how the health of your friends are. My family are not well. I am not well myself. I am bad off with the rheumatism altho I attended the meeting every day but the first. I was in a great deal of pain but the excitement helped to keep me up. Olivia[35] is quite unwell. Edward[36] is sick a bed with the membraneous sore throat. Several of brother Burches[37] family had the fever during the meeting but still they attended the meeting nearly all the time. Your brother[38] had the fever at the first of the meeting but he was at the church one day with the fever, after that he stayed at home 2 days and took quinine and broke it. Your Aunt Annah[39] could not attend all of the time for her baby was so young[40] that she could not stand the fatigue. Hannah Burch[41] was baptised with a chill on her. She said she did not feel the least cold after she came out of the water and she has not had a chill since. It seems that the water broke her chills. Josephs[42] family are all well. Cousin Betsey Hepburns[43] health is bad. Do Lauretta write to me as soon as you can. I received a letter from Caroline[44] two weeks back. She said they were well. I received one from Mary Ann Lide[45] the same day. She said all of the family were well but your aunt.[46] She had a flow of blood to the head that brought on apoplectic spasms. She said that she was some better than she had been but far from well. I would be very glad to get a letter from Louisa[47] too. I have not got one in some time. I shall write to her in a few days. You must excuse bad writing and all mistakes for I have wrote all of this letter lying down and in a hurry for I have so many to write that I wish to write as soon as I can for it is not at all times that I can write for there is times that I am in so much pain that I cannot. Mary[48] sends her love to you and cousin Davy[49] and all of the children and accept of the same from your affectionate Aunt

                Elizabeth B Pettigrew

P S   Lindy[50] says tell Miss Lauretta and Mass Davy a heap of howdeys and tell them her health is some better. Tell them that she will be very glad to hear that both of them are baptised. James Burch[51] was converted at his sister Marthas[52] grave. He went there to pray and while there he felt that his sins were forgiven. I have been sick all this week and am no better. I have to keep my bed nearly all the time. I think I took cold during the meeting for I went two nights to meeting. The rest of the family are all well at this time.

                Oct the 5 1850

FOOTNOTES

[1] George R. Pettigrew in Annals of Ebenezer indicates that this was the greatest revival effort since the establishment of Ebenezer Baptist Church and indicates that 70 blacks and whites were baptised during this period.

[2] James E. Burch (2/11/1826--4/11/1882), nephew of Elizabeth, son of her sister Joanna White Blackwell and Edward S. Burch. His wife was Mary Jane Sinclair (9/22/1829--8/29/1854).

[3] Hannah M. Burch, daughter of Joanna White Blackwell and Edward Sebrey Burch was a niece of Elizabeth Blackwell Pettigrew.

[4] Elizabeth T. Burch, was a younger sister of Hannah Burch.

[5] John Hamlin Blackwell, MD, brother of Elizabeth.

[6] James Hepburn, born about 1824, was the son of Robert and Elizabeth (Cousin Betsy) Hepburn.

[7] Isabella Olivia Wingate born, 3/22/1825 was the daughter of Elizabeth's sister Isabella Ann Blackwell and her husband, William W. Wingate.

[8] Anna Eugenia Pettigrew (September, 1835--April, 1892), daughter of James and Elizabeth Blackwell Pettigrew.

[9] Sarah A. S. Pettigrew (1830--1913), daughter of Robert A. and Elizabeth (Pearce) Pettigrew.

[10] James R. Gee, called "Redden", (b. 1825).

[11] Benjamin Burris and Tabitha Burris.

[12] Marcus Booth, (b. 1817 in VA), shown in 1850 Darlington Co., SC census with Cephas Cole who was to later marry Mary Annah Blackwell, Elizabeth's niece, daughter of Samuel Blackwell, III. and Sarah Harrell Blackwell.

[13] Elizabeth (Betty) Smoot, daughter of Thomas W. and Sarah Thomas Smoot married Lafayette Gandy, son of Abel Gandy in 1860.

[14] Joseph Louis Harrell, Elizabeth's son-in-law, husband of her daughter Eleanor.

15 William Edwin Dargan (7/13/1811--12/11/1851), son of Timothy Dargan, III. and Lydia Keith and brother of Rev. J.O.B. Dargan. He was a deacon in Ebenezer Baptist Church and first cousin of James Alexander Pettigrew.

16 John Culpepper was co-pastor of Ebenezer Baptist Church along with Rev. James Morris in 1850.

17 Samuel Blackwell McBride.

18 Samuel Blackwell McBride.

19 Elim Baptist Church, located on Lynches Creek in Darlington Co.

20 Joseph Louis Harrell, husband of Mary Ann Eleanor Pettigrew Harrell.

21 Joseph Edward Wingate, (1830--1888) son of William W. Wingate and Isabella (Blackwell) Wingate, Elizabeth's sister. Joseph Wingate later married Elizabeth's daughter, Anna Eugenia Pettigrew, his first cousin 10/26/1856.

22 Isabella Ann (Blackwell) Wingate, widow of William W. Wingate.

23 Joseph Louis Harrell.

24 Isabella Olivia Wingate, (b. 3/22/1825), daughter of Isabella (Blackwell) and William W. Wingate was a niece of Elizbeth B. Pettigrew.

25 James Alexander Pettigrew, Elizabeth's husband.

26 John Orr Beasley Dargan, son of Timothy Dargan, III. and Lydia Keith Dargan. He was pastor of Black Creek Baptist Church for 43 years and a first cousin of James Alexander Pettigrew.

27 John Culpepper, co-pastor of Ebenezer Baptist Church.

28 Possibly Rev. Robert Napier, pastor of Mispah Baptist Church for 40 years who married as his second wife, Elizabeth Blackwell Lane, daughter of James Lane, Jr. and Martha Eleanor Adair.

29 Rev. James Morris had been providing pastorial care for the people of Ebenezer Baptist Church since 1841.

30 Swift Creek Baptist Church was located about 8-10 miles east of Camden, SC.

31 Mispah Baptist Church at Mars Bluff, was constituted in 1834.

32 Angelina (possibly a Lane).

33 Possibly Edmund Lane, son of James and Eleanor Adair Lane.

34 Ebenezer Baptist Church.

35 Olivia Pettigrew (7/23/1833--8/4/1852), Elizabeth's daughter.

36 Joseph Edward Pettigrew (9/7/1841--5/28/1909), Elizabeth and James Pettigrew's youngest child.

37 Edward Sebrey Burch, Elizabeth's brother-in-law, husband of Joanna White Blackwell Burch.

38 Samuel Blackwell McBride.

39 Joanna White Blackwell Burch (5/15/1804--5/19/1884) married Edward Sebrey Burch, 10/15/1823.

40 The baby, Ada Burch, was born 23 July 1850.

41 Hannah M. Burch, daughter of Joanna Blackwell and Edward Sebrey Burch.

42 Joseph Louis Harrell.

43 Elizabeth S. Hepburn, wife of Robert Hepburn.

44 Caroline McBride Baker, Lauretta's sister and Elizabeth's niece, lived in Union Co., NC.

45 Mary Ann Lide (11/10/1831--6/25/1879), Elizabeth's niece, was the daughter of Eli Hugh Lide and Martha Blackwell. The Lide family was living in Dallas Co., AL.

46 Martha Johnson (Blackwell) Lide (6/13/1811--12/16/1880) was Elizabeth's half sister, the daughter of Mary Ann Hamlin and Samuel Blackwell, II.

47 Louisa McBride Woodward, Lauretta's sister.

48 Mary Brown.

49 David Gulledge, Lauretta's husband.

50 Lindy was a house servant.

51 James E. Burch (2/11/1826--4/11/1882), son of Edward Burch and Joanna White Blackwell.

52 Martha Isabella Burch (10/31/1835--8/11/1842), daughter of Edward S. Burch and Joanna White (Blackwell) Burch is buried in the Blackwell family cemetery on the former plantation of her grandfather, Samuel Blackwell, II.

Elizabeth Blackwell Pettigrew to
Lauretta McBride Gulledge

Feb the 23   1851

My dear Lauretta

    I got up this morning in a great deal of pain with the rheumatism; put on my clothes and lay down on the bed and was thinking about you and Louisa[1] being so far from me and how glad I would be to see all of you. At that time Zilphy[2] came in at the end door with a letter from you which informs me of the distress that you are in. You know that I truly simpathize (sic) with you for my dear sisters[3] children feels (sic) almost as near to me as my own. I hope by this time if consistent with the will of our maker that cousin Davy[4] is fast recovering and I hope that your brother[5] is with you before this. Lauretta my dear child, the Lord is wise in all of his dealings with the children of men for he doeth not afflict willingly nor grieve the children of men. Endeavor to cast your care upon the Lord for he careth for you and if your husbands life is spared be thankful to the Lord and should he be taken recollect that the Lord giveth and he has a right to take when he pleases altho it is like tearing the heartstrings asunder. All that I can tell you or the best advice that I can give you is to put your trust in the giver of every good and perfect gift for he is a present help in every time of need. I feel truly glad that your brother went out to see you at this time. I was glad when he started altho I hated to part from him but I am ten times gladder now for I know it is a great satisfaction to you. I am in hopes that he got there before Louisa left. I am truly sorry that Tommys[6] people would not let him alone and let you and your sister be in reach of each other. Tell Samuel to write me soon. My family are all well but myself. I am still suffering with rheumatism. Mary Brown[7] has the sick headache. Josephs[8] family are well. Eleanor[9] will be confined in April. Do Lauretta, if Louisa does move off when she writes to you do write to me and let me know where to direct letters to her. Lauretta I am truly sorry that I had nothing to send to you and Louisa by Sam but I had nothing at that time and I was not able to go to a store to get anything. If Mr. Pettigrew had of had his cotton sold I would of given $[10] money to of got some things in town for both of you. You must excuse bad writing for I can hardly write I have the rheumatism so bad in my hands and I have wrote this letter in a hury (sic) for if I don't write today I will not have the opportunity of getting a letter to the office in a week. Give my love to Sam. Give my love to Cousin Davy for I hope he will be well when you get this. Give my love to all of the children. Tell them that Aunty loves all of them and hopes they are good children. Eugenia[11] is not at home. She has been at the village[12] a fortnight today. She will come home this evening. Olivia[13] sends her love to all of you. The boys[14] send their love to all. Mary Brown sends her love to all. Do my dear Lauretta write as soon as possible, you or your brother, for I am very anxious to hear and will be until I do. I must close by subscribing myself your affectionate aunt.

                       Elizabeth B. Pettigrew

Olivia says that she will write to you this week so you will get a letter from her a week after you get this. Do write soon for you have not been out of mind since I got your letter. Dear Louisa, I feel sorry for her. She will be so far from all of her relations. When both of you were near enough to see each other now and then I felt better satisfied.

FOOTNOTES

1   Louisa McBride Woodward, Lauretta's sister.

2   A servant.

3   Mary Jane (Blackwell) McBride, Elizabeth's sister and Lauretta's mother, died before 1831. In addition to Lauretta, her children included Louisa who married Thomas Woodward; Samuel Blackwell McBride who married Joanna Louisa Burch, Feb., 1854; Caroline who married William P. Baker in Nov-Dec, 1849. and Ellen who married William Rufus King in October, 1850.

4   David Gulledge (9/4/1813--9/14/1895), Lauretta's husband.

5   Samuel Blackwell McBride.

6   Thomas Woodward, Louisa's husband.

7   Mary Brown lived with the Pettigrew family.

8   Joseph Louis Harrell, Elizabeth's son-in-law.

9   Mary Ann Eleanor Pettigrew Harrell, Elizabeths daughter, and wife of Joseph Harrell was pregnant and due to deliver about April of 1850.

10   Samuel Blackwell McBride had evidently gone to Jasper Co., MS to visit his sisters, Lauretta and Louisa.

11   Anna Eugenia Pettigrew, daughter of Elizabeth and James Pettigrew.

12   The city of Darlington was a village at this time. Eugenia was evidently visiting one of the families of the many relatives living there at the time.

[13] Olivia Albertina Pettigrew, Elizabeth's daughter.

[14] Thomas Jefferson, George W., and Joseph Edward Pettigrew were the Pettigrew boys living at home at the time.

Elizabeth Blackwell Pettigrew to
          Lauretta McBride Gulledge

                   January the 15 1852

My Dear Lauretta

    I expect you have come to the conclusion that I have entirely forgotten you but you may be well assured that I have not. I have been very bad off with the rheumatism. The weather is so changeable. I have (been) in bed nearly half of the time since the middle of Nov. The rest of my family are well. I hope these lines may find you and your family in the enjoyment of good health. Josephs[1] family are all well. Sarahs[2] family are all well but herself. She is not. She has been in Chesterfield[3] ever since the first of November until Christmas day. Her mother[4] and her sister Eugenia came down with her. I was at Josephs[5] when they got there. Her mother is perfectly restored to her right mind. No one would know that she had ever been in the situation that she has. Your brother[6] left here yesterday. He is quite well. He moved his trunk from here yesterday up to Dr. Smiths[7] where he is to oversee this year. He is to get $225, his bread and meat, and cows to furnish him with milk and a negro to cook and wash and tend his garden but he will be so lonesome living by himself. It makes me feel sad when I think of him all alone. I know he feels bad after leaving all

of us. He has been more with us this year than
he ever was. I had one of my mothers[8] nephews
to visit with us this fall. Cousin James
Commander[9] of Georgetown. If you recollect I
saw his name in the almanac when I was sick at
the other place. He was then sheriff of
Georgetown. The way that we became acquainted,
Samuel[10] wrote to him to get him a place to
oversee. He replied to the letter, said they
were relations and that he would aid him in
getting a place. I replied to his letter,
invited him and his family to visit us. He
then replied to my letter, said that he would
try to come when he was on his way to Marion C
H to the encampment and that his wife wished to
correspond with me. I then wrote to her. She
then wrote to me a very affectionate letter,
expressed great desire to see us, said she had
never seen any of her husbands relations of his
fathers[11] side. Said that she entertained for
me and my children the warmest sentiment of
affectionate regard and altho we were utter
strangers to each others features or
dispositions that it appears that she had long
known me and that she longed to see the girls.
Cousin James came on his way to the encampment.
He stayed two nights and a day with us. He was
very glad to see us. Said that I was almost as
near to him as a sister, that I was the nearest
relation he has on earth except his wife and
children. I sent for Sam[12] as soon as he came.
S was not here. He was off at a job of work
for Mr. McLocken.[13] Mr. Pettigrew likes cousin
James very much. Says he is a smart man. He
is a fine looking man. He is a portly man;
weighs the same that Mr. Pettigrew does; has
blue eyes, light auburn hair. He has three
children, two sons and a daughter. He has lost
two sons, the two eldest children. He got Mr.
P to promise him that we would pay him a visit
which we would of done before this if I had of
been well enough at the time we contemplated
going. Olivia, Eugenia,[14] Sarah Pettigrew,[15]
and Samuel[16] went. They arrived at his house

the 9 of Dec which was on Tuesday and stayed until the saturday before Christmas. All of them were delighted with their visit. Say they had quite a pleasant time of it. They are much pleased with cousin Eliza[17] James wife, also with her mother Mrs. Hull.[18] I will go down in the spring when Mr. Pettigrew goes to Charleston if I am well enough, and stay with cousin Eliza until he returns. He will go from Georgetown in the boat. Mr P could go from Mars Bluff in the boat but if I can go down I am afraid to go by water.[19] I received a letter last week from cousin Margaret Withers[20] formerly Margaret Walker. She lives in Charleston. She says her family consists of only herself, one single daughter and one granddaughter whose mother died when she was but a few days old. Her granddaughter is the child of one of her daughters. Her son[21] lives near her. He has five children, one son and four daughters. Cousin Margaret said in her letter that she would be very glad to see all of her relations and that I must remember her to all of them. If Mr P goes to Charleston next year I am in hopes that he will carry the girls for the railroad will be finished by then and he has promised the girls that he will take them down when the cars get to running. The depot will not be more than two miles from us.[22] Olivia has received a letter from cousin James Commander since they came from their house. He said that cousin Eliza said that she did not think that the girls would of left her house until January if they had of known how dreary the house looked after the light of their countenance. The girls say that cousin Eliza is a sweet woman; Mrs Hull quite a neat old lady. I have not told you how Eugenia suffered when she was in Georgetown. She had a whitlow on the finger that her thimble goes on. It was lanced twice and they had to call in a physician. She could not sleep the pain was so severe unless she took morphine. They were all of them very attentive to her. Mrs Hull and

Mrs Vernon, Mrs Hull's sister would sit upstairs with her nearly all day and hold her hand when she was in so much pain with her finger and get up with her when she could not sleep at night. Her finger is not well yet but much better. Joseph[23] has sold Calvin.[24] He would not stay with him. He was in the woodyard before last (sic) nearly all the time they were making the crop last year from May 10 until Dec the 11. I am truly glad he has got rid of him for he worried Joseph so much. He has been more expense than profit. Eleanor says the Joseph is agoing to make over Ginny[25] to her in Calvins place, that she would rather have a woman than a fellow. I suppose that you have heard that cousin Margaret Pettigrew[26] is dead? Her children all lives together and is agoing to carry on the farm. Cousin Edwin Dargan[27] died very sudden. He ate a hearty supper and died at three o'clock. He was sick only five hours from his first complaining. His wife[28] says that he was very cheerful that night before he was taken sick. The first he complained of was giddiness. Said that he would go in the room and lye (sic) down. Went in pulled off his coat, lay down, took a newspaper, read for an hour as he was in the habit of doing of nights before he stripped and went to bed. Stopped reading all at once. Clapped his hands on his head and said that he thought that he knew what pain was before but that he thought that he never had such a headache in his life. Cousin Sarah[29] sent off immediately for his brothers[30] and for some of the neighbors but no one got there until after he was dead but Solomon Wilson, Koon, and Booth.[31] I don't think that I ever had such a shock in my life. The boy got here at five o'clock. The first that I heard, Mr. Pettigrew woke me by saying very low that Dr. Edwin Dargan is dead. He had been talking to the boy some little time but I was asleep. When I woke up he was still questioning the boy, but the shock was so great on me that I hardly knew what he said to the boy or the boy to him. I was certain that he said that his mistress was not at home. I knew that she was at Cheraw on Sunday but she had got uneasy knowing that he had two attacks before with his head. She started home on Monday and got home that night. So she was with him two nights. She says that she has felt all of last year that there was some distress before her but she thought it was one of her children. She would live or she would die herself. He was warm so long but it was useless for the spirit had flown. Poor cousin Sarah. I truly sympathize with her. She takes his death very hard. He will be missed in the Church[32] very much indeed. Do Lauretta excuse this bad letter. I thought that every (torn) was (smeared) when I found it was not I could not get a pencil. I tried the pen that spoilt the looks then I tried the handle of a teaspoon. You must not let any person see this. Mary Brown sends love to you, says that she reckons you have forgot her; that you must not let Zilphy[33] forget her. The children sends love to all. Give my love to all and accept of the same from your aunt

      Elizabeth B. Pettigrew

Answer this soon. Tell the children I want to see them so bad. Oh how tired I am. I can hardly hold the pen. Olivia[34] has received your letter. So you have another daughter? Old Cinder[35] is dead. She died the 11 of Nov.

FOOTNOTES

[1] Joseph Louis Harrell, husband of Eleanor (Pettigrew) Harrell, Elizabeth's daughter.

[2] Sarah Perkins Harrell Blackwell, widow of Elizabeth's brother, Samuel Blackwell, III.

[3] Chesterfield Co., SC, was her mother's home.

[4] Sarah's mother was Mary Hollingsworth (Burch) Harrell, (8/29/1799--6/29/1875). She was the daughter of Joseph Burch, Jr. and Elizabeth Thomas and the granddaughter of General Tristan Thomas and Mary Hollingsworth. Mary Burch married James H. Harrell on 1/5/1815. He died 9/16/1822.

[5] Joseph Louis Harrell, Elizabeth's son-in-law.

[6] Samuel Blackwell McBride.

[7] Probably Dr. Thomas Smith (1/9/1793--3/8/1875) of Society Hill, SC, one of the wealthiest men in Darlington District at the time.

[8] Elizabeth's mother was the daughter of James Commander I, a planter in Georgetown, SC. Elizabeth's mother died about 1802, at or shortly after her birth.

[9] James M. Commander, born 1818, was the son of Samuel Commander and Elizabeth Allston. James M. Commander owned a large rice plantation on the N. Santee and was a brigadier general in the militia.

[10] Samuel Blackwell McBride, Lauretta's brother.

[11] James M. Commander's father, Samuel Commander was the brother of Elizabeth Pettigrew's mother. Samuel Commander was born sometime between 1755-74 in Georgetown District, SC. He married Elizabeth (Allston) Vereen, a widow on 7 May 1812 in Georgetown.

[12] Samuel Blackwell McBride.

13   Evander McLauchlin (b. 1817) with wife Mary (b. 1817) and daughter Margaret lived in the vicinity of the Edward S. Burch family.

14   Olivia and Eugenia Pettigrew, Elizabeth & James Pettigrew's daughters.

15   Sarah A. S. Pettigrew (1830-1913), daughter of Elizabeth Pearce and Robert A. Pettigrew Jr. Robert and James Pettigrew were first cousins.

16   Samuel Blackwell McBride.

17   Eliza Howle.

18   probably Mrs. Howle.

19   The trip from Mars Bluff, near the Pettigrews would have been down the Great Pee Dee River to Georgetown, SC.

20   Margaret (Walker) Withers, born about 1794 was the daughter of John Walker and Margaret Commander. Margaret Commander, daughter of James Commander, I. was the sister of Elizabeth's mother.

21   William Withers.

22   The North Eastern Railroad Co, which was to connect present day Florence, SC with Charleston actually made its first passenger run on October 5, 1857. The depot it shared at that time with the Wilmington and Manchester and the Cheraw and Darlington lines was located at the intersection of Church and Front Streets, in Florence, SC.

23   Joseph L. Harrell.

24   Slave.

25   Slave.

26 Margaret Pettigrew's relationship to Elizabeth is unknown.

27 William Edwin Dargan, MD (7/13/1811--12/11/1851) son of Timothy Dargan, III. and Lydia Keith. Married Sarah Thomas Dubose in Oct, 1838. He was a grandson of Timothy Dargan, II., a founder and first pastor of Ebenezer Baptist Church. He was ordained a deacon in Ebenezer Church in 1850 and was a brother of J.O.B. Dargan, pastor of Black Creek Church.

28 Sarah Thomas DuBose, daughter of Isiah DuBose and Gillie Benton.

29 Sarah Thomas DuBose Dargan.

30 His brothers were: George Washington, Timothy J. K., Jeremiah, J.O.B., Julius Alfred, Sidney R. F., Theodore Alonzo, and Charles A. Dargan.

31 Koon and Booth were slaves.

32 Dr. Edwin Dargan was an active member of Ebenezer Baptist Church. He was a deacon, the Church clerk; organized the first Bible study classes and became the Sunday School Superintendent.

33 Zilpha Ann Gulledge, Lauretta's daughter.

34 Olivia Albertina Pettigrew.

35 Lauretta's new daugher was Martha Adeline Gulledge, born 10/13/1851.

36 A slave.

Elizabeth Blackwell Pettigrew
          to Lauretta McBride Gulledge

                May the 19 1852, Darlington

Dear Lauretta

     I expect by this time you have almost come to the conclusion that Aunty has forgotten you but I have been so bad off this spring that I could not write.   I have several letters to answer from others of my friends but it will be some time before they will be all answered.   I feel much better at this time than I have for months. The rest of my family are well. Mary Brown has been very sick but she is so that she is going about again but has not regained her strength entirely.   She was taken with a sore throat in a few hours. She was so that she could scarcely be understood when she spoke. She has never been as bad off since she has been living with us. Her mother died while she was so sick. She came to see Mary on Saturday, spent the day and night, went home on Sunday morning as well as usual, was taken on Monday evening with inflamation of the windpipe and died Tuesday.   You may judge it was a great trial to me to let Mary know that her mother was in eternity when she was so ill herself. We received a note written to her a few hours or two after her mothers death with the intelligence but we did not let her know until the next day. It was a great shock to her for she had not heard that she was dead. There has been a great deal of sickness and a great many deaths this spring and in the winter. We have lost four negroes and had several very sick for two months. Brother John[1] traveled here very regular. The negroes we lost are old Cinder, Ceny, Chany, and Chany's baby, that she left just a week old when she died.   I took it in the house with us the day its mother died and attended to it and had it attended to with as

much care as if it had been my own but it only
survived the mother 6 weeks. Josephs[2] family
are well.   Sarahs[3] are well.   My boys[4] are
boarding at Josephs, going to school to a Mr
Norwood.[5]   Caroline Lide[6] was here last night
and today. This is the second time she has
been here since she came out. She expects to
return in September. She is very like her
mother.[7] Miss Martha Langston is married and
you can't guess who to, an old man old enough
for her grandfather, Old Bob Campbell. His
wife died the 26 of January and he was courting
4 or 5 weeks after her death. He tried the
widows first. Said he would not marry a young
girl for she would only marry him for his
property. Mrs Langston is dead. Stephen
Meadows[8] married Isabella Cole[9] winter before
last and left her last January, a few days
before she gave birth to a fine son. He took
Thomas Gees daughter Caroline with him. Took
the cars[10] and was gone until April. He
returned and brought Caroline back to Mr.
Harpers in the neighborhood of her father where
he took her from when they went off. A few
days after their return she was taken sick very
suddenly and died before they could get a
physician to her. James Hepburn[11] was sent
for. He lives a few miles from Harper. But
she was dead and laid out before he got there.
It is thought she poisoned herself for she was
nearly black after she died and very much
swollen. Her mother died two days before she
returned. I have not seen Samuel[12] in several
weeks. He was quite well when I saw him last.
Says that Dr. Smith[13] is well pleased with him.
I hope he may remain there several years altho
it is a good ways from me that I cannot see him
as often as I did last year. He is in good
business and he don't forget to come to see
Aunty. If he can't stay long he knows that I
am always glad to see him and I believe he is
as glad to see me. He is very different to
what he used to be. He is quite at home when
he is here. You know that is a great pleasure

to me. Well Lauretta your Aunty is in a comfortable house and tolerably well furnished, four large bedrooms and one small shed room, a dining room and a parlor, two piazzas, four passages, two above and two below and a better kitchen than I ever had. You must not think that I am boasting for you know that I have been very badly situated altho in a leaky house and a sooty one as I wrote you word that Mr. P[14] was having one built. I knew that you would like to know that it was finished and we in it, just three weeks last Saturday we moved in.[15] It is much nicer that cousin Marthas.[16] The man that built cousin James Lanes[17] superintended the building of this. What do you think, Aggy[18] has a great mullateo (sic) boy just a fortnight old day after tomorrow. There now you will say I know that Aunty is mad but what can't be helped has to be endured but she will never have another here for her master is resolved to be as good as his word for both of us have always said that if one of that color was born ours, that it would not remain ours not longer than the mothers recovery and we could find sale for both mother and child. Give my love to cousin David[19] and all of the Children. Tell the children Aunty wants to see them very bad. Tell Blackwell, Mary and Zilphy[20] that they must be good children and help father and mother all they can and be obedient to them and that they must love their books. Tell Sarah[21] she must too. Eugenia[22] and Mary[23] sends love to all. Olivia[24] and the boys[25] are at Josephs.[26] I must close by subscribing myself your affectionate aunt

        Elizabeth B. Pettigrew

P S Samuel[27] has been here today but he did not stay long. He came down to preaching and came home with us and stayed an hour or two.

FOOTNOTES

1   John Hamlin Blackwell, MD (11/12/1815--1/15/1891), practiced medicine in Darlington and Florence Counties for over 40 years. He was a member of the SC State Legislature in 1850-1 and 1860-1 and a deacon in Ebenezer Baptist Church.

2   Joseph Louis Harrell (11/14/1818--11/14/1877), husband of Mary Ann Eleanor Pettigrew, Elizabeth's daughter.

3   Sarah Amanda Perkins Harrell Blackwell, (2/11/1822--11/5/1863) widow of Samuel Blackwell, III., Elizabeth's brother who died 7/26/1847.

4   Thomas Jefferson, George W., and Joseph Edward Pettigrew, James and Elizabeth Pettigrew's sons.

5   An advertisement in *The Darlington Flag* edition of 3/19/1851 states: "WANTED: A gentleman qualified to teach Latin, higher English and Mathematics to take charge of a school in a healthy and pleasant location in upper Darlington, S. C. Salary, $300 and board, or the profit of the school. Apply Joseph Norwood or Thomas C. Law, Hartsville."

6   Caroline E. Lide (1/20/1833--9/11/1884), daughter of Eli Hugh Lide and Martha Johnson Blackwell Lide, Elizabeth's sister. Caroline and her family had moved from Darlington in 1835 and were living in Dallas Co., AL. She was evidently back in SC visiting the relatives possibly her father's sister, Hannah Lide Coker and her family of Society Hill, with whom they were very close.

7   Martha Johnson Blackwell Lide married Eli Hugh Lide, son of James Lide and grandson of Major Robert Lide on 19 July 1830. At that

time Eli Hugh Lide had been a widower twice.

[8] Stephen Meadows (b. 1838) was a school-teacher.

[9] Isabella Cole (b. 1838), daughter of Issac and Elizabeth Cole.

[10] Railroad.

[11] James W. Hepburn, son of Robert and Elizabeth S. (Cousin Betsy) Hepburn.

[12] Samuel Blackwell McBride, Lauretta's brother.

[13] Dr. Thomas Smith of Society Hill. Samuel was the overseer for Dr. Smith's property.

[14] James Alexander Pettigrew.

[15] This beautiful home built by James A. Pettigrew still stands on Cherokee Road in Florence, SC. It has passed through each generation from one lineal descendant of James and Elizabeth to another and is currently owned and occupied by a fifth generation of Pettigrew descendants. The original home on this site burned in the 1840's while James Pettigrew was buying furniture in Charleston. Hence Elizabeth's reference to living in a sooty and leaky home. Parts of the original foundation are still visible on the site. The current home as described by Elizabeth was built near the previous one.

[16] Martha Eleanor (Adair) Lane (born 11/1/1794) widow of James Lane, Jr.

[17] James Lane, Jr. (11/24/1790--8/20/1844) was the son of James Lane and Rachel Blackwell, sister of Samuel Blackwell, II, Elizabeth's father. James Lane, Jr. was Elizabeth's first cousin.

18   Slave.

19   David Gulledge, (9/4/1813--9/14/1895) Lauretta's husband.

20   David and Lauretta's children: Samuel Blackwell Gulledge (2/6/1840--7/5/1863), Mary Eleanor Gulledge (12/17/1841--1873), Zilpha Ann Gulledge (9/12/1844--12/1/1881).

21   Sarah Lauretta Gulledge (12/11/1845--3/21/1878).

22   Anna Eugenia Pettigrew.

23   Mary Brown.

24   Olivia Albertina Pettigrew.

25   Thomas Jefferson, George W., and Joseph Edward Pettigrew.

26   Joseph Louis Harrell.

27   Samuel Blackwell McBride.

Elizabeth Blackwell Pettigrew
            to Lauretta McBride Gulledge

January the 29 1853

My Dear Lauretta

    I seat myself for the purpose of once more addressing a few lines to you hoping they may find you and you and your family in the enjoyment of good health. My family are not all well. Cousin Elizabeth Pettigrew[1] is sick with sore throat and fever. I am suffering a good deal with rheumatism. A good many negroes are sick from colds. I don't know when we ever had as many sick ones. Bad colds are quite prevalent. The weather is so very cold that nearly everybody has a cold. I wrote to you in August and have got no answer whether you received the letter or not. I don not know but I wonder why my dear Lauretta has not wrote to me before this. I think it has been a year since I received a letter from you. I though when I wrote the last that if you received it you would reply as soon as you could as I was passing through deep waters of affliction for my dear Olivia[2] had a few weekds before bid adieu to this world. I wrote you all the particulars respecting her death and her obituary. She died on the 4 of August in full hope of immortal glory. My dear Lauretta if you could of been here to of seen her and heard her conversation when the world was receding and eternal things in reality gathering thick around her, you would say let me die the death of the righteous and let my last end be like hers. She was perfectly in her senses to the last, perfectly calm, had all called to her bedside, said that she had a great deal to say, that she was afraid that her strength would fail before she said all that she wished to say. She talked a great deal, said several times that she wished no tears shed for her. Said that Jesus was near her that she was going where she had long wished to go, to her God. She said I wish to see him as he is. She was asked if she wished to see him just as he is. She said yes, just as he it. She would say with such honestness, yes he died for me. Said she was not afraid to pass through the dark valley of the shadow of death. Would say O Lord be pleased to draw nigh to thy little one. Would hold up he hands and look at them and say come Lord Jesus, come quickly. Sent for her father. He was downstairs. Told him to read his Bible more, to bring up his children in the fear of the Lord, to pray with them and for them and meet her in heaven. Said that she had been 19 years with us but the time had come that she would soon leave us. Told her Uncle John[3] that he had a faithfull (sic) part by her that she hoped he would be rewarded. Had the glass brought to her. Looked at herself. Said she was pale. Said that she would soon be where all sins and sorrow would be done away and all tears would be wiped from her eyes. Said that she would soon be with her little brothers and sister.[4] She talked for three hours. She did not live more than a quarter of an hour after she stopped talking. She requested that all of her friends should be told that she wished them to meet her in heaven. I believe she was impressed for several months that her time on earth was short and she was willing to depart I believe, months before she did. Lauretta you must know that I miss her very much and that my distress is great but I sorrow not as those as that have no hope. I feel that it is impossible for me to be thankful enough to the giver of every good and perfect gift that he has blessed me and my child in drawing sensibly near to her in her last moments and calming every fear for I have every reason to believe that not a doubt did arise to darken her sky or drive for one moment God from her sight. O Lauretta, there is a pleasure mingled with the pain to see a friend or relation die in the triumphs of faith in the savior. I never in all my life witnessed such a death. Manly Wingate and his wife[5] was here. He says that he would not of missed witnessing the scene for anything. He conversed a good deal with her. He read the 23 Psalm and prayed at her bedside a few minutes before she left this world of trouble. She requested him to do so. Lauretta I expect you will say I wonder how Aunty bears it. If it was not for the unshaken belief that she is peerfectly happy and the hope that I have that we will be reunite in a better world where parting is no more it seems that it would nearly take my life. Altho it lacks but a few days of six months there is time that it is fresh in my mind as if it had taken place but a few days ago. How glad would I be if it was so that I could be with you to tell you all about it but that pleasure of our being together in this world is not for us but let both of us entreat of the Lord that we may meet our dear Olivia in his Kingdom, there to join her in praising Him for redeeming grace and dying love. T. Jefferson[6] is gone to Greenville to school.[7] He took the cars[8] last Wednesday night. Was to get there on Friday night. He won't return home until November and return in January again. Then George and Edward[9] will go back with him. Then we won't have but one child with us. Eugenia will be the only one if she don't take it in her head to marry. But I reckon she will before her brothers get through with their education for it will take seven years before they will graduate. Their father intends for to keep Tommy there until he gets through. He will only be at home during the vacation. It will be the same with the othe two when they go next year. George would of went this year but Edward could not bear the thought of being separated from him and Edward is too small to go so far from home.[10] Eugenia, Sally Pettigrew, Mary Ann Nettles, Olivia Wingate, and brother John[11] are all at the depot ready to take the cars in the morning for Charleston. James Hill has built near Mrs. Whites. The depot is near Hills. They are all of them at Hills tonight. Brother John and Sally Pettigrew is to be married the last of March or the first of April.[12] They will be married here. They have gone down to get things for the wedding. Sarah Blackwell[13] is married to James Owens.[14] Crecy[15] died last April. Left five children. Left an infant two months old. Sarah was married in December. Don't you write to anyone about brother Johns going to be married for they may not like it. I know they won't mind your knowing it so that it is not known about here but I don't believe any person writes to you from about here but myself and your brother. Your brother[16] was here this day week. He had the shingles. He lives with Mrs McLeneghan. Oversees for her. She is to give him $300. Well Lauretta I must close as it is late at night, a bad pen and bad light, and I am tired. George and Edward send love to the children, particular to Blackwell[17] also to cousins Davy[18] and Lauretta. Mrs. Parker is here sitting near me. She sends love to cousin Davy, to all of the children and to yourself. Give my love to each member of your family and accept a great portion yourself. No more at present but remain your affectionate aunt.

        Elizabeth B. Pettigrew

  Excuse bad writing and all mistakes for I was in a hurry. Cousin Elizabeth[19] is very sick tonight. Aneky[20] has two children, a boy and a girl. Nancy[21] has four, only one girl. Peggy[22] is in a family way. Josephs[23] family are not well but they are all up. Ellen[24] is on the way again. She lost two or three last year, brother John thought. Old Maria[25] is dead. She died this day week. Sam Burch[26] and Eugenia Sinkler is married. They live with sister Sinkler.

FOOTNOTES

[1] Elizabeth Sparks (Pearce) Pettigrew (5/14/1812--7/4/1884), wife of Robert A. Pettigrew, Jr., son of Robert A. Pettigrew, Sr. and Ann Dargan. Ann Dargan was the daughter of Timothy Dargan, II. and Ann Beasley.

[2] Olivia Albertina Pettigrew (7/23/1833--8/4/1852), daughter of James Alexander and Elizabeth Blackwell Pettigrew died at age 19. She is buried in the Blackwell family Cemetery, along with her grandfather and brothers, sisters and other family members at Burches

Crossroads, 3 miles from present day Florence, SC. The engraving on her tombstone in words and style, attest to the great loss, Elizabeth felt at the time.

3 John Hamlin Blackwell, MD, Elizabeth's brother.

4 William A. Pettigrew (5/24/1822--9/23/1823), John Alonzo Pettigrew (12/6/1825--10/11/1827), James Robert Pettigrew (11/10/1828--8/30/1831), Samuel B. Pettigrew (6/15/1830--8/31/1831) and Isabella Susannah Pettigrew (3/27/1831--7/17/1832), all preceded her in death and are buried in the Blackwell family cemetery.

5 Washington Manley Wingate, son of William W. and Isabella Ann Blackwell Wingate, Elizabeth's sister, was a Baptist Minister. His wife, Mary Elizabeth Webb was originally from North Carolina.

6 Thomas Jefferson Pettigrew was 15 1/2 years old at the time.

7 Furman Institute in Greenville, SC was a popular school of higher learning for the sons of the Darlington families at that time.

8 Thomas J. Pettigrew travelled by the recently completed railroad from what is now Florence, SC to Greenville.

9 Thomas' brothers.

10 George W. Pettigrew was 14 years old and Edward was 12 when their brother Thomas went to Greenville.

11 The group consisted of Eugenia Pettigrew, Elizabeth and James Pettigrew's daughter; Sarah Pettigrew, daughter of the late Robert A. Pettigrew, Jr. (James first cousin) and Elizabeth Sparks Pearce; Mary Ann Nettles,

daughter of Joseph B. Nettles and Hannah M. Blackwell, Elizabeth's sister; Olivia Wingate, daughter of the late William Wingate and Isabella Blackwell, another sister of Elizabeth; and Dr. John Hamlin Blackwell, Elizabeth's brother.

[12] This was the second marriage for John Hamlin Blackwell. His first wife Aletha Windom of Alabama had died leaving him with a son and daughter.

[13] Sarah A. Harrell Blackwell (2/11/1822-- 11/5/1863) was the second wife and widow of Samuel Blackwell, III, Elizabeth's brother.

[14] James Owens was a widower with five children. Sarah had three of her own.

[15] A slave.

[16] Samuel Blackwell McBride.

[17] Samuel Blackwell Gulledge, Lauretta's son

[18] David Gulledge, Lauretta's husband.

[19] Elizabeth Sparks (Pearce) Pettigrew, widow of Robert A. Pettigrew, Jr., first cousin of James Alexander Pettigrew.

[20] Slave.

[21] Slave.

[22] Slave.

[23] Joseph Louis Harrell.

[24] Mary Ann Eleanor Pettigrew Harrell.

[25] Slave.

[26] Joseph Samuel Burch (7/13/1828--4/15/1889), son of Edward Sebrey Burch and Joanna White Blackwell, Elizabeth's sister.

Elizabeth Blackwell Pettigrew
          to Lauretta McBride Gulledge

                 July the 1   1853   Dar Dis So Car

My ever dear Lauretta

     I have received you very welcome letter of the 29 of May and am truly glad to hear from all of you but sorry to hear of your bad health. I think that you should make no delay but procure medicine from a physician immediately before the disease becomes permanently sealed. My family are all well. I still suffer with the rheumatism but not as bad as I have. Josephs[1] family are well. Ellen[2] is near her confinement. Brother John and Sally Pettigrew[3] was married the 2 of March. They were married here. We gave them quite a large party. Brother John has had quite a snug house built. All the fault I find with it is that it is rather small. It is in the shape of a T. The stem of the T is the dining room. It is not two story. It has five rooms. It has two shed rooms. Brother John has his children[4] with him. He carried them home when he carried Sally. His family are well. Brother Burch[5] is in very bad health; has the dispepsia as bad as I ever knew any person to have it. He has no more mind than that of a child. The rest of the family are well the last I heard from them. Sister Isabellas[6] family--Joseph[7] had been quite sick but was on the mend--the rest were well. Manly[8] and his wife are at Wake Forest. They have been there all the year. Mary[9] stays with her mother. Believe Manly is agent for some board therefore he is very little with Mary. He is riding from place to place nearly all the time. Mary hates very much being separated from him so much for she is a devoted wife. So is he to her. She is an excellent woman. They were both of them well the last I heard from them. Brother Josephs[10] family are all well. I suppose you heard that Sarah Blackwell[11] and James Owens were married in December. He has 5 children. She has 8 to do for now. I like Mr Owens very much. He appears to be a fine man. He is a class leader in the Methodist Church. He is considered to be a pious man. Sarah appears to be quite happy. He is kind to her and to her children. She and her children were well the last I heard for them. Your brother[12] was here last Sabath (sic). He was well. I see him every week. He will be here tomorrow. I would like to know if you got the letter I wrote you soon after my dear Olivia's[13] death. I wrote you a long letter and wrote her obituary[14] in the letter. My dear Lauretta you know not what deep sorrow I was in when I wrote that letter. Work was a thing I could not do. I was better satisfied while pursuing by Bible or some other good book or conversing on paper to some one of my dear friends that I knew would sympathize with me. Yes Lauretta I know you felt deeply for me for you are a mother yourself and yo can form some idea how trying it is to us poor mortals to be bereft of our dear offspring. But she was only lent to me and her heavenly father has a right to call her home to himself when he saw best. We poor shortsighted creatures would have our offspring with us always. We dread the separation so much but the Lord removes them for this world of sin and sorrow in love to them and us poor mortals too. I think, not only think but I know, that I have great reason to be thankfull (sic) to my creator if I have been bereft of 6 children, I have every reason to believe they are all safely housed in that house not made with hands eternal in the heavens. O Lauretta, if you could of seen her in her last you would have been constrained to say Lord grant that my last moments may be like hers. Do my dear Lauretta never, no never, forget her dying words for it was one of her last requests that all of her friends should be told that she wishes them all to meet her in heaven. We will never meet her on earth again but I hope my dear Lauretta has chosen that good part which shall never be taken away from her. If so she is only gone to those blissfull (sic) mansions a little before you. If you have not as yet chosen whom you will serve I entreat of you to make no delay for time is always on the wing. Who of us thought this day 11 months that in four days time that dear one would be in eternity. What if she had of procrastinated until then, how awful would her situation of been forever. What a terror death would have been to her instead of being a welcome messenge as it was. You may think that I have all that I could wish for. What more could I wish for than to see her leave this world strong in the Lord and to see her faith triumph over death, hell, and the grave for she had no fear of either. She died relying on the merits of a crucified Savior. She would say yes he died for me with all the earnestness that she could, but still I grieve. The flesh is weak but I sorrow as I would if I had no hope. I do not wish her in this sinfull (sic) world but I long to join her above. I have the degarotype (sic) that was taken better that a year before she died. It is the express image of her. Thomas[15] is in Greenvile going to school. He has been there since the last of January. Won't return until Nov. He is getting along very well. We hear from him every week or two. We get a circular from the professor of the institution every month. Thomas is pleased with Greenville. G and Edward[16] boards at Josephs[17] and goes to school in the house that we lived in. It is all taken away but my room and that much of the piazza remains. Well Lauretta I have been to Charleston. Started on the cars three o'clock at night and reached the city 4 o'clock in the evening of the same day. Saw cousin Margaret Withers.[18] She passed the hotel we put up at just as were conducted to the room we occupied. Eugenia[19] knew her for she saw her when she was down in February with brother John and Sally[20] just before they were married. I wrote to cousin Margaret to let her know they were agoing down. She sent to two hotels enquiring (sic) for them but they were not at either for brother John said that they would go to the Charleston Hotel but he changed his mind and went to the Merchants Hotel. But cousin William Withers[21] looked over the papers that contained the list of persons at the different hotels and in that way found where they were the day before they left town. Cousin Margaret and cousin Harriet, cousin William's wife; that is cousin M(argaret's) daughter-in-law, came immediately to the hotel to see them. Said they were very much disappointed in not finding them sooner for they anticipated a great deal of pleasure for they had made preparation for them to stay at their houses all the time they stayed in the City. To stay at cousin Williams in the day but...(page cut off)..it was so that the girls did not visit them but when I went down in April, cousin Margaret, her daughter and daughter-in-law came to the hotel and I went home with cousin M and stayed all the time with her. Only one day at her sons and one night with Martha Pegon. I enjoyed myself very much. Cousin M, her children and grandchildren were all very glad to see us. Cousin M said that she had felt for many years like a lone one to her self; that she had no relations but her children for she had heard that sister[22] and myself were married and gone clean off. Cousin M has but two children, one son and daughter. Her daughters name is Resolve. Her son[23] has five children, 4 daughters and one son. Cousin M's family consists of herself, her daughter, one grandchild the daughter of her youngest child who died a few days after the birth of her child. Cousin M has had the child ever since her daughter's death. It is 13 years old, a very smart child. I am expecting a letter from Cousin M to let us know when she will be up. She promised us that she and her daughter and granddaughter would visit us this summer. Lauretta this letter has been commenced several weeks. I have been quite sick since I commenced it. Had it not of been that I was very sick it would of been in your hands by this time. Had it not of been detained on the way. You must excuse bad writing blots and all mistakes for I am hardly able to write for I am quite weak. My disease was bowel affection and derangement of the liver. There was a very sudden death in our family while I was sick. Cousin Nancy Orr[24] died quite unexpected to all of us. Brother John[25] was her physician or he had been called to her once the night before she died. He did not think her dangerous. Said she would be up in a few days. She said she was better not more than 20 minutes before her death. I was sick lying in the room with her. Eleanor and Lindy[26] was sitting in the room. Cousin Nancy had went (sic) to sleep. She got to making a noise in her sleep as she very often did. Lindy went to her and called her and asked her what made her go so. She gave no answer but appeared to be asleep; no change in her countenance at that time. She turned over twice after Lindy went to her, as strong as ever and was dead in a few minutes. I do not think she had the least idea that she would die for she talked and laughed not more 2 hours before her death. She died on the 16 July 11 o'clock in the morning. I must now draw to a close as I have to make some preparation to start to Josephs[27] early in the morning as I have just received a note from Ellen.[28] She was taken sick this morning. I feel very uneasy about her for she has been more helpless and more complaining. All sends love to all of you. Give my love to cousin Davy[29] and all of the children and accept of the same from your affectionate Aunt.

      Elizabeth B Pettigrew

July the 29 1853

Kiss all of the children for me. Peggy has a fine son, three weeks old. Brother Burch[30] is better. Samuel,[31] your brother was well last Sunday. Mary Brown sends her love to all of you.

Aug 8

Ellen[32] has a fine son born the 30 July. They have named it Julius Dargan.[33] Joseph[34] has received cousin Davids[35] letter. You must not think hard of me that this letter has not been sent off yet for Geny[36] is from home and I did not know where the envelopes were as she had put them away and her keys were not here.

FOOTNOTES

[1] Joseph Louis Harrell (11/14/1818--11/14/1877) had married Mary Ann Eleanor (Ellen) Pettigrew (11/8/1823--8/25/1903), Elizabeth's daughter on 11/4/1840.

[2] Eleanor Pettigrew Harrell would deliver her son Julius Dargan Harrell on July 30.

[3] John Hamlin Blackwell, MD (12/12/1815--1/15/1891) son of Samuel Blackwell, II. and Mary Ann Hamlin took Sarah A. S. Pettigrew (1830-1913), daughter of Robert A. and

Elizabeth Sparks Pearce Pettigrew on 3/2/1853, as his second wife.

4   Probably Edward John Burch Blackwell and Carrie Aletha Blackwell, children by his late first wife, Aletha Windom.

5   Edward Sebrey Burch (12/30/1806--9/6/1864).

6   Isabella Blackwell Wingate (born 9/21/1823), widow of William W. Wingate, who had been Darlington District Sheriff and a representative to the State Legislature. He died 7 June 1845. Isabella's family living at home at that time included Joseph Edward Wingate and Isabella Olivia Wingate.

7   Washington Manley Wingate (6/28/1828--2/27/1879), another son of Isabella and William Wingate was a professor at Wake Forest College in NC at the time. He was later to become the president of that institution.

8   Mary Elizabeth Webb and Manley Wingate had married about 1850.

10   Joseph Burch Nettles (9/4/1804--3/5/1886) son of James and Mary (Burch) Nettles. Born on Lower Fork Jeffries Creek, moved to Darlington Village in 1823. He married Hannah Mara Blackwell, widow of Edmund Gee in 1832.

11   Sarah Amanda Perkins (Harrell) Blackwell, second wife and widow of Samuel Blackwell, III.

12   Samuel Blackwell McBride.

13   Olivia Albertina Pettigrew (7/23/1833--8/4/1852).

14   "Died in this District at her fathers residence August the 4th, of congestive fever, Miss Olivia A. Pettigrew, daughter of James A and Elizabeth B Pettigrew, age 19 years."

[15] Thomas Jefferson Pettigrew was James and Elizabeth's oldest surviving son at that time.

[16] George W. and Joseph Edward Pettigrew, James and Elizabeth's two other sons.

[17] Joseph Louis and Eleanor (Pettigrew) Harrell lived in Darlington Village at the time, while Elizabeth and James lived South of present day Florence, SC, a distance of about 12 miles. George and Edward were living with their sister and brother-in-law and their family while attending school.

[18] Margaret (Walker) Withers was the daughter of John Walker and Margaret Commander, who was Elizabeth's mother's sister. Elizabeth and Margaret Withers were first cousins.

[19] Eugenia Pettigrew, James and Elizabeth's daughter.

[20] John Hamlin Blackwell, MD and Sally A. Pettigrew.

[21] William Withers, son of Margaret (Walker) Withers.

[22] Mary Jane (Blackwell) McBride, Lauretta's mother.

[23] William Withers.

[24] Nancy Orr, daughter of John and Mary (Dargan) Orr. Mary Dargan was the sister of James Alexander Pettigrew's mother, Susannah Dargan. Nancy Orr and James Pettigrew were first cousins.

[25] John Hamlin Blackwell.

[26] A slave.

[27] Joseph Louis Harrell.

28 Mary Ann Eleanor (Pettigrew) Harrell, Elizabeth's daughter.

29 David Gulledge, Lauretta's husband.

30 Edward Sebrey Burch, husband of Joanna White Blackwell, Elizabeth's sister.

31 Samuel Blackwell McBride.

32 Mary Ann Eleanor (Pettigrew) Harrell.

33 Julius Dargan Harrell (7/30/1853--1854/5).

34 Joseph Louis Harrell.

35 David Gulledge.

36 Eugenia Pettigrew.

Elizabeth Blackwell Pettigrew
         to Lauretta McBride Gulledge

                August the 8 1854   Darlington

My Dear Lauretta

   I fear by this time you have come to the conclusion that I have forgotten you as I have not replied to your letter before this but believe me I have not been well enough to undertake the task of writing, not that it is not a pleasure to write to my friends for it is a great pleasure to me to write to you, also to receive letters from you; but I have suffered more with the rheumatism this year than I have in two years and the weather has been so excessively hot and I so weak that it is all that I can do to lye (sic) on the bed and fan. Indeed the weather has been so oppressive that

well hearty people could scarcely do anything.
There has been several persons sunstruck in
Charleston and I expect the weather has been as
oppressive here for it is a general complaint.
Old persons say they have never experienced
such weather. We had some rain last night and
it has been cloudy today which makes it more
pleasant. The rest of my family are all quite
well. I was truly sorry to hear that cousin
David[1] has been so ill but glad to hear that he
was on the mend. I have not seen your brother[2]
in some time. I have heard from them. They
are well. I suppose you have heard that he is
married. He has married Lou Burch.[3] They were
married in February. He oversees for John
Witherspoon.[4] He gets $200, a cook and a boy
to wait in the house and all of his provisions
found him but sugar, coffee and flour. Sam and
Lou are both of them well pleased there. Lou
says that she would rather live there at that
price than to live at other places and get
more. She says the woman they have for a cook
is such a good negro. I have heard that Mr.
Witherspoon is well pleased with Sam. If so he
will raise his wages another year and I do not
doubt but what it is so for Sam is very
attentive to his business. Sam says that he
has very little trouble there for he has a
negro drive. Josephs[5] family are well.
Brother Johns[6] are well. Brother Johns wife[7]
will increase his family before this year is
out. She is a looking right bunchy. Mary Jane
Burch[8] has had no child yet but she is
expection (sic) to be confined. I do not
expect there ever was two people better pleased
than James[9] and Mary Jane. They have been
married so long and had no child until both of
them are very anxious for one. James bought a
crib several months ago. Sister Isabellas[10]
family are all well. Mr. Pettigrew[11] was there
today. Brother Josephs[12] family were well,
all but Anna[13] and she is better. Brother
Burches[14] health is not good and Hannah[15] has
been quite sick but she is much better. The

rest I believe are well. Ma[16] suffers with rheumatism. Brother Lide[17] is dead. He died in Texas. He was moving there but died with cholera; he and 9 of his negroes before they reached the place that they expected to stay at this year. He had not bought land. He had only rented until he could purchase. A widow lady was kind enough to invite dear Sister[18] and the children to her house and welcome them to stay as long as they wished. Mary Ann[19] and Caroline[20] neither of them was along. Caroline is married and Mary Ann is staying with her in Arkansas until fall and Dawson[21] the man Carry married intends moving to Texas. Cousin Margaret Withers,[22] her daughter,[23] and granddaughter came up from Charleston and stayed a month with us in the spring. Cousin Margaret is my mothers sisters daughter. How glad she would have been to of seen all of your mothers[24] children. She thought so much of your mother. They were children together and she was living with my mother[25] when she died. Sam and Lou[26] stayed here one night when she was here. She was very glad to see him and said that she liked her cousin Sams wife very much. Little Samuel McCowns[27] wife died about a month ago. Dr Jarrots wife[28] died a short time before Mrs McCown. Margaret was near her confinement. She had been complaining of her head for some time the night that she died. The Dr was unwell. He was lying on the bed. She went in the room and said that her head felt bad and she felt blind. He told her to go lye (sic) down. As soon as she lay down she took a fit. The Dr tried to hold her on the bed but she fell off of the bed. He got help and got her back on the bed and to his astonishment she was a lifeless corpse. Cousin James Commander has moved to East Florida.[29] I have received one letter from him since he settle(d) there. He gives a favorable account of the lands there. Mr. Jacquiling G[30] has just returned from East Florida. He has purchased lands with the intention of settling there. Cousin James got there the 3 of March last year right in a forest for the land he purchased has no improvements. He had to go to building and clearing land to plant and he made two bales of sea island cotton to the land that he said would bring hims 40 cents per pound. It is a healthy country, never very cold or very hot. They very seldom have frost there. I wish cousin David[31] would go there. I think he would like the country and you would be near cousin James and he thinks so much of his fathers[32] relations. If you could see the letters that he wrote to me and Sam[33] before he saw us and the letter his wife wrote to me before and since he was here, I know that you would like to live near them. When he was here he told me that I was the nearest relation that he had on earth but his immediate family, i.e. his wife and children. He said to me cousin we are almost as near kin as brother and sister. Mary Brown[34] says that cousin David must move to Florida for she wants to see you and the children and if you move there perhaps she may see you for she has the Florida fever. Says that she won't be satisfied until she sees Florida. Eugenia[35] says that she intends going home with cousin James Commanders wife[36] when she comes to see us this winter. Cousin James wrote me that his wife was acoming this winter, that it would take but two days to get to Charleston on the boat but one from there on the cars. Jefferson[37] is still in Greenville going to school. The Furman University is moved there. They have two hundred students this year. Next year they will have 400 students. Jefferson goes off the last of January and does not return until the second week in November. George[38] will go next when Jefferson goes back. Mr Pettigrew and Eugenia just got home from Greenville last week. The Baptist Convention was held in Greenville. They went to the Table Rock and to Caesars Head. Eugenia went up on the Table Rock. She had to go up 200 steps nearly perpendicular to get up and when she got up she said she did not know (how) she would get down, it was so dangerous, but she got someone to help her down. Tell Blackwell[39] he must be smart and help his father all that he can. Tell him Aunty sends her love to him and I hope he will be a good boy and make a smart man. Give my love to Mary, Zilphy and Sarah[40] and tell them that their Aunty wants to see them very much. That they must be good children and mind what their father and mother says to them. Tell the other children[41] that their Aunty loves them too and that she wants to see them all. I have said nothing to you to let you know how Sarah[42] is getting along. She and Mr. Owens is getting along very well. I think Sarah is happily married. Me, Eugenia, and Edward[43] paid them a visit not long since. We stayed from Wednesday until Saturday. Enjoyed the visit very much. Sarah will soon have two daughters grown. Mary Anna[44] and Elizabeth[45] is nearly as tall as Sarah. Mary Anna has the rheumatism very bad. Mary[46] sends a heap of love to you and the children. Says that she often thinks of all of you. George and Edward[47] send much love to Blackwell and love to all of you. Give my love to cousin David and tell him that I wish that all of you was back in Darlington. Tell him that Mr Pettigrew has the best crop that he has ever had but he has guannoed a good deal of it but not all. Well my dear Lauretta I must close as it is getting late. May the giver of every good and perfect gift bless you and yours both in your souls and body is the sincere prayer of your aunt.

       E B Pettigrew

FOOTNOTES

1 David Gulledge, Lauretta's husband.

2 Samuel Blackwell McBride (1821--12/1877).

[3] Joanna Louisa Burch (3/9/1832--11/3/1832), daughter of Joanna White Blackwell and Edward Sebrey Burch was Samuel's first cousin. His mother, Mary Jane Blackwell was the half-sister of Joanna White Blackwell.

[4] Col. John D. Witherspoon (3/17/1778--4/2/1860), son of Gavin Witherspoon was a noted attorney and lived in Society Hill.
He owned Lowther's Lake plantation of some 2400 acres on Witherspoon Island adjacent to the Great Pee Dee River.

[5] Joseph Louis Harrell, husband of Mary Ann Eleanor Pettigrew Harrell, Elizabeth's daughter.

[6] John Hamlin Blackwell, MD.

[7] Sarah A. S. Pettigrew (1830--1913), daughter of Elizabeth Sparks Pearce and Robert A. Pettigrew, Jr., married John Hamlin Blackwell on 3/2/1853 in the home of James and Elizabeth Pettigrew. John and Sarah Blackwell's first child, Robert James Blackwell was born 12/10/1854.

[8] Mary Jane (Sinclair) Burch (9/22/1829--8/29/1854), wife of James E. Burch, died shortly after this letter was written.

[9] James E. Burch (2/11/1826--4/11/1882), son of Edward S. and Joanna White Blackwell Burch ran the plantation of his grandmother Mary Ann Hamlin Blackwell, widow of Samuel Blackwell, II.

[10] Isabella Blackwell Wingate, widow of William W. Wingate.

[11] James Alexander Pettigrew.

[12] General Joseph Burch Nettles, husband of Hannah Mara Blackwell.

13   Anna Nettles (b. after 1850).

14   Edward Sebrey Burch, husband of Joanna White Blackwell.

15   Hannah M. Burch, daughter of Edward & Joanna.

16   Mary Ann (Hamlin) Blackwell (10/8/1786--11/20/1869).

17   Eli Hugh Lide (4/15/1796--4/18/1854), son of James and Jane (Holloway) Lide, originally from Darlington Co., SC and a graduate of SC College had answered the "call to the West" in 1835 and moved his family to Dallas Co., Alabama. After 19 years, he felt compelled to move further West and died in Louisiana while in route to Texas. He was buried in Woodville, Tyler Co., Texas.

18   Martha Johnson (Blackwell) Lide (6/13/1811--12/16/1880), was the third wife of Eli Hugh Lide, and mother of 9 of his 11 children.

19   Mary Ann Lide (11/10/1831--6/25/1879), eldest daughter of Eli Hugh and Martha (Blackwell) Lide.

20   Caroline E. (Lide) Dawson (1/20/1833--9/11/1884), daughter of Eli Hugh and Martha (Blackwell) Lide.

21   Lawrence Edwin Dawson, Jr. (6/20/1831--11/19/1897), son of Lawrence Dawson and Mary Huger, all former South Carolinians who had moved to Dallas Co., AL in the 1830's. After his marriage to Caroline Lide in December 1853 he moved to Camden, Ouachita Co., AR. The Dawson family remained in AR and never moved to Texas. They would later be joined there by Martha Blackwell Lide and four of her children: Sarah E., James Eli, Hannah Mariah, and Samuel

Blackwell Lide.

[22] Margaret (Walker) Withers, daughter of John Walker and Margaret (Commander) Walker who was a daughter of James Commander.

[23] Resolve Withers.

[24] Elizabeth's mother was the first wife of Samuel Blackwell, II, and also a daughter of James Commander.

[25] Mary Jane Blackwell McBride.

[26] Samuel Blackwell McBride and his wife Louisa Burch McBride.

[27] Samuel O. McCown (b. 1833), son of Anna McCown, a neighbor of the Edward S. Burch family in 1850.

[28] Dr. James Howard Jarott.

[29] James M. Commander, Sheriff of Georgetown and Brigadier General of the militia was a wealthy rice planter. He was the son of Samuel Commander brother of Elizabeth Pettigrew's mother. James and his family moved to Ocala, Marion Co., FL.

[30] Jackquilling Gee (b. 1799) was a neighbor of the Pettigrews.

[31] David Gulledge.

[32] Samuel Commander.

[33] Samuel Blackwell McBride.

[34] Mary Brown lived with the Pettigrews.

[35] Eugenia Pettigrew, Elizabeth's daughter.

[36] Eliza Howle Commander.

37   Thomas Jefferson Pettigrew, Elizabeth's son.

38   George W. Pettigrew, another son.

39   Samuel Blackwell Gulledge, Lauretta and David's son.

40   Mary Eleanor Gulledge (12/17/1841--1873); Zilpha Ann Gulledge (9/12/1844--12/1/1881); Sarah Lauretta Gulledge (12/11/1845--3/21/1878).

41   Lauretta's other children in August 1854 included: Thomas Huntley (10/14/1847--10/15/1864); Elizabeth Louisa (11/19/1849--1881); Martha Adeline (10/13/1851--1/28/1901); and Albert Joseph (11/17/1853--12/1/1903).

42   Sarah Amanda Perkins (Harrell) Blackwell, widow of Samuel Blackwell, III., Elizabeth's brother married as her second husband, James Owens, a widower.

43   Joseph Edward Pettigrew.

44   Mary Annah Blackwell (5/29/1841--6/25/1877) daughter of Sarah and Samuel Blackwell, III.

45   Elizabeth Isabella Blackwell (11/11/1842--1923), also a daughter of Sarah and Samuel Blackwell, III.

46   Mary Brown.

47   George and Edward Pettigrew, Elizabeth's sons.

Elizabeth Blackwell Pettigrew
           to Lauretta McBride Gulledge

           March the 27 1855   Darlington So Car

My dear Lauretta

Tis with an aching heart that I seat myself for the purpose of addressing a few lines to you to let you know that Death has visited our family circle again. Yes my dear Lauretta our dear Thomas[1] is now numbered with the dead. His remains were brought home from Greenville where he and George[2] was going to school last Tuesday. On Wednesday, he was laid by the side of dear Olivia[3] there to rest until Gabriels trumpet shall awake the sleeping dead. He was taken with a chill on the 11 after breakfast. A physician was sent for. He thought Thomas was taking the measles but after some day of so found that it was pneumonia. He bled him, his brain and lungs. Then he became congested. He breathed his last on Friday night there at 12 o'clock. We received a letter from George on Sunday the 18 stating that his brother was sick. Mr Pettigrew and myself were making preparations to start to see him on Tuesday but on Monday, sister Isabella[4] received a letter from one of the students which brought the sad intelligence of his death. Eugenia[5] was at brother Joseph Nettles.[6] Sister Isabella sent for her as soon as she received the letter and she and sister Martha[7] came down with Eugenia. My feelings were indescribable when I saw sister Isabellas carriage. I knew that they had heard sad news of my dear child. The evening Mr Pettigrew received a letter from James Furman[8] which stated more particulars respecting his death. Brother Furman is one of the professors of the institution. He was by my dead child to the last. I will give you Brother Furmans own words as in his letter. At times he had been quite rational so much so that I was able to converse with him. He seemed to feel very clearly his need as a sinner and the necessity of his dependence upon Christ for salvation. He wished me to pray for him. When I had offered prayer he continued praying himself pleading for mercy. His last petition was in these words, O my father take me to thy vest. George[9] and John Blackwell[10] says that after he stopped praying that he sang the hymn As on the Cross the Savior Hung; about two verses and his strength failed, that he could sing no more. They told me also that he told one of the students that was by his bed that he was perfectly resigned to death for he knew that he would go to heaven. I will also write you the tribute of respect that was published in the Greenville paper and sent to us. TRIBUTE OF RESPECT. At a meeting of the students of the Furman University held for the purpose of giving an expression of their feelings in reference to the death of T J Pettigrew the following preamble and resolutions were unanimously adopted: Whereas it has pleased Almighty God to remove from earth our young friend and fellow student T J Pettigrew who by upright conduct and amiamble qualities had won the regard of his companions. Therefore Resolved first: that while we mourn his death we humbly submit to the will of God and endeavor to make the event profitable to ourselves. Resolve second: that we tender to the parents and friends of the deceased our sympathy and in their behalf implore the sustaining grace of the most high. Resolve third: that we wear the usual badge of mourning 30 days. My dear Lauretta altho you must know that it is a great trial to all of us not to be with him in his last moments but it is the hand of him that erreth not and we must be still for he is God. He had a right to dispose of me and mine as he pleases. I have been so far wonderfully supported taking all things into consideration. That day 6 weeks that he left home in the bloom of health, his remains started back to us. Just imagine for a moment what our feelings must of been when we met dear George bowed down with grief but he says that he had as kind friends as if they were his relations. We were not denied the priviledge of beholding his face in death. He was placed in a metallic coffin with glass over his (torn)...looked very pleasant and quite natural. Eleanor[11] is near her confinement. I expect to go there this evening but I will return tomorrow for George is taking the measles. I will finish this letter when I return.

29   I have returned from Josephs. I will finish this letter. They are all well at Josephs but a man that is helping to paint Josephs house, he has the measles but he stays upstairs and none goes where he is but those that has had them. All of the children has had them but the 2 youngest.[12]   Eleanor will be confined before you receive this.[13]   George[14] is still in bed with the measles. They have not come out good yet. Mary Brown is in bed today with a bad cold. Cousin Hepsey Woods[15] dropped dead the day after Jefferson was buried which was this day week. The dear old soul was here. Yes she came to see us in our distress and truly sympathised (sic) with us. She was quite infirm. She had been upstairs conversing with me not more than 20 minutes before she dropped dead. She was anxious to start home and all of us opposed her as the day was very cold and cloudy. Cousin E. Pettigrew[16] came upstairs in the room where we were. Aunt Hepsy got up and told her to go with her. I thought they had only stepped in one of the other rooms until I heard the screams downstairs. I heard Eugenias[17] voice first. The first thought that struck me was that Eugenia was on fire. I went down and there was Aunt H on the floor in the dining room and both White and Black round her doing all they could to bring her to, but all

in vain. Her spirit had taken its flight. Mary[18] says that she gave only three very faint gasps. She was just eating a soft boiled egg and was standing by cousin E Pettigrew. About 6 weeks before, she fell and was apparently dead for some time. Cousin Ann[19] told me there was a great struggle in the system when she was coming to. If she had of started home the day she died I don't know what Joe Brunson would have done, no one with her but him. I feel thankful that she was here. The hands of the Lord was (torn)...it all for cousin Ann and Mr. Backhouse[20] was just going to start to her home. Cousin Ann had her bonnet on to start and if Aunt H had of been at home what would they have done there. Rosanna[21] at the schoolhouse perhaps for it took place at 11 o'clock, Maria in the field at work. There would of been no one by but Martha Hunter. I suppose you have heard that brother Lide[22] and 8 of his negroes died of Cholera on their way to Texas. All of the family had cholera, white and black, but three. Sister Martha[23] and two of her children are out here on a visit. They intend to stay all the year. I think she will move and settle in Darlington for she has no land in Alabama and nothing to induce her to settle there. She was rejoiced at getting with all of us again. Dear child, she passed through a great deal of stress last year in a strange land and no one to even seek provisions for her family or to direct her what to do until her son-in-law[24] come to her. He is a son indeed for he was sick when he got her letter but he went to her and brought them back altho he had to be months from his wife and child. Sister Martha is fat and harty. Eugenia sends her love to all of you. Mary Brown sends love to all. George and Edward sends their love to all. Tell Blackwell[25] he must write to George and Edward. Tell him I will get Edward to write to him soon. Tell him it won't be long until he has the measles bad. Tell Mary[26] I will write to her soon. Well

Lauretta I about know that you can make out all of this scroll but I hope you can for I love to write long letters to you. Give my love to Cousin David. Tell him that I hope he is striving to prepare for that awful change that waits him, to think on the two in the bloom of youth that has left this family never to return and that they loved him. Does he not wish to meet them where parting is no more? Tell him I entreat of him to seek the Lord with his Heart and he will be found of Him. Give my love to all of the children and accept of a great deal from your dear Aunt.

E B Pettigrew

I have received no answer to my last. Do write soon.

FOOTNOTES

[1] Thomas Jefferson Pettigrew (7/1/1837--3/17/1855), up to that time was the oldest surviving son of Elizabeth & James Pettigrew.

[2] George W. Pettigrew (9/29/1838--5/21/1910), James and Elizabeth's second oldest son.

[3] Olivia Albertina Pettigrew (7/23/1833--8/4/1852), sister of Thomas. Many of Elizabeth and James Pettigrew's children are buried in the family plot on the old Samuel Blackwell, II. plantation property at Burches Crossroads, 3 miles south of Florence, SC.

[4] Isabella Blackwell Wingate.

[5] Anna Eugenia Pettigrew.

[6] General Joseph Nettles, husband of Elizabeth's sister, Hannah Blackwell Gee Nettles.

⁷ Martha Blackwell Lide, who was widowed in May, 1854 while moving to Texas from Alabama was evidently visiting her sister Isabella in Darlington at the time.

⁸ James Clement Furman (12/5/1809--3/3/1891), was the son of Richard Furman, founder of Furman University. He married Harriet Dargan, daughter of Timothy Dargan, III. and Lydia Keith. Harriet Dargan Furman was the first cousin of James Alexander Pettigrew, whose mother Susannah Dargan was the sister of Timothy Dargan, III.

⁹ George W. Pettigrew.

¹⁰ John Caroline Blackwell (4/11/1837--3/22/1910), son of Samuel Blackwell, III. and his first wife, Caroline Matilda Hunter.

¹¹ Mary Ann Eleanor Pettigrew Harrell.

¹² William Lewis Harrell (b. 1852) and Julius Dargan Harrell (b. 6/30/1853).

¹³ Eleanor Pettigrew Harrell delivered her son Thomas Jefferson Harrell in April, 1855.

¹⁴ George W. Pettigrew.

¹⁵ Hepzibah (Dargan) Woods (1781--3/22/1855), daughter of Rev. Timothy Dargan, II. and Ann Beasley and wife of Joseph Woods. She was the aunt of James A. Pettigrew, the sister of his mother Susannah Dargan.

¹⁶ Elizabeth Sparks Pearce Pettigrew, widow of Robert A. Pettigrew, cousin of James A. Pettigrew.

¹⁷ Eugenia Pettigrew.

¹⁸ Mary Brown.

[19] Edith Ann Woods Backhouse, daughter of Hepzibah Dargan and Joseph Woods, wife of John A. Backhouse, and member of Ebenezer Church.

[20] John A. Backhouse, Baptist Minister, in 1844 had been associated with Rev. James Morris at Ebenezer Baptist Church.

[21] Rosanna E. Woods, daughter of Hepzibah Dargan and Joseph Woods, operated a boarding school in the Doneraile section of Darlington.

[22] Eli Hugh Lide.

[23] Martha Johnson Blackwell Lide.

[24] Lawrence E. Dawson, Jr., husband of Caroline E. Lide, Martha's daughter, evidently left his home in Camden, Ouchita, AR when his father-in-law, Eli Lide died in route to Texas to bring the family back to their former home in Dallas Co., AL.

[25] Samuel Blackwell Gulledge.

[26] Mary Eleanor Gulledge, Lauretta's daughter.

Elizabeth Blackwell Pettigrew
          to Lauretta McBride Gulledge

        Darlington So Car   June the 13 55

My dear Lauretta

    I received your letter on the 12 and am truly glad to hear from you all but sorry to hear of the distress that you are in. I am truly sorry to hear that cousin Davys[1] health is so bad for well do I know what bad health is but I know that it must be very distressing to both of you when you look around on your dear children that are wholy (sic) dependant on both of you for a support and their father not able to assist you. Lauretta you know that I am a true friend to you and yours and was it in my power to assist you and your family in any way you know that I would not hesitate one moment for when it is known to me that you are in distress I am distressed too. You know that not one of those that closes my bowels of compassion against those that are flesh and bone of my bone. Was is it in my power my ever dear Lauretta to put you in possession of every requisite means for you and your family to get from where you are and place you in a more comfortable situation most gladly would I do it. You must not think hard of me for writing in this way for I am only expressing the sincere feeling of my heart. Yes you may be well assured that there is one heart that will ever share in your joys and sorrows until it ceases to beat. I have no doubt if you get to Florida but what it will be of infinite service to Cousin Davids health for the climate is said to be so mild none of those sudden changes from cold to hot to hot to cold. It is neither very hot nor very cold. There is very seldom frost. There is game in abundance, oranges a-plenty, groves of them in the woods. Cousin Margaret Withers[2] has ate some that grew near cousin James.[3] She says they were nice. Cousin Margaret is here at this time. I expect she will spend the summer and fall with us. She is delighted that she has got with some of her mothers[4] relations. She sends her love to you. Cousin James Commander started a barrel of oranges on a boat to me; directed the barrel to the care of Mr Pettigrews factor; wrote to Mr P's factor to direct the barrel to the depot near us and have it put on the train but I suppose from what I have heard the boat took them to Savannah instead of to Charleston so I have not received them. I will write to Cousin James as soon as I can but I am scarcely able to write this scroll of a letter to you. I feel and have felt for several days as if there is a spell of sickness before me. it is all I can do to keep up. Dysentery is prevaling in this country. There has been and still is a good many cases in our family. I do not know that there is a family in this neighborhood but what some of the family has it. The measles has been in our family. I believe it was the measles that my dear son Thomas[5] had that caused his death. They did not come out on him but fell on his lungs. George[6] took them a few days after he got home. They went very hard with him. He is not entirely over the effects of them. At one time I began to think they would teminate fatal. It was after the measles had disappeared for weeks, he was nearly all the time with bowel infection. It seems to me that I never knew the effects of the measels to remain in the system so long after them as it has with all that has had it here both black and white. We have the Whooping Cough among our little negroes. I am fearful it will go very hard with them as it is so short a time since they had the measles. We lost one with the measles, Marys youngest. Aneky has a baby just two weeks old. Irene has a daughter a few days older. Sary[7] has a daughter a few weeks older. I fear if they take the cough, particular Anekys for hers is such a delicate looking little thing that they will hardly get over it. Your brother[8] has a pretty little boy.[9] He is a fat little fellow; grows finely. They were quite well when I heard from them. It is seldom that I see them. I am very anxious for you to move to Florida. True I would like to have you near me but I believe from all the accounts that I have heard of Florida I think Cousin Davy could do better there than here. The last letter that I received from cousin James he wrote to me to direct letters to Orange Lake, Florida. I will write to him as soon as I can but you must not wait to receive a letter from him or me. Write to him as soon as you get this. Let him know that you are a sister to Sam. He has seen your brother. He went to Georgetown with Eugenia and Olivia[10] and stayed two weeks at Cousin James house. You must not be backward in writing to Cousin James. I may write to him before you get this. I will write him as soon as I feel better. The last letter I received from him he said he would soon write Eugenia a long letter giving her a description of the neighbourhood (sic) he lives in. He is delighted with the country. He thinks if I would visit them and spend one winter with them that I would be freed from rheumatism. He wrote me word that if a man would go there and exert his energy with the Blessing of Providence he might attain to the highest round in Fortune's ladder. Josephs[11] family are all well but two of the children has the whooping cough. Eleanor[12] has a fine son a little better than two months old. They have named him Thomas Jefferson.[13] Brother Johns[14] family are well. I received a letter from the old Lady that my dear Thomas[15] boarded with. She writes very cheering news as it respects the state of his mind on the subject of religion. She says that he was under deep concern when he first went to live with her; that she spoke of it to Brother James Furman[16] hoping that he would talk to him. I have not room to write all of letter here but I will copy it off soon and envelop it and send it to you for your satisfation and you must copy that and send to Louisa.[17] Have you got my letter that bore the intelligence of Thomas death. You said not a word about it. The family join me in love to all of you. I will now have to close. Your true friend and affectionate Aunt.

E B Pettigrew

FOOTNOTES

[1] David Gulledge.

² Margaret Walker Withers, daughter of John Walker and Margaret Commander and a widow.

³ James M. Commander was born in 1818, the son of Samuel Commander and Elizabeth Allston, and grandson of James Commander, I. Samuel Commander was the brother of Elizabeth's mother.

⁴ Margaret Commander Walker was the daughter of James Commander, I. and sister of Elizabeth's mother.

⁵ Thomas Jefferson Pettigrew (7/1/1837--3/17/1855) had died while attending school in Greenville, SC.

⁶ George W. Pettigrew (9/29/1838--5/21/1910).

⁷ Mary, Aneky, Irene, and Sary were slaves.

⁸ Samuel Blackwell McBride had married Joanna Louisa Burch his first cousin in February, 1854.

⁹ James Burch McBride was born 11/24/1854.

¹⁰ Anna Eugenia Pettigrew and the late Olivia Albertina Pettigrew, daughters of Elizbeth and James, along with Samuel McBride, their cousin had visited James M. Commander and his family at their old home in Georgetown, SC in December, 1851.

¹¹ Joseph Louis Harrell.

¹² Mary Ann Eleanor Pettigrew Harrell, wife of Joseph and daughter of Elizabeth and James Pettigrew.

¹³ Thomas Jefferson Harrell, born April, 1855 was obviously named for Eleanor's brother Thomas Jefferson Pettigrew who had died in March, 1855.

[14] John Hamlin Blackwell, MD.

[15] Thomas Jefferson Pettigrew.

[16] James Clement Furman, Baptist minister and professor at Furman University, was the son of Richard Furman, the founder. He married Harriet Dargan, first cousin of James A. Pettigrew.

[17] Louisa McBride Woodward, born 5/22/1823, Lauretta's sister, married Thomas Woodward and moved to Jasper Co., MS.

Elizabeth Blackwell Pettigrew
            to Lauretta McBride Gulledge

            Darlington Dis So Car Nov the 24 1855

My dear Lauretta

           I have been thinking for some time that I
would write to you but I have been so unwell
that I put it off from time to time hoping that
I would feel better, but I am still suffering a
good deal with the rheumatismm but I try to
bear it patiently knowing that every pain and
every affliction that I have passed through or
may have to pass through is all appointed by
Divine Wisdom. Therefore it is my will to bow
in humble submission to his holy and righteous
will knowing that all things shall work
together for good to them that love the Lord.
The rest of the family are all well. Mr
Pettigrew[1] is as fleshy as he was when you left
here but he cannot stand the fatigue that he
could a few years back. I think he has failed
a great deal since the death of our dear
children.[2] Josephs[3] family are all well.
Eleanor[4] is quite fleshy. Her little boy[5]
grows finely. He is a pretty baby but not
prettyer (sic) than dear little Julius[6] the one
that died last winter. I never felt my heart
twine around a child more in my life than it
did around that dear little one that was so
soon to be taken and transplanted in a fairer
garden. Mr. P[7] often cautions me about little
Thomas. He says that he is afraid that we are
a going to love him as we did Julius and he
will not be raised. Brother Johns[8] family are
all well but Cousin Elizabeth Pettigrew[9] is
quite sick. Brother Johns daughter[10] professes
to be converted. She has not joined the Church
yet. She says that she was seriously impressed
for some time before the death of my dear
Thomas but after his death that her convictions
were deepened when she would think how short a

time it had been since he had been with her and
to think that he was then in eternity. Brother
John is a very pious man. He makes very good
prayers. He has prayers regular in his family.
Your brother[11] has a pretty little boy.[12] I
expect he can walk by this time. Cousin
Margaret Withers,[13] Betty Harrel,[14] Edward,[15]
and myself went to Sams[16] in September. They
were all well and getting along very well.
Lou[17] said that Mr and Mrs Witherspoon[18] was
very kind to them. Mrs Witherspoon brought her
plates, spoons, cups, saucers, tumblers, sheets
and I think knives and forkes. They let Lou
have a nurse for her baby and a nice negro
woman to be about the house and cook; also a
boy. I have not heard from them since I was
there, but I hope I shall soon. Harriet
McElvene[19] is a widow. Her husband died in
July. She has five children and will have
another in two or three months. Ursula
Muldrows[20] husband died in July. She has four
children. Amelia Lane,[21] cousin Eleanor
Lanes[22] youngest daughter is dead. Cousin
Jerry Dargan[23] died very sudden. He started
from the Village[24] to come to Ebenezer Church
Meeting and stopped at Oliver Cogshells where
Sam Green formerly lived on some business.
Before he got in the house he began to throw
up. There was no one at Cogshells but the
servants and before anyone could be got to him,
altho the servants sent after their master and
after Theodore and Julius,[25] he was dead before
any of them got there. No white person was
present when he died. There has been a great
revival at the Village lately. There was 40
persons immersed, two of cousin John Dargans[26]
sons, one of cousin Edwins,[27] 2 of Juliuses[28]
and Samuel Blackwell[29] were a part of the
number. Sister Isabella[30] has been quite sick
but was on the mend when I last heard from her.
Manly Wingate[31] has another daughter. He lives
at Wake Forest. He is one of the professors of
that institute. I have written cousin James
Commander[32] and have received an answer. He

said in his letter that he had not written to you. That I did not say in my letter to him whether you was a relation of his or not and that he did not know how to address you; that he might of give offence had he not of addressed you as a relation. I was under that impression that I had written him that you and Samuel McBride are brother and sister. I do not know how it was that I did not for that was one thing that I wished him to know for he expressed so much pleasure to me at meeting with his fathers[33] near relatives but I now that I must of made the mistake for I recollect that I was quite unwell the day that I wrote to him for I had put off writing to him so long that I felt that I must try to write. I have written to him and let him know that you are as nearly related to him as my children. As it respects Florida he says it is a great poor mans country. Nowhere is there a better return for labour. He says his neighbourhood is healthy. He says that pneumonia or pleurisy is seldom in that climate. He says that he heard a Physician who has practised there for 18 years say that he never knew a case where flannel was worn next the skin. As I am in so much pain that I cant write all that Cousin James wrote to me I will envelope his letter to me and send it to you and you must be sure to write him. I have just received a letter from Cousin Margaret Withers.[34] She spent the summer with us; returned home last month. One of her granddaughters is to be married soon. She told me when ever I wrote to you or any of sisters[35] children to be sure to send her love. She is very anxious to see all of you. Give my love to Cousin David[36] and all of your children and accept of the same yourself from your Aunt.

                          E B Pettigrew

P S I have Olivias[37] and Thomases[38] degarotypes (sic) that I can look at. They are the express image of them. I know were you to see them you would know whose they were. Eugenia[39] is at Josephs.[40] Mary Brown and George and Edward[41] sends love to all of you. Tell cousin Davy that George is as tall as he is. Edward is rather on the chunky order. Betty Harrel[42] is as tall as her mother. Mary Harrel[43] is little and slim.

FOOTNOTES

[1] James Alexander Pettigrew.

[2] Six of James and Elizabeth's 11 children had died, the most recent being Thomas Jefferson on 3/17/1855 at age 17 and Olivia Albertina on 8/4/1852 at age 19.

[3] Joseph Louis Harrell.

[4] Mary Ann Eleanor Pettigrew Harrell.

[5] Thomas Jefferson Harrell, born April 1855.

[6] Julius Dargan Harrell (7/30/1853--Winter 1854/5).

[7] James Alexander Pettigrew.

[8] John Hamlin Blackwell, MD.

[9] Elizabeth Sparks Pearce Pettigrew (5/14/1812--7/4/1884), widow of Robert A. Pettigrew who was a first cousin of James A. Pettigrew.

[10] Carrie (Caroline) Aletha Blackwell, daughter of John Hamlin Blackwell and his first wife Aletha Windom. Caroline Blackwell was baptised at Ebenezer Church in September 1857.

[11] Samuel Blackwell McBride.

[12] James Burch McBride (11/24/1854--7/29/1924).

[13] Margaret Walker Withers, daughter of Margaret Commander and John Walker.

[14] Elizabeth Susanna Harrell, born in 1842, Elizabeth's granddaughter, daughter of Eleanor Pettigrew and Joseph Louis Harrell.

[15] Joseph Edward Pettigrew.

[16] Samuel Blackwell McBride.

[17] Joanna Louisa Burch, daughter of Edward Sebrey Burch and Joanna White Blackwell, Elizabeth's sister, was the wife of Samuel McBride, her first cousin.

[18] Col. John D. Witherspoon (3/17/1778--4/2/1860) of Society Hill and his wife Elizabeth Boykin (1786--9/1861). Col. Witherspoon owned 2400 acres on Witherspoon Island in Lowther's Lake. Samuel McBride was the overseer for him and received the use of a house as part of his job.

[19] Harriet McIlvane (b. 1815) wife of H. W. McIlvane, (b. 1823), in 1850 had children: Elizabeth (b.1843), Sarah (b. 1844), Mary (b. 1846), James L. (b. 1848) and Martha E. (b. July, 1850).

[20] Ursula Muldrow (born 1826), the wife of Samuel W. Muldrow (born 1822).

[21] Amelia Lane, daughter of James Lane Jr. (11/24/1790--8/20/1844) and Martha Eleanor Adair (born 11/1/1794).

[22] Martha Eleanor Adair Lane.

[23] Jeremiah Dargan (1808--8/4/1855), son of Deacon Timothy Dargan, III and Lydia Keith,

brother of Rev. J.O.B Dargan, and a deacon in Ebenezer Baptist Church.

24 The present city of Darlington, SC.

25 Theodore Alonzo Dargan, MD. (8/15/1822--9/10/1881) and Julius Alfred Dargan (1816--3/1861) an attorney, were brothers of Jeremiah Dargan. All were sons of Timothy Dargan, III. and Lydia Keith.

26 John Orr Beasley Dargan, Baptist Clergyman and brother of Jeremiah, Theodore, Timothy, Edwin, George, Sidney, Charles, and Julius Dargan. J.O.B. Dargan and his wife Margaret Jane Lide had 5 sons and 2 daughters.

27 William Edwin Dargan (7/13/1811--12/11/1851) married Sarah Thomas DuBose in October, 1838. They had 4 sons and 2 daughters.

28 Julius Alfred Dargan married Martha J. Woods.

29 Samuel Issac Blackwell (10/11/1834--9/3/1898) was the son of Samuel Blackwell, III., Elizabeth B. Pettigrew's brother, and his first wife Caroline Matilda Hunter.

30 Isabella Blackwell Wingate, (b. 9/21/1805) widow of William Wingate.

31 Washington Manley Wingate (7/28/1828--2/27/1879), son of William and Isabella B. Wingate married Mary Elizabeth Webb.

32 James M. Commander, son of Samuel Commander and Elizabeth Allston was Elizabeth's first cousin, both being grandchildren of James Commander, I.

33 Samuel Commander was the brother of Elizabeth Blackwell Pettigrew's mother.

34 Margaret Walker Withers, whose mother, Margaret Commander was a sister to Elizabeth Pettigrew's mother.

35 Mary Jane Blackwell McBride.

36 David Gulledge.

37 Olivia Albertina Pettigrew who died 8/4/1852.

38 Thomas Jefferson Pettigrew died 3/17/1855.

39 Anna Eugenia Pettigrew.

40 Home of Joseph Louis Harrell and Eleanor Pettigrew Harrell, sister of Eugenia.

41 George W. and Joseph Edward Pettigrew.

42 Elizabeth Susanna Harrell (born 1842) daughter of Joseph Louis and Eleanor Pettigrew Harrell. Elizabeth Blackwell Pettigrew's granddaughter.

43 Mary Eugenia Harrell (born 1844), also a daughter of Joseph and Eleanor Harrell.

Elizabeth Blackwell Pettigrew
        to Lauretta McBride Gulledge

        Sept the 9 1856   Darlington

My ever Dear Lauretta

I have received your very welcom (sic) letter and was truly pleased to hear from you for it has been a long time since I have heard from you or Louisa[1] and as for Sam[2] I have not seen him in better than a year and Cousin Maggy,[3] Betty Harrel,[4] and myself went to see them but if Sam does not care for me it is not worth my while to let it fret me. I know he is closedly confined overseeing but he could come to see me once in a year. Lauretta I hardly know to commence to let you know what distess I have passed through this year for I do not wish to murmur for it could have been a great deal worse and I feel that the Lord has been merciful. I was so bad off with the rheumatism in the winter and the winter was so severe that I had to keep my room from the first of Feb until April. In the last of May I went to Josephs[5] and I was taken very bad off there with inflamation of the womb and had to stay there for a month and then had to be brought home in the carriage on a mattress. In a few days after I got home Mr Pettigrew was taken sick and he never had such a spell in all his life. Everyone that saw him thought he would die. His disease was inflamation of the brain. He had high fevers with it. He was for two months confined to bed. Brother John[6] and Dr Jarrott[7] attended him. They had to keep the room dark and the house as still as possible. All the time he was so sick I was not able to be out of bed, only to go from one room to the other and lye (sic) down. Brother John said if he had not of had the best of nursing that he would of died. Sister Isabella[8] has been very kind. She came and stayed with us the greater part of of the time that Mr. Pettigrew was at the worse and nursed him by day and by night. If she had of been his own sister she could not of been any kinder. I know I shall never forget her for her kindness. I am still suffering greatly with the rheumatism. I fear that I will never be any better for it is a task for me to write all the writing that I do. I do it lying down. Aneky[9] died on the 6 of August. She left 3 children. She left an infant daughter three months old. Dice[10] died the 17 of September. They were both of them perfectly resigned to death. I miss them very much for Aneky was a good seamstress and Dice was the one that waited on me, helped me to dress and attended to me when I was sick. John[11] died the 5 of this month. You recollect Senys[12] youngest child. He was the one that Mr Pettigrew kept about the yard to get his horse for him and to go on errands and do any little job about the yard or lot. Mr Pettigrew will miss him very much. John was not 15 but he was nearly a man in size. Mr Pettigrew has not entirely recovered from his sickness but he has got so that he can ride about. Eugenia[13] is well. The boys[14] were well the last I heard from them. Cousin Margaret Withers is here. She is well. She sends love to you and your children. Mary Brown is not well today. Eleanor[15] had a son born on the 29 of Sep.[16] You wish to know the names of Eleanors children: Elizabeth Susana; Mary Eugenia; James Alexander; Sarah Ann, she is dead; John Edward; Samuel Joseph; William Lewis; Julius Dargan, he is dead; Thomas Jefferson; George Washington. You see Eleanor lacks but one of having as many as I have. Well Lauretta, Aunty will soon have no single daughter for Eugenia and Joseph Wingate[17] is to be married on the 19 of Nov. There is several weddings to take place. Eugenia sends love to you, cousin David and the children. Give my love to cousin Davy and all of the children. Tell them that I wish to see them very much. Let me know if you have ever wrote to Cousin James[18] and if he answered your letter. Well Lauretta I must now close by sending much love to you.

       Elizabeth B. Pettigrew

FOOTNOTES

[1] Louisa McBride Woodward (born 5/22/1823), sister of Lauretta and Samuel.

2   Samuel Blackwell McBride.

3   Margaret Walker Withers.

4   Elizabeth Harrell, Elizabeth's granddaughter.

5   Joseph Louis Harrell, who lived in Darlington Village.

6   John Hamlin Blackwell, MD.

7   James H. Jarrott, MD., was a prominent landowner in Florence.

8   Isabella Blackwell Wingate.

9   Aneky was a slave.

10   Dice was also a slave.

11   A slave.

12   A slave.

13   Eugenia Pettigrew.

14   George W. and Joseph Edward Pettigrew were away at school at Furman Institute in Greenville, SC.

15   Eleanor Pettigrew Harrell.

16   George Washington Harrell. Elizabeth Pettigrew must have written this letter in stages as she frequently did since it is dated 9 September 1856 and she indicates Eleanor's son was born 29 September.

17   Joseph Edward Wingate (1830--1888) was the son of Isabella Ann Blackwell, (Elizabeth's sister) and William W. Wingate. Eugenia Pettigrew was his first cousin.

[1] James M. Commander, who was living in Ocala, FL.

Elizabeth Blackwell Pettigrew to Lauretta McBride Gulledge

Sep the 1 1859 Darlington So Car

My dear Lauretta

Several months has passed since I received your last letter. I have been quite sick since. I was taken with severe bowel affection and fever. I had but little hope that I would ever be able to be up again. Brother John[1] visited me every day for a week and for two weeks every other day and after that not so often. I have had very sore eyes ever since then. It will take several days for me to write this letter for I cannot look at anything long. I still suffer a great deal with rheumatism. Mr Pettigrew has been quit complaining for some time but keeps up. The rest of the family are well but our family is quite small for Eugenie[2] has gone to houskeeping so we have but one of our children with us. George[3] is with us. He attends to the farm this year. Next year he expects to keep batchlors (sic) hall. His father has had a small house built on the hickory hill between the mill place and where we use to live. His father has given the mill place and the place where we lived to him and Edward.[4] You know Joseph Harrel[5] bought as far as the branch before the house. The rest of it with the mill place he says is for them. So George is a going there to try his luck at farming. Edward is in Greenville. He has entered college. He says he will go until he graduates. George got tired and quit. He did not get through.

Edward will make a hansome (sic) man. He has improved very much in his looks within a few months and he conducts himself so well that he is thought a great deal of by all that know him. He is a steady boy. He reads his Bible everyday and never goes to bed without falling on his knees first. He has followed this for better than four years. There has been many changes taken place since we saw each other last. My children were none of them grown but Ellen.[6] Now they are all grown but Edward, that is a living, and he is almost grown. Eugenias[7] little girl[8] is a running all about and tries hard to talk. She can say a few words. She is sick at this time with a sore mouth and fever. The rest of their family is well. Joseph Harrells family are well. Eleanor will get down in October. That will be 12 for her, one more than I have had. She is fat and harty. I have not seen your brother[9] in nearly two years. He is still with Mr. Witherspoon.[10] I suppose you have heard of the death of your sister, Caroline.[11] She died quite happy. Said she wished no tears shed for her. She died with the disease your mother[12] died with.[13] She left an infant a few weeks old and three other children. She had been a member to the Baptist church for better than two years. I have heard that the minister that preached her funeral sermon and preached at the church where she held her membership has taken the infant. His name is Stought. They have no child of their own. Cousin Betsy Hepburn[14] is numbered with the dead. She died on the 22 of Aug just before sunset. Ursula sent for me the day she died. I got there about 2 hours before her death. She was speechless when I got there. I sat by her and saw her breath (sic) her last, in less than a week after Ursula lost her youngest child. He was better than 4 years old, a beautiful child, the prettiest she had. Cousin Ursula Cogdel has broke up housekeeping. She lived with cousin Betsy last year and this. I am truly (glad) that yourself and Mary[15] has obtained a hope in Christ and united with the people of God. May the Lord be with both of you and bless you with the influences of his Spirit to assist you in loving and serving him in an acceptable manner. You know that I could hear nothing from you that could give me as great pleasure. How is it with cousin David. I hope he is in search of the Good Old Way. Does he not wish his fathers God to be his? What would it profit him if he could gain the whole world and lose his immortal soul. I hope he will strive to enter in at the straight gate. Tell him I hope he is trying to prepare to meet his God. You said in your lettr that you did not (torn) all of the Baptist Doctrines. I s(torn) what ones you disapprove of. If it is what is called Close Communion I do not think they should be censured for not communing with persons that have not been baptised as it would laying aside baptism as an ordinance. Blackwell Burch[16] has been here since I began this letter. He was in Chesterfield when your sister died. He says her infant is a son. She left two others,[17] a son and a daughter. He said he heard her funeral sermon preached. It was preached by the man that has taken her infant to raise. Blackwell said he preached an excellent sermon and that he is a nice looking man and that his wife is a nice lady. Blackwell would of went to Carolines burial but he did not know on what day she was to be buried. Solomon Wilsons wife died day before yesterday. I hope she is gone to rest for he treated her dreadfull (sic) bad. Mrs Hewet died before Cousin Betsey. Give my love to cousin David and all of your children. I hope if we never meet on earth that we may meet on Cannons (sic) happy shore where parting will be no more. I will put the mulberry seed in this (torn) for Mary.[18] Mary Annah[19] (torn) married to Sephus Cole.[20] I wish you (torn) write as often as you can to your affectionate Aunt

       E B Pettigrew

Sept the 7

Today I am fifty seven years old. Edward[21] is 18.

FOOTNOTES

[1] John Hamlin Blackwell, MD.

[2] Anna Eugenia Pettigrew, Elizabeth and James daughter, married her first cousin, Joseph Edward Wingate on October 26, 1856.

[3] George W. Pettigrew.

[4] Joseph Edward Pettigrew.

[5] Joseph Louis Harrell, Elizabeth's son-in-law.

[6] Mary Ann Eleanor Pettigrew Harrell.

[7] Anna Eugenia Pettigrew Wingate.

[8] Jenny Wingate, probably born about 1857, died young.

[9] Samuel Blackwell McBride.

[10] Col. John D. Witherspoon of Society Hill, SC.

[11] Mary Caroline McBride Baker, wife of William Baker of North Carolina.

[12] Mary Jane Blackwell McBride.

[13] Caroline and her mother each died probably of postpartum complications.

[14] Elizabeth Hepburn, widow of Robert Hepburn.

[15] Mary Eleanor Gulledge, Lauretta's daughter.

[16] John Blackwell Burch (5/11/1837-- 3/12/1913), son of Edward Sebrey Burch and Joanna White Blackwell, Elizabeth's sister.

[17] In this same letter, Elizabeth says Caroline left three other children, in addition to the newly born infant.

[18] Mary Eleanor Gulledge, Lauretta's daughter.

[19] Mary Annah Blackwell (5/29/1841-- 5/25/1877), daughter of Samuel Blackwell, III. and his second wife Sarah Harrell.

[20] Cephus Cole, b 1828, VA.

[21] Joseph Edward Pettigrew.

Elizabeth Blackwell Pettigrew
             to Lauretta McBride Gulledge

                    Florence   June 27 1861

My dear Lauretta

    I have written to Blackwell[1] now I wish to write to you. My family are all well but myself. Both of my daughters family are well. Eleanor[2] has been the mother of nine sons and three daughters. Eugenia[3] has been the mother of one son, two daughters. Both of her first were girls.   Ellen,[4] her second is a very interesting child.   William Pettigrew[5] the youngest is a fine grothy (sic) child. He will be ten months old on the 3 of July. Eleanor[6] is fat and healthy but Jenny[7] is pale and lean. She is her mother in constitution. I do not think she can now stand what I could at her age. I was with Ma[8] at Joseph Harrells[9] last week. She was quite sick at brother Johns[10] when I came home. I went to your brothers[11] when I came on home. The are all well. He has very pretty children. They are pretty behaved also. Lou[12] makes them obey. Lou is a smart industrious woman. Your brother had just received a few lines from your father[13] requesting him (Sam) to go up as quick as possible for he was near his last with a heart affection. Sam went up on Monday. You said in your letter that (illegible) he would have to go to Virginia thinking he might meet with some of his relations there. Edward Nettles[14] is the only one who has gone there yet but Sebry Burch[15] expects to go there in a few days. He has volunteered for three years or during the war. All of the single relations went down to guard Charleston harbour. They went down on the third of January and was discharged the last of April. Edward[16] is at school in Greenville. He will be at home in a few weeks. Their vacation will come on by the middle of July. He made an open profession of religion about three week ago by following his Lord and master into the Baptismal stream and uniting with his people. He is very anxious to go to Virginia. The last letter he wrote me he said he felt miserable when he thought of his countrymen that are in danger and he in safety. He was anxious for the company that he is in to be called out when his brother[17] was on the Island but the Governor said he would not call out students. The company that George[18] was in was called The Darlington Guards. They numbered 104. George was on the Island when THE STAR OF THE WEST was fired into; also when Fort Sumter was taken. I will now write the name of those of the (?) that was in the company. Brantley Pettig,[19] Blackwell Burch,[20] Sebe Burch,[21] R Hepburn,[22] Clem Hepburn,[23] Burch Blackwell,[24] Robert Nettles,[25] Moore that married Mary Ann,[26] Jack Branson who married Hannah Burch,[27] Elihu Muldrow who married Betty Hepburn.[28] All of your Aunt

Annas[29] daughters are married but the youngest.[30] Emma is married to John Blackwell.[31] Not long since she gave birth to twins, a boy and a girl but they were untimely. Mary Ann[32] has no child. Her health is bad all the time. She has a good husband. Hannah[33] has one little girl. Betty[34] has 3, one boy, two girls. James Burch[35] has a girl and a boy. Sam Jo Burch[36] has 4 but one girl. They had two girls but the oldest got burnt so it died. Martha that lived with you a while has become a useful woman. She is married but has no children. Her health is bad. She is thought well of by people of the highest standing. She is in the Baptist church. Has been a member for several years. All of brother Sams[37] children are married but James.[38] Mary Anna[39] has a daughter. Betty[40] has a son and a daughter. Amantha P[41] that was, has a son and a daughter, the son the youngest. Cornelia[42] has no child. Brantley[43] is still single. He lives at his mothers place. Emma Nettles[44] married Joseph McCown[45] two weeks ago, James McCowns[46] son. Lou Nettles[47] that was, has three sons. Robert[48] has a son and a daughter. Edward Nettles[49] is married to Simses[50] daughter. Mary Brown and all of the family join me in love to you and all of your family. Write soon to your affecionate Aunt

                    E B Pettigrew

    I have wrote this letter with a pencil because it is the easiest for me. Mary B[51] has a headache today. Martha Russ (possibly Bass) has one child. How pleased I would be to see you for I cannot write hardly as (*illegible*) oldest child and two of Laney Bransons sons are in Virginia. They are in Greggs regiment. Laney has one son in Custers Regiment and two in Greggs. The last foray was at Vienna. Greggs men killed a good many.

FOOTNOTES

1 Samuel Blackwell Gulledge (2/6/1840--7/5/1863), Lauretta and David Gulledge's son. At this time Blackwell had joined the Confederate Army and was in Union City, TN.

2 Mary Ann Eleanor Pettigrew Harrell.

3 Anna Eugenia Pettigrew Wingate.

4 Ellen Wingate, born about 1859/1860.

5 William Pettigrew Wingate born 5/3/1860, died young.

6 Eleanor Pettigrew Harrell.

7 Eugenia Pettigrew Wingate.

8 Mary Ann Hamlin Blackwell (10/8/1786--11/20/1869), widow of Samuel Blackwell, II.

9 Joseph Louis Harrell (11/14/1818--11/14/1877) husband of Eleanor Pettigrew.

10 John Hamlin Blackwell, MD (12/12/1815--1/15/1891).

11 Samuel Blackwell McBride (1821--12/1877).

12 Joanna Louisa Burch McBride (3/9/1832--11/3/1902).

13 William McBride, MD (1/27/1784--8/2/1861).

14 Joseph Edward Nettles (8/24/1836--6/21/1899), son of General Joseph Burch Nettles and Hannah Mara Blackwell, Elizabeth's sister.

15 Sebrey Burch born 1839, son of Edward Sebrey Burch and Joanna White Blackwell, sister of Elizabeth.

[16] Joseph Edward Pettigrew.

[17] George W. Pettigrew.

[18] George W. Pettigrew.

[19] William Brantley Pettigrew (1832--1884), son of Timothy Dargan Pettigrew and Martha L. Lane. Grandson of Robert Alexander Pettigrew and Ann Dargan and James Lane and Rachel Blackwell. His father Timothy Dargan Pettigrew was a first cousin of James Alexander Pettigrew.

[20] John Blackwell Burch (5/11/1837--3/12/1913), son of Edward Sebrey Burch and Joanna White Blackwell.

[21] Sebrey Burch (born 1839), son of Edward Sebrey Burch and Joanna White Blackwell.

[22] Robert Hepburn (born 1836), son of Robert and Elizabeth "Cousin Betsey" Hepburn.

[23] Clement Cogburn Hepburn (7/22/11839--8/9/1921), son of Robert and Elizabeth "Cousin Betsey" Hepburn.

[24] Edward John Burch Blackwell (born 1839), son of John Hamlin Blackwell, MD and his first wife Aletha Windom.

[25] Robert B. Nettles (born 1835), son of General Joseph Burch Nettles and Hannah Mara Blackwell.

[26] Mary Ann Burch (born 1825), daughter of Edward Sebrey Burch and Joanna White Blackwell.

[27] Hannah M. Burch, sister of Mary Ann Burch.

[28] Elihu Muldrow (1831--1907) married Elizabeth S. Hepburn (2/17/1832--11/17/1894), daughter of Elizabeth and Robert Hepburn.

29 Joanna White Blackwell Burch.

30 Ada Burch (born 7/23/1850) was evidently the only single daughter at this time.

31 Emma S. Burch (10/30/1842--9/24/1904) married John Caroline Blackwell (4/11/1837--3/22/1910), the son of Samuel Blackwell, III. and his first wife Caroline Matilda Hunter. They were first cousins.

32 Mary Ann Burch married a Mr. Moore.

33 Hannah Burch married Jack Branson.

34 Elizabeth T. Burch (born 1836).

35 James E. Burch (2/11/1826--4/11/1882). His first wife Mary Sinclair Burch died 8/29/1854.

36 Joseph Samuel Burch (7/13/1828--4/15/1889) married Eugenia Sinkler about 1852.

37 Samuel Blackwell, III (3/17/1807--7/26/1847) had married first Caroline Matilda Hunter and second Sarah Amanda Harrell.

38 James Harrell Blackwell (1/8/1844--5/13/1928), son of Samuel and Sarah Harrell Blackwell. He was to marry Martha Isadora Timmons on 3/1/1865.

39 Mary Annah Blackwell, daughter of Samuel and Sarah Harrell Blackwell, married Cephas Cole in 1859.

40 Elizabeth Isabella Blackwell (11/11/1842--1923), daughter of Samuel and Sarah Harrell Blackwell, married James Tazwell Bristow.

41 Amarintha B. Pettigrew (11/6/1836--8/23/1907), daughter of Timothy Dargan Pettigrew and Martha L. Lane, married Joseph E. McKnight in 1858.

[42] Cornelia Manning Pettigrew (born 1830), daughter of Timothy and Martha Pettigrew, married James A. Tillman circa 5/27/1856.

[43] William Brantley Pettigrew (1832--1884), son of Timothy and Martha Pettigrew, later married Mary Ella Tillman on 7/11/1865.

[44] Emma Nettles, daughter of Joseph Burch Nettles and Hannah Mara Blackwell.

[45] Joseph John McCown (b. 1831), son of James and Hannah McCown.

[46] James McCown (born 1803) son of John and Sarah McCown.

[47] Louisa H. Nettles (born 1833), daughter of General Joseph Burch Nettles and Hannah Mara Blackwell, married Benjamin Catesby Norment, MD (4/25/1833--1/9/1903) on 5/7/1857.

[48] Robert B. Nettles (born 1835) son of Joseph B. and Hannah Blackwell Nettles, married Eugenia Mochelle McCall.

[49] Joseph Edward Nettles (8/24/1836--6/21/1899), son of Joseph B. and Hannah Blackwell Nettles, married Gertrude Lydia Sims (12/6/1839--10/3/1891) on 2/7/1861.

[50] Alexander Dromgoole Sims (6/2/1803--11/22/1848) and Margaret A. P. Dargan, daughter of Timothy Dargan, II., and Lydia Keith, were the parents of Gertrude Lydia Sims.

[50] Mary Brown who lived with the Pettigrews.

The remaining letters in this section which Lauretta had saved are from other members of the family. They are included here as they provide additional information about the family and the times in which they lived.

William McBride[1]
        to Lauretta McBride Gulledge

South Carolina Chesterfield Dist Sept 2 1852

     Yours of the 25th July came duly to hand. We are all well at this time through Mercy. You wish to know something about Carolines[2] illness when I seen her about the first June she was as (torn) as I ever saw anyone to be alive. Her child was three or four months old and she had never been well from the time of confinement untill (sic) she was taken down with a bowel complaint & a bad dry cough. I & my wife[3] went & stayed a week with her and by good nursing & the means or course her physician had her on or was put on after we went. It pleased kind providence to somewhat restore her so that she has visited us and stayed three or four weeks during which time she mended much. And I hear she continues to mend. But I am well satisfied that she will never enjoy health again. I believe her lungs are effected (sic) with tuberculosis & so say her physician who is man of first rate eminence. I think she possibly may live a few years but I think if she is ever again in a situation to be confined that she will not live long afterwards. Our crops are the most promising I ever seen. We have had a very rainy August but the clouds are gone & we have a clear sky.
                             Wm McBride

FOOTNOTES

[1] William McBride, MD (1/27/1784--8/2/1861), Lauretta's father.

[2] Mary Caroline McBride, daughter of William and sister of Lauretta.

[3] Harriet (Bryan) McBride, second wife of William and Lauretta's step-mother.

J. William McBride[1]
        to Lauretta McBride Gulledge

        Chesterfield C H S C   June 1 1878

Dear Sister,

    Your letter of April 25th has been to hand some time. We were very glad indeed to get a letter from you again and very glad to receive the pictures of James & Albert[2] but cannot say which is which. You know it has been seventeen years since I saw them & the features have no doubt changed since then. They both I think have honest good looking faces. The one with the hat on looks like there is mischief in his eye. The other looked more serious when the picture was taken but you know you cannot form correct opinions from a picture to tell whether the subject is lively or solid for the same face may at different times make a dozen different expressions. I think I remember Albert was about four years old when I was with you. I remember how Mary, Dippie, Sallie Lou, Thomas and Blackwell[3] looked also how you and Mr Gulledge[4] looked, but do not remember any of the other faces. Tell the boys I thank them for their pictures & I had some taken a week ago; all my family, viz. my own, wifes, Flora,

Emma, Cora, Sallie, and Jim Burches, my baby. You will see him by looking closely in his mothers lap. He is the only boy we have. He is seven months. Whatever you do please send me yours and Mr Gulledges pictures as you look now. I send you mine, Elizas and Floras now. It seems from the tenor of your letter that you did not know brother Samuel[5] is dead. He died last December. One of Sam Joe Burches[6] sons was up here Christmas and told it. They say he was a good man. He told me 2 1/2 years ago he had then had heart disease 15 years & said he had been compelled to controll (sic) his temper to prevent death. Told me then he had not had a difficulty with anyone during that period enough to give him any trouble. He had bought land since the war & nearly paid for 300 acres land. (i.e. when I saw him). I heard recently his wife was teaching school. Ned[7] was there 1 year ago & told me they were good livers. I don't know what to tell you about mother's[8] death. (I am one who believes that not a large proportion of the human race will be saved). Besides it is hard to tell from appearances here now as the Doctors stuff all their patients when very sick on opium. She was partially under the influence of both opium and chloroform as she died shortly after the Drs quit using the knife on her for you remember they cut her to try to relieve her of Hernae. I will send my picture next time I write you. It was taken too near night & after he painted it I did not want it.

          JWM

All my children had Whooping Cough when the pictures were taken. Makes them look dull.

FOOTNOTES

[1] J. William McBride was Lauretta's half brother, the son of William McBride and his second wife Harriet Bryan.

[2] James Alexander Gulledge (6/21/1856--4/18/1944) and Albert Joseph Gulledge (11/17/1853--12/1/1903) were sons of Lauretta McBride and David Gulledge.

[3] Children of Lauretta and David Gulledge. Mary Eleanor (12/17/1841--1873), Zilpha Ann "Dippie" (9/12/1844--12/1/1881), Sarah Lauretta "Sallie Lou" (12/11/1845--3/21/1878), Thomas Huntley (10/14/1847--10/15/1864), Samuel Blackwell (2/6/1840--7/5/1863).

[4] David Gulledge (9/4/1813--9/14/1895), Lauretta's husband.

[5] Samuel Blackwell McBride, lived in Darlington Co. and married his cousin Joanna Louisa Burch in February, 1854. He is mentioned frequently in Elizabeth Blackwell Pettigrew's letters to her niece Lauretta.

[6] Joseph Samuel Burch (7/13/1828--4/15/1889), son of Edward Sebrey and Joanna White Blackwell Burch was the brother of Louisa Burch McBride, Samuel's wife.

[7] Possibly his brother, Edward H. McBride, (b. 8/30/1849), a doctor.

[8] Harriet Bryan, married William McBride, MD, 8/10/1831 as his second wife.

J. William McBride[1]
            to Lauretta McBride Gulledge

                Chesterfield   Aug 21st 1879

Dear Sister,

     Your letter dated 2nd August came to me yesterday. We were very glad to hear from you; very sorry you have suffered so much from drought. I read in my New York Newspapers of the drought over entire state of Texas and also over many other states of the Union. I have one brother and five sisters in Texas.[2] You and Thom[3] are about the only ones who write to me every year. Thomas is more prompt to write than you. I have had only two letters from Ellen[4] in 17 years tho she seems to think and has told some of my friends in Texas that she thinks a great deal of me & ask if ever I put my foot on Texas soil she intends to see me.
Sister Louisa[5] never writes to me of late years. Please when you write hereafter always say something about her and family. Hennie[6] has written to me twice since she has been in Texas and then on business mostly. Sally[7] don't write. Every sister and brother of mine (except you) now owes me a letter and I never had an answer to my last I wrote you. With great pleasure will I write to you about twice a year as you requested & will I think send in this letter one of my little girls picture. The types of the ones I have of my own is entirely too large and I am not willing to send such ones. The next time I see an artist I will think of you & send you mine. Duncan McGregor of Anson County[8] died recently.
Also Mrs General Hanna of Chesterfield. Perhaps you knew these. Many other citizens have died. Very much more fatal sickness in our county than has been in (a) long time. Old Mrs Becky Hancock's son Joe Pete came in last of July from Alabama to see his old mother. She is mother (of?) Bill Hancock's wife. Pete

has not been here in 14 years & what I stated to say is he says this county is one hundred percent better farming country that when he left here first. He left here in 65/4. Sherman's Army had ruined us temporary. We have improved by manure by using principally guano. We get of an average per acre 200 to 250 pounds in lint cotton, use $4.00 per acre in manure and use geese to pick the grass from the cotton.

I lost much by my move West and have made it back and now have a prospect of living better than I have ever been. I (?) over 3 head of horses I think would (torn) form my (torn) and give 12 bales. I have never (used) my guano myself but one year and that was in a very (easy) one--1871--and I did not pay which caused me never to use any more. I now see so plain that many are making by it. I intend using it next year on my entire farm. I make 18 bales. Corn has been selling in this market for 3 years at 79 cts per bushel cash. Bacon 6 to 12 cts, everything else is likewise. Land can be bought from 11 cts to five dollars cash. Most common cash price for land is $2 to $2.50 per acre. Not much selling for cash. This country is fast returning from a (ruinous?) credit to a cash system of trade on personal and merchandize (sic). Many thousands have been ruined by buying on credit but people are fast learning to live on the cash system (torn) are making money. Write soon.

I am your brother,

J W McBride

FOOTNOTES

[1] J. William McBride son of William McBride and Harriet Bryan was a Confederate veteran.

² Lauretta and David Gulledge had moved from Mississippi to Texas in 1866.

³ Thomas J. McBride, also a son of William and Harriet Bryan McBride, lived in Red River Co., TX.

⁴ Ellen McBride (6/17/1830--9/12/1915), married William Rufus King 10/17/1850, and was living in San Saba Co., Texas in 1880.

⁵ Louisa McBride (b. 5/22/1823) married Thomas Woodward.

⁶ Henrietta McBride married David J. Green (b. 1838, NC) and lived in Collin Co., Texas in 1880. Their children at that time were: Mary A. (b. 1867, NC), Charles D. (b. 1870, TX), Francis R. (b. 1872, TX), Hattie B. (b. 1875, TX) and Addie (b. 1875, TX).

⁷ Sallie E. McBride was living with her sister Henrietta McBride's family in Collin Co., Texas in 1880.

⁸ Anson Co., NC was Lauretta's husband, David Gulledge's home, as well as the birthplace of her father, Dr. William McBride.

Elizabeth Louisa McBride Woodward[1]
    to Lauretta McBride Gulledge

      Jackson La Mar 24 1866

Dear Sister,

  It is with pleasure I again write you a few lines which will inform you myself and family are all well except Crawford, my youngest son, he is having chills.

I received a letter from you about the 8th of Feb written on Oct 11, I think. Mr W and Billy² was both fortunate enough to get back home & if the war had lasted one month longer I do not think either of them would have got home. Thos.³ had been in bad health for 6 or 8 months with diareah (sic). Had liked to died after he came home. He never got entirely well for several months. Billy was real sick when he came home and had a severe spell of pneumonia which like to have taken him off. Had he been in service I am confident he would have died. He is not sound yet tho (sic) he has fleshed up, he has chills occasionally. He is as tall as brother Billy⁴ I think. He is 6 foot & 1 or 2 inches high. Lauretta⁵ is half head taller than I and very straight & slender, a pretty figure if she is tall. She is boarding off from home near enough to come every Friday evening & return Sunday evening. She is going to Miss Laura Spivey. All of the boys are going to school at Douglass. Anna is going to Miss Laura's sister. I fear you will disappoint us in coming to this country. You can't imagine how pleased the children was. I hope you will make a good crop that you will be enabled to move next fall. Thos. says he would be glad that you would come. He says he will help you what he can. Dr Jack W⁶ says he will write to you soon. None of our negroes is with us. Norice is with Stucky where his wife is. I would not keep Lyd. She had two children & was very trifling. We have here at home 5 hands employed & on our other plantation 5 hands. I have a cook hired at 8$ per month. The others here feed and cloth themselves, pay their Drs bill. We find stock, tools & feed for the stock and give them half they make. On the other place they find themselves in everything i.e. what we let them have they pay us for we get one fourth of corn & one fifth of cotton. They built houses to live in & dig a well as they (sic) was no buildings on the land which fell to Thos. His portion which he drew was in land & stock of all kinds. He got nary darkey & I am not sorry of it. If you know anything about fathers family and estate let me hear of it. I have written but have not heard from them yet. I know not whether the Yankees destroyed the place or not. We received a letter from Jesse Woodward[7] last but heard nothing of my relatives. Thos. is at work at a steam mill. He is copartner in the mill with Mr. Busby. You must write soon. The children sends their love to all of you & family. I am fearful you will suffer. It is bad enough here & I know it is bound to be a great deal worse where you are. The army was passing & around you so long I cannot see how the inhabitance (sic) subsist on that side of the river. I think they are borned (sic) to suffer. You will excuse bad writing as I am in a great hurry to send it to the office. Thos. sends his respects to you and family. I remain as ever your most affectionate sister.

           E L W

FOOTNOTES

[1] Elizabeth Louisa (McBride) Woodward (b. 5/22/1823), daughter of Mary Jane Blackwell and Dr. William McBride, married Thomas Woodward.

[2] Thomas Woodward (b. 1822), Louisa's husband and son William McBride Woodward (b. 1848) both served in the Confederate Army during the War.

[3] Thomas Woodward.

[4] J. William McBride, son of Dr. William and Harriet Bryan McBride.

[5] Eleanor Lauretta Woodward (b. circa 1850), daughter of Louisa and Thomas Woodward.

[6] Jack Woodward, brother of Thomas.

[7] Jesse Woodward, brother of Thomas.

PART TWO

LETTERS FROM BLACKWELL

Samuel Blackwell Gulledge, called Blackwell, was the eldest son of David and Lauretta (McBride) Gulledge. He was born in Darlington Co., SC, 6 February 1840 and died of wounds received in the Battle of Gettysburg on 5 July 1863. Wounded, he was carried from the battlefield to Gettysburg Hospital by ambulance by James Gibbs, the night of 1 July. He never regained consciousness.

The obituary in his parent's family Bible reads: "Samuel Blackwell Gulledge departed this life 5 July 1863, aged 23 years 4 months and 29 days. He was mortally wounded in Pennsylvannia during the Battle of Gettysburg. Thus fell one in youth for the Liberty of his Country and died as a Christian at his post. He was much beloved by his family as well as by all others who knew him."

These letters, to Lauretta and David Gulledge, his parents, reflect the thoughts and feelings of a young man: his longing for home, his concern for his family's welfare, his life in the "camps", and his pride in his country. They have been copied as received by the editors, with some slight modifications, such as punctuation for the sake of clarity and better understanding. In a few instances words were inserted ( ) by a previous editor when omissions were apparent.

SAMUEL BLACKWELL GULLEDGE

(2/6/1840--5/5/1863)

Corinth, Miss. May the 17th, 1861

Dear Mother and Father,

I take the opportunity of writing to you a few lines to let you know that we are in Camps. We are all messed out. I will tell you who are in with me, A.B,[1] John and Van Gilbert, Jim and Joe Gibbs, Grinner Gilbert and Martin. We have plenty of flour, bacon, sugar, coffee and beans. Each of us has two blankets. There is about 3,000 troops at this place; we do not expect to stay here long. The probability is we will go to Virginia. We are sure to fight and my only hope of safety is God and that is a great hope, too, if it only holds out. If I live to serve out my twelve months I expect to come home and go to school. Tell Riley[2] that I saw some of the richest land I ever saw as I came on. Give my respects to all the young ladies. So nothing more. Write as soon as you get this letter as we expect to leave her soon. Direct to Corinth, Miss.

We belong to the 13th Regiment of this State.

S B Gulledge

FOOTNOTES

[1] A. B. Stone

[2] Riley W. Wyatt, husband of Blackwell's sister, Zilpha Ann Gulledge (9/12/1844--12/1/1881), and evidently a close friend of Blackwell's as well.

Corinth, Miss. May 24th 1861

Dear Mother,

I received your letter this evening. I was glad to hear from you. I have been sick but am getting better. There was some of our boys sick but not dangerous. You need not fear that I will be a drunkard for it is the most abhorable habit in life. I hope that Pa has put by this time. I wrote you in my last letter that I was satisfied with my mess, but I was mistakened. Martin is the most disagreeable person I ever saw; nothing can please him. We was mustered into the Confederate service yesterday. We are going to Union City, Tenn. in 20 miles of the enemy. We expect to have a battle there....(the letter is cut away at this spot).

There was three Companies passed here today. They was from Mobile. Corinth is about three times as large as Enterprise. It will someday be a large town. I expect to come back to Old Newton in twelve months. I do not believe that I was born for a Yankee to kill me. You need not write until I write again, so nothing more except excuse bad writing. Your most affectionate son.

S B Gulledge

June 2nd 1861

Dear Mother,

As I have an opportunity of sending you a few lines by one of our Company it is with great pleasure I undertake the task. I am well. There is 5,000 soldiers here. I have not received but one letter from Newton since I left. I want you to write soon. Direct it to Union City care of Captain Carlton, R N.

                                                S B Gulledge

(letterhead torn off), Tenn. June 14th 1861

Dear Father,

    I take the present opportunity of writing you a few lines as I believe you will like to hear from me. I have nothing of importance to write but I think it is my duty to write. I am well except for a bad cold. My Dear Father I want to see you all very much but I will put my trust in the Lord that we will meet on earth again. As for being killed by a Blue Bellied Yankee I do not believe that I ever was born to die in that way. A. Stone wrote a letter to his Pa and stated in it that we expected to be ordered to Columbus to engage in a battle, but we have not been yet. He wants you to tell his people about it. I want you to tell all of my friends to write to me for nothing can please me better than to get a letter from them. Martin is sick today but not dangerously. I think I will come to see you all about the 15th of Sept. if we are not too tightly engaged. Tenn. is out of the Union by a large majority. Write as soon as you get my (torn)....the news generally. I want you to tell me where Little Lizzie[1] was buried and tell Riley[2] and Dip[3] I wrote a letter to them yesterday and sent it by Mr. N. Doby. Give my love (to) Mother and all the children, also Dip and Riley and yourself. I will come to a close. Your affectionate son.

                                                S B Gulledge

FOOTNOTES

[1] Possibly a child of Riley and Zilpha Ann (Gulledge) Wyatt.

[2] Riley W. Wyatt, his brother-in-law.

[3] Zilpha Ann (Gulledge) Wyatt, called "Dip" or "Dippy", Blackwell's sister.

Union City, Tenn. June 18th 1861

My Dear Mother,

I received your letter of the 7th yesterday evening with great pleasure. You wrote to me you was afraid I was sick but I was not. The cause of my letter being so short was that Mr. D. Johnston was going home and I did not know that he was going till a few moments before he left. So you must excuse me for it being so short. I am well at present. I wrote a letter to you and Riley a day or two after I got to this place and a few days after it left here it came back to Union. I was very sorry to hear that sweet little Lizzie was dead for I loved her and often thought of her. We are in 4 miles of the Kentucky lines 13 miles from the Mississippi River and 35 miles from Cairo. There was one of the Volunteers died here yesterday. His remains was sent home for burial. One night last week an alarm was given that the enemy was near. Each and every man must now be at his post. We formed a line of battle with loaded arms but it was all a false report. Our chance here is worse than a negroes. We are drilled about 6 hours a day and have to (haul) water 12 miles, wait on the sick, and so on. There is about 75 men sick at the hospital from our regiment. There is about eight thousand volunteers here and about 13000 at Corinth. I said we were being treated worse than negroes but I am perfectly satisfied with my treatment if I only can get a Yankee skalp (sic). We got plank today to floor our tents. Our Captain has been to Memphis and got his Company another uniform. We are to get a regimental uniform before long. The 12th regiment is camped in sight of ours. They have a dance about once a week. The Kentucky ladies come down to the dance. We expect to get our monthly wages on the 23 of this month. If I can obtain money enough I will try to come back to Newton about 15th September. So nothing more at present. Write as soon as you get this letter for nothing can afford me more pleasure than to get a letter from home. I remain your affectionate son.

            S B Gulledge

This letter was written on the back of the previous one.

Dear Father,

  You must excuse me for not writing to you before now for we are kept so tired we have so much to do that it is seldom I can get to write so I hope you will comply with my request. I have written all the news that I know of. I want you to write to me in person. You need not think because I write to Mother personally that I do not think of you. If you do, it is a mistake. I think of you often though we (are) a long way apart. Tell Riley and Dip[1] that I will write to them in a day or two. (Tell) all of them that I an very sorry to hear of their misfortune.[2] I want you to write to me and tell me what sort of crop you have and the news generally.

So nothing more for the present, only write as soon as this come to hand and often. I remain your affectionate son.

            S B Gulledge

FOOTNOTES

[1] Riley W. and Zilpha Ann (Gulledge) Wyatt

[2] Possibly referring to the death of Little Lizzie from the previous letters.

       Union City June 28 61

Dear Mother,

I received your very welcome letter yesterday evening and was glad to here (sic) from you once more. I received a letter from Riley[1] at the same time. You spoke something about sending me some cloths but you need not send them yet as I have as many as I could carry if we were to leave here shortly. We got those vegetables you sent to us and was very glad to get them. You said something about wanting to see my likeness. If you want to see it just ask Miss C. to let you have it two or three days but it is my sincere request that she should have it. Two soldiers died day befor yesterday but we are in very good health at the present. Mr. Graham is going home tonight and I will send this by him. I want you to find out when he is going to start back and send a letter back by him. We have to go out on drill parade and I must close. Write often. I must remain your affectionate son.

            S B Gulledge

FOOTNOTES

[1] Riley W. Wyatt, his friend and brother-in-law.

                      Union City, Tenn. July 3th 61

Dear Mother,

     I received your letter of June the 30th and was glad to hear from you. I am well at this time. I have nothing of importance to say. Mr. C. Childs went to the state line (torn off)...ong since he staid (sic) over his time a (torn) men was sent to arrest him. (He) was brought back and was court-martialed by order of the Captain. He was put under guard two days before his trial came on then sentence was passed on him, 4 hours under guard. There is great dissatisfaction in our Company on the part of the Captain. Last Saturday we went to wash. While gone we held a convinsion (sic), appointed a committy (sic) of five to ask the Captain to resign his office, but he has not done it yet. The measles is in our regiment. Joe Gibbs has them but not dangerous. I have quit my first mess as no man can live with John and Van Gilbert. I now mess with A. B.,[1] Jim, and Joe Gibbs, N. McGee and J. McDaniel. I wish I could be at Newton on the fourth but so it is I cannot be. I have written two letters to Riley[2] and have not received an answer yet. I want you to tell me if you have heard from Uncles Evander[3] and William[4] and tell me where they are what they are doing. There is about 11,000 soldiers at this place, Kentucky has voted a Union ticket by 11,000 majority. I was on guard last night and I am so tired I must come to a close. Write often.
I am your affectionate son.

                                            S B Gulledge

FOOTNOTES

[1] A. B. Stone

[2] Riley W. Wyatt

[3] Evander Calhoun McBride (born 1837), his mother's half brother was killed in 1861.

[4] J. William McBride, brother of Evander C. McBride and half-brother of Lauretta, was serving in the Confederate forces, 12th Louisiana Regiment.

                              Corinth, Miss   July 12   61

My Dear Mother and Father,

    I received a letter from you this evening and was glad to hear from you. We left Union City yesterday expection (sic) to go to Jackson, Tenn. but when we got there we received orders to go to Richmond, Va. So this morning we left Jackson T and are in our old state Miss. once more, but we have to lieve (sic) here in the morning for Richmond. I received a letter from aunt Pettigrew[1] a few days ago. I want you to write her and tell her that I got the letter she wrote to me. I have not had the chance to write her but when I get to Va I will. I fear that I will never get a letter from you anymore for it is such a long ways from home. We are going where there is fighting to do but we are willing to do it. My Dear Parents, it may be that we will never meet on earth again but if we do not I hope that we will meet in that world that is all pleasure, peace and joy. My belief is that I was not born for a Yankee to kill me and then go to everlasting punishment. God forbid that it shall be so.

Mother, I think of you all very often but thank the Lord my faith is strong that we will meet once more on earth. Tell Riley and Dippy[2] that I often think of them. I wrote two letters to Riley and have not rec'd an answer yet. I am well tonight as common I must close. So Farewell my Mother. I am truly your affectionate son.

S B Gulledge

FOOTNOTES

[1] Elizabeth (Blackwell) Pettigrew, his great aunt, sister of the grandmother (Mary Jane Blackwell McBride) that he never knew.

[2] Riley W. Wyatt and Zilpha Ann (Gulledge) Wyatt (called Dippy), his brother-in-law and sister respectively.

Leesburg, Va. Aug 25th 1861

Mr & Mrs Gulledge

Dear Pa and Ma,

    It is with the greatest of pleasure that I write to you. I am improving very fast. I have had the measles but I am now ready for service. We are sending home for our winter clothing. I wish you to (send) 1 pr of pants, 1 coat, 1 vest, 2 pr of drawers, 2 or 3 pr of woolen socks and one pare (sic) of good casse boots or shoes and have my name put on all of my cloths (sic). The collar of the cloth gray if convenient. Everything is very high here and we have not been payed as yet. Send them to Newton Station by the 10th of October. You will put Brass buton (sic) on the Coat and Vest if they are convenient. You will please tell Mr Stones family that Ab is dead. We regret the death exceedingly bad. The most of us will have to go in some way or in fact all. He was the first (to) take with the measles and the (illegible) the Phit(illegible) fever. I wrote to you by Mr. Taylor and have not received an answer as yet. You may look for me next Spring...

    Tell Riley W(iset?) and his wife wrote to me. Give my love to all of my acquaintances...The reason that I got this letter wrote is that my (illegible) is so bad from being sick that it is impossible to write myself. Goodby your son.

                                          S B Gulledge

P S   There will be some of the company at Newton to bring me the cloths (sic).

Leesburg, Va   Sept 11th 1861

My Dear Mother and Father,

    Once more I embrace the opportunity of writing to you but to tell you the truth I do not know hardly what to say. I recd a letter from you and from Riley[1] sent by Mr. Wash. I got all the cloths you sent me. I was glad to know that I have such a kind Mother. Those five pair of socks you sent with names marked on them I got. Tell Dippy,[2] Mary,[3] Sally,[4] and Gracy, I thank them all kindly for such a present. Joe Gibbs, John Gibbs, Battle and Tom Watts got here about 2 weeks ago. Joe and John has had the measles. Joe is up. John is very sick and I think will die. The health of our regiment is improving. I am as well as I ever was and as fat as a buck. You wrote you could not help fretting about me. I want you not to be uneasy for if I am to be sick it cannot be helped but I hope we will live to meet again for I trust that him that made me is on our side. Now I must tell you something about the War. We are in four miles of the Maryland line. The Yankees aare still there. We expect a fight at Arlington Heights in a few days but our regiment is so torn up that we will not be there. I reckon the clothes you sent me will last me through the winter so don't send me any more yet. I can think of nothing more so I will close. Write often for I love to hear from you. Your affectionate son.

                                            SB Gulledge

Direct to Leesburg

FOOTNOTES

¹ Riley W. Wyatt, Blackwell's brother-in-law.

² Zilpha Ann (Gulledge) Wyatt, Blackwell's sister.

³ Mary Eleanor Gulledge (12/17/1841 Chesterfield, SC--1873, Van Zandt Co, TX), Blackwell's sister, who married William Pendergrass in January, 1872.

⁴ Sarah Lauretta "Sally Lou" Gulledge, (12/11/1845, Jasper Co, MS--3/21/1878 Van Zandt Co., TX), Blackwell's sister who married Robert W. Coker in 1866.

           Leesburg, Va. Sept the 27th 1861

My Dear Mother

    As Mr. Gibbs is going back home I will write you a few lines to let you know that I have not forgotten you. I am well and hearty as I ever was. Our Company got paid off yesterday. I got thirty eight dollars and twenty five cts. I am going to lend Joe Gibbs $20. and he promised to pay it to you for me in gold. I want you to get it and keep it till I come home and if I never come it is yours. I have no news to write. Mr. Gibbs will tell as much and more than I can write so I will close.

                         Your affecionate son

                                S B Gulledge

Leesburg, Va.   Sept the 29th 61

Dear Mother and Father

    As Mr Wyatt is going to start back home I will write you a few lines to let you know that I am well. I hardly know what to say for we are where we here (sic) no news scarcely. Battle recd a letter from J. R. Johnson stating that he was appointed by the community at Newton to bring Clothing for the Company. If you get this letter time enough I want you to send me the largest potato you can get for a show. Our Captain is under arrest and will be tried tomorrow for mutiny. If he is condemned it will go very hard with him I think. Pa you must not think hard of me for not writing to you oftener for I write to Mother and you can here (sic) from me but if you will write to me I will write to you often. I want you, mother and Riley to send me a letter by Mr. Johnson. I am doing fine and better satisfied than I have been since I left home. Nothing more at present.   I   remain   your   affectionate   and beloved son.

                                            S B Gulledge

Leesburg, Va.   Nov 21   61

Dear Mother and Father

    As Mr. Brown is going home in the morning I will write to you. I am well and hearty as you ever saw me. I read your letter a few days ago and was glad to hear from you. I was sorry to hear that you was sick though I am in hopes you all have once more gained your health. It keeps me all the time uneasy when I hear you are sick. I received a letter from Uncle William.¹ He was at Columbus, Ky at the time he wrote.

We had a fight with the Yankees at Leesburg on the 21st of last month. They crossed the river with about 3,000 strong but we fought them bravely and finally drove them back with great loss on their side. We did not loose (sic) one man in our company and but 4 killed and 14 wounded in the Regiment. I did not have the pleasure of being there myself for I was sick about 40 miles from our regt. In your letter you said you heard that I found some kin. It is a mistake. I don't know of any of my kin being in Va. You wanted to know if I would like to (have) an overcoat, shirts and blankets. I would like very much to have them if you can get anyway to send them. Martin got his things you sent. He is sick but not dangerous. I can think of nothing more at present. I want you to write as soon as you get this for I shall be uneasy till I get an answer.

Direct letters Leesburg, Va. Care Regt. Carlton Newton Rifles 13 Regt Miss. Vol.

Your affectionate son
S B Gulledge

FOOTNOTES

[1] J. William McBride, Lauretta's brother.

Leesburg, Va Nov 29th 1861

My Dear Mother

    I received your kind letter of the 19th inst day before yesterday and was very glad to hear from you once more. I an not very well but am up. At the time John Gilbert told you that I was sick I had an attack of pleuracy (sic) but have recovered. I have nothing new to write. The troops are all still at this time but we are expecting an attack every day. We have a good deal of sickness in our regiment at this time. The disease is mumps and the itch. There was a man in the regiment went to bed last night well and hearty and got up this morning. He said he felt bad and went back to bed and in a little while he was dead. Jim and Joe Gibbs is well. The old Captain has come back and took command of his company. All the Company is very much dissatisfied with him. I would like very much to see you all but I cannot expect to see you before next June if we both live which I have the same hope that I did when I left Newton Station. Those 20 dollars I sent home by Mr. Gibbs get it as soon as you can and keep $15 of it till I come home and I will make you a present of five dollars out of the twenty if it can be called a present...you have done much more for me than a son could expect of a Mother so kind. So anxious are (sic) such a mother for the welfare of her son. I hope My Dear Mother the day is near that I can by the help of my Maker pay you back for your kindness. I wrote to you by Mr. Brown. Nothing more. Yours most truly.

                                      S B Gulledge

Direct to Leesburg, Va.

Leesburg, Va   Dec the 15th   61

Dear Mother and Father

    It is with pleasure that I endeavor to write you a few lines to let you know that I am enjoying very good health at this time and hope that these lines will find you in the same great blessing.   I received a letter from Riley[1] two or three days ago which stated that you were all well.   I have not got a letter from you since Mr. Norman got to the regiment. I wrote to you by Henry Brown and I hope you have got it before now and have written by mail twice since he left.   I have been throwing up brestworks at Leesburg.   Last night the 18th Miss. Regt. worked at it.   We are expecting another attack shortly at this point but we are ready for them at any time.   Our first General was Evans of South Carolina but last Monday we had a review and the General bade as he said his brave brigade adieu and General Griffith who was formerly Col. of the 12th Miss. Regt. took command.   Mother I am proud to say to you that for several evenings on parade this brigade have got great praise for bravery in the Leesburg fight.   The Adjutant read to our Regt from the Gen. that this brigade was the bravest and best soldiers in the world.   I wrote you a few lines in a letter that Joe Gibbs sent home by mail but I do not know whether you got it or not.   Joe, Jim and J. Mc.[2] has sent for them a comfort apiece and I wrote in that letter for you to send one to me of which I would be glad to get.   I have nothing to cover with these colds nights of my own but one single blanket but the Captain says they will be sure to come.   Our Company is in very good (health) with the exception of a few cases of Pneumonia.   I suppose Gov. Pettus has ordered out ten thousand for sixty days.   When you write tell me who all is gone from our settlement that I know.   I had almost forgotten to tell you that my mess has got smart enough to build us a nice chimney to our tent. It is the greatest invention that we have made since we have been in Camp. Mr Humphrey sends his best respects to you and Father. I can think of nothing more that is worth writing this evening so I will come to a close by asking you to write as soon as you get this letter. So Mother direct your letters to Leesburg, Va in care of Lt. Walkins Co E 13th Regt Miss Vol. I remain your affectionate son until death.

            S B Gulledge

FOOTNOTES

[1]   Riley W. Wyatt, his brother-in-law.

[2]   J. McDaniel.

       Leesburg, Virginia   Jan 1 1862

My Dear Mother and Father

  I received your kind letter a few days ago and was very glad to here (sic) from you and to here (sic) that you were all well. I am enjoying good health at present. Our Company is near the Potamoc (sic) on picket. You wanted to know if I got the testament. I did so and tell Miss Martha[1] I thank her very much for her kindness. I also got the socks, gloves and potatoes and the two apples Sue sent to me and was very glad of them. I have no news to write of interest. Van Gilbert is dead. You wrote that you heard there was a premium offerred to twelve months volunteers and for me not to accept of their offers. Now I don't want to trouble your minds for I have got my belly full of soldiering...if I live to serve my time out. Although it is not as bad as some people think it is. You also wanted to know what sort of Shoes Joe Alexander sent to me. They was just common homemade ones. There was a fight at Drainsville last Friday week of which our forces was victorious as is usual. I received a letter from Uncle William[2] in September. I was taken sick directly afterward and did not write to him until day before yesterday. I explained the case to him but I want you to write to him and also tell him about it. Tell him to write to me. Pa I don't want you to think I have forgotten you for I do think of you often. Don't think because I don't write to you individually, when I write home I write to all. I wrote a letter to Riley and you by Mr Gardner which I hope you have got. The boys is all well that you know. I can think of nothing more at present. Calvin Doolittle sends his respects to you and family, also Riley and Zilpha.[3] Give my love to Riley and Dippy[4] and accept of the same yourselves from your affectionate son.

S B Gulledge

FOOTNOTES

[1] Martha Woodham

[2] J. William McBride, his mother's brother.

[3] Riley W. Wyatt and Zilpha Ann (Gulledge) Wyatt, his brother-in-law and sister.

[4] Zilpha Ann was called Dippy.

Leesburg, Va   Jan the 17th 1862

My Dear Mother and Father

   It is with pleasure that I again endeavor to write to you although I have no news of interest to relate but I deem it my duty to write when circumstances will admit. I am well and hope this will find you enjoying the same great blessing. I have not recd a letter from you in two or three weeks and I have written two letters and havent got an answer yet. I want you to write how much you made last year, also write what produce is worth. The health of the Company is very good at present. A goodly number of our Regiment is going in for the War. There is some twelve or fifteen of our Company gone in. There is a Bounty of $50 and Sixty days furlow given to them. Thirty eight out of a company is allowed to go home immediately to return in the time limited. Out of the names of this Company is W J McDaniel, H McGehee, Martin[1] and others. I want to know what per cent could gold be got for Confederate bills in our State. I havent got the box you sent me yet but I hope when the wagons go to Manassas I will get it. We are on the river on picket yet but we expect to be relieved in a short time. Our time lacks not quite four months of being out and I hope that I will live to get back and see you all again. Tell Riley[2] I have written two letters to him and havent recd an answer yet. I want you all to write every chance you get for nothing affords me more pleasure than to get a letter from home. We are looking for an attack at this point soon but I hope we will be able to give them the same reception that we did on the 27th of Oct last. I can think of nothing more. Be sure to write as soon as you get this. So nothing more at present. I remain your affectionate son until Death.

                                 S B Gulledge

FOOTNOTES

1 Martin Watkins?

2 Riley W. Wyatt, his brother-in-law.

Leesburg, Va. Feb the 27th 1862

Dear Mother and Father,

    I received yours of the 19th yesterday evening and was very glad to hear from you once more. I was very sorry to learn the great misfortune the sixty day troops met with, especially when they had left all that was near and dear to them, to go forth and defend their Countries (sic) rights. It is true a soldiers life is a hard and dangerous one but when they think of their Mothers, their fathers, their brothers, their sisters, and their rights they will spill the last drop of blood in their veins before they will Submit to the Federal Government. I expect to come home if I live to see my time out but I know not how long I will stay with you for if my Country needs me and call on me to go to the field of battle I cannot, I must not hesitate a moment but shoulder my gun and go forth to meet the foe; let the result be what it may on my part. I had rather die the Death of a brave and truehearted Southern Soldier than to see my Country troden down by the Northern invader. My feeling is so much touched by hearing of the Federal Victory at Somerset, Ky that I had almost forgotten to say that I was well. The health of the Regt is very good at the present time, though it does not seem strange that we enjoy as good health as any Regt in the Confederate service. When we turn our eyes to our brave and noble Colonel I can say with true earnest that we have got the best and most feeling Colonel in the Army. We don't drill or stand guard duty day or night. As for War matters everything is still at this time here. I don't expect we will have any fighting to do until Spring and do not know whether we will then or not but if we do we are ready and willing at a moments warning to get our guns and march to the field of battle. The Reg. will draw their money in a few days. We will draw forty seven dollars apiece and I have notes on good men in the Company amounting to $35. which in all will make eighty. That is what I have saved since I have been in the Army. Martin asked me to say to you that he got the pants that Miss Martha Woodham sent him in John Gilberts bundle and that he thanked her very much for her kind present. I also thank her kindly for the testament she presented to me but from being sick I unfortunately lost it but I bought another. Tell Riley[1] to write to me. I have written several letters to him and have not got an answer yet. Be sure to write to me often for I love to get a letter from home. So no more at this time My Dear Parents. From your son most affectionately.

S B Gulledge

FOOTNOTES

[1] Riley W. Wyatt, his brother-in-law.

Orange C H Va Mar 28th 62

Dear Mother and Father

    I seat myself to answer you kind letter which came to hand a few days ago. I also received a letter the day before we left Leesburg but did not have an opportunity of answering it. I was very glad to hear from you all and to here (sic) you were all well. There is nothing new here. We are ordered to keep 3 days rations cooked and expecting to move every minute but I know not where to. I am not very well this morning nor have not been for several days but I am not dangerously sick. You need not expect an interesting letter from me as a Soldier has a bad chance to gain any news of interest. I have no knowledge of where we will march to at all. I suppose we will not be allowed to carry our tents with us. I received a letter from Uncle Samuel McBride[1] a day or two before we left Leesburg but have not answered it yet. It was dated Feb 24th. His family were well when it was wrote. He is living in sight of Mars Bluff Station overseeing for Joseph Gregg. It also stated that Aunt E. B. Pettigrew[2] died last November. You wanted to know if I had plenty of clothing to do me. I can make out I recon for if I had any more I could not carry them when we went to march. M L Stewart was left at Middleburg sick when we were retreating and was not able to be hauled in an ambulance. Middleburg is about 15 miles from Leesburg. I have never heard from him since he was left there. I don't know whether he was taken prisoner, is dead or has been sent on to Richmond but I hope he was sent on. I was very much surprised to hear that Mrs. S. L. R. had taken such an active part in a matter wherein I don't think she was concerned. In reference to that as soon as I get settled, if I ever do before my time expires, I shall write to Miss C. immediately if possible. So I shall bring my letter to a close very soon. I had like to forgot to tell you that I never have nor I recon ever will receive that box of goods you sent to us as we are not settled here. You need not write to me anywhere until you receive another letter from me as I don't know where to tell you to direct your letter to. C H Doolittle sends his compliments to you both and family, also to Riley[3] and family. So tell everybody Howdy for me and nothing more.

To E L & D Gulledge[4]

S B Gulledge

FOOTNOTES

[1] Samuel Blackwell McBride (c. 1821--12/1877) of Darlington Co., SC, brother of Blackwell's mother, Lauretta (McBride) Gulledge.

[2] Elizabeth (Blackwell) Pettigrew, his great aunt, half sister to his grandmother, Mary Jane (Blackwell) McBride.

[3] Riley W. Wyatt, his brother-in-law and friend; husband of his sister Zilpha Ann (Gulledge) Wyatt.

[4] Eleanor Lauretta and David Gulledge, his parents.

Va April the 18th 1862
(Chimborayo?) Hospital

My Dear Parents

As I have been sick I have not had the chance of writing to you before now. I will endeavor to write you a few lines this morning. I am well except cold. I have been at this hospital in Richmond for twenty days. My Regt is at Yorktown on the James River about fifty miles below this place. We are expecting a great battle there every day. The French Minister arrived in this City day before yesterday but we have not yet heard his business. The Yankee papers are speaking of peace. Nothing would please me any more than to hear of peace being made for I want to see you all so much. It has been twelve months since I left you to join the Army and at that time if it was the will of the Lord to spare me I expected to return to see all my Dear Relatives and friends. I will not admit it at the present but I hope in a few weeks I will be granted a furlough to go home and see you all. Congress has passed an act to keep all the twelve months volunteers in the Service for over eighteen and under thirty five years of age for two years longer unless the War be sooner ended. There is nothing that I hate about the Act only the name of being pressed into service but there is a battlion (sic) of Cavalry making up in Richmond and I now think I will reenlist in it and get my bounty of fifty dollars and furlough for sixty days and come home. Dear Parents when you get this letter write soon. Direct to Yorktown Co. E, 13th Regt Miss Vols. From your son

S B Gulledge

Williamsburg, Va   Apr the 27th 1862

Dear Mother

    I seat myself this morning to write you a few lines in answer to your kind letter which come to hand a few days ago. I was very glad to hear from you all. I have got to the Company now and I am well now. Our Company elected new officers yesterday. Tom Thurman is our Capt. now. There is no use in talking about us coming home now for Congress has pressed us in for the War or 2 years. They say we are allowed a 50 day furlough whenever the Secretary of War sees fit to give it and it is uncertain whether he will see fit at all or not. Our boys are taking it pretty well though but some men swear they will go home or die. Still I think that is foolishness. You need not really look for me home really until the war ends. I shall get a transfer if I can to where Riley[1] is. If I can't of course I shall have to serve here. Calvin Doolittle wants you to see his people and tell them the news for it is almost impossible to get paper here to write on. He says for you to tell them he is going to get a transfer to the 10th Regt. Miss. Vols. if he can as soon as this fight is over. They are expecting the greatest battle here that was ever fought on this Continent in a few days. Also the Gibbs boys, John Gilbert and J. McDaniel says for you to send their people word how they are getting along. So I shall close soon. When you write to me Direct your letters to Williamsburg, Va in care of Capt. Thurman. Calvin Doolittle sends howdy to the family also to Dip.[2] Tell his folks to Direct their letters to him in the same way. So nothing more but write to your affectionate son.

                                        S B Gulledge

Co E 13th Regt Miss. Vols.
in care of Capt Thurman

I shall send this letter by Lieut. Smith also I shall send $100 by him. So nothing more.

S B Gulledge

FOOTNOTES

[1] Riley W. Wyatt, his brother-in-law, who had evidently joined the army by this time also.

[2] Zilpha Ann (Gulledge) Wyatt, called Dip, was his sister and Riley's wife.

Richmond Va   June 8 1862

Mrs E L Gulledge
Dear Mother

I received yours of 20 and 23 of last month contents noted. I was truly glad to hear from home and to learn that all was well and getting on so well. We are expecting a big battle here every day. Everyone is anxious for it to come off. We had a considerable fight here on the last of the past month. Our Regiment was ordered in but just got to the field at dusk. The enemy threw their grape shot and miney balls thick over our heads. We never returned the fight at all. We had only one of our Regiment wounded and that was one of our Company. Martin Watkins[1] got shot through the left hand, lost his two middle fingers which was taken off up to his wrist. He may lose his arm yet. I got a letter from Riley[2] a few days ago. I want you to write him and tell him that I have no chance to write as we are on picket duty all of the time and as for the cloths you spake of, it would be impossible to get them here without someone was passing, so I will be compelled to (do) by my cloths unless we go on furlough soon...

I wish you to let my money out on interest and take the note in my name and if I should never return I want the money to be yours. This is a written certificate to show that the money is yours at my death. I would like to hear from you all as often as possible. Give my respects to all of the nabors (sic). My love to the family.

Your son

S B Gulledge

FOOTNOTES

[1] This may be the Martin, referred to in many of the previous letters.

[2] Riley W. Wyatt

Richmond, Va   June the 18th 62

My Dear Mother

I received yours of June the 7th yesterday evening which gave me great pleasure and satisfaction for nothing gives me more pleasure than to get a letter from home. I am well and I thank my maker for the protection and great mercy he has shown me while enduring this hard soldiers life for I assure you no one knows what a hard life is till they try a soldiers life but we must endure our trials and tribulations with cheerfulness and we will in the end I hope, be victorious. I got Mr.

Watkins[1] to write to you for me a few days ago about the money. We are here in a mile of the enemy expecting an attack every day and when the fight begins it will be the most dreadful battle ever fought in modern times. You wanted to know who was in my mess. I will name them to you. Joe Gibbs, J. McDaniel, Martin and a young man by the name of Poore. Martin is at the hospital in Richmond with the rheumatism. The Gibbs boys, Calvin[2] and Ben Wells is well. In fact the Company in general is in good health. Tell Pa I would like very much to be with him and talk with him about my travels since I last saw him. Tell him not to think that I have forgotten him because I have not written to him personally for when I write home I write to all of the family for we are moved about so often that it is a bad chance to write a letter atall (sic). When you write tell me how large John and Fanny is and tell me if John is broke to plow. I also want you to state to me just how you are getting along. Tell Dippy[3] I still have her likeness but I am sorry to say I have broken the top glass off the picture but tell her not to think hard of me for that for if I live to return home in peace I will have it drawn anew. Tell her I would also like to see her fine son.[4] I would like very much to get a furlough in two or three weeks and come home but times is two (sic) critical for me to even think of such a thing at present. You wrote if the Capt. would send a man home we could get cloths. That is impossible. Col. Barkdale himself can't go to Richmond, a distance of 7 miles without a pass signed by his Major General and I heard him say that he would not leave his Regt one half mile for his right arm under the present circumstances. H H McGeha told me to say to you that he wished to get you to make him 2 pares (sic) of jeans pants and a short coat and wants to know what they will cost. He says he will send the money to you by letter or pay it to me here. He wants them made the size you made for me, only the pants a little shorter. Write to me my dear Mother, for it is a pleasure to me to get a letter from you and you have a better chance of writing than I do. Farewell for the time my Mother.

from your son

S B Gulledge

FOOTNOTES

[1] Father of Martin Watkins, whose injury was mentioned in Blackwell's last letter?

[2] Calvin H. Doolittle.

[3] Zilpha Ann (Gulledge) Wyatt, his sister and wife of Riley W. Wyatt.

[4] John H. Wyatt, son of Riley and Zilpha (Gulledge) Wyatt, was born April, 1862.

Richmond, Va   July the 14th 62

My Dear Parents

I received your letter of July 1st and was very glad to hear from you once more. Dear Mother I have glorious news to tell you. Our Army in Richmond has attacked and completely whipped McClellans Grand Union Army. The fight lasted nearly six days. It was the most (??) struggle known in modern history. The fight commenced on Thursday the 25th of June and lasted till Tuesday July the 1st. The battlefield was about sixteen miles long. Our brave boys would charge their batteries and drive them from their entrenchments in every instance. On the 29th our brigade was ordered to the battle field after it had gone about a mile and a half. Gen. Griffith our Brigade General was killed by a shot thrown from the enemies battery. On the first our regt got into the fight. There was 1810 killed and wounded. Our company was very fortunate. There was three killed and five wounded slightly. I will give you the names of the killed. Joe Harrell, John Allen and Joe Laman. The wounded was W. Johnson, Jesse Railey, J McDaniel, D Graham, and W B Norman. There was several thousand prisoners taken with 51 fine peices (sic) of artillery and a large quality of small arms ammunition, mules, wagons, commisary stores, etc.

    I am well as usual. Tell Mr Gibbs, Jim and Joe is well. Martin has just got from the hospital. When you write to Uncle William[1] tell him to write to me and I will write to him. Calvin Doolitte sends all his respects to you all. Write soon. Nothing more. I remain your affectionate son until death.

                                              S B Gulledge

FOOTNOTES

[1] J. William McBride, his mother's half-brother who was in the 12th Louisiana Regiment, CSA.

Richmond, Va   Aug the 5th 62

My Dear Mother

    I received your letter a few days ago. I was very glad to hear from you once more. I am in good health at present. Our regiment is encamped about four miles from Richmond. We have good water and are in tolerable good health but my Mother, we have the tightest command. Col. Barksdale has command of our Brigade and our Lieut. Col. was wounded in the fight so the Major has the regiment in charge. Every man that does not answer to his name at roll call is sent to the guard house unless he has a good excuse. We have to drill four hours a day in a very hot old field but I am willing to stand all of that if the Lord will spare me to get back home. All is quiet around Richmond now but we are expecting every day to hear of Stonewall Jackson and Pope having a fight at Culpepper C H. Each one has a large army and I feel it will be a hard fight when it comes off. We was paid $40 dollars last Saturday and we will get our bounty before long and if I can get a chance I will send you some money to buy salt and shoes as you said you did not know how you would do about getting them. I have been thinking about sending some money in a letter. Write to me how you think it would do. If you think it will go I will send it. Write to me what salt and shoes is selling at. If you can make me any winter cloths and it not two (sic) much trouble make them grey and the coat a frock. I dont like a short coat. When I write letters I will send you a sheet of paper and an envelope and as soon as I can get them I will send you some stamps and then I am sure you will write to me oftener. I would be glad if you would write to me once a week anyhow. I can think of nothing more so I will come to a close. Your affectionate son.

                                        S B Gulledge

Leesburg, Va   Sept 5th 1862

My dear Parents

    It is with pleasure that I embrace the opportunity of droping (sic) you a few lines to let you know where I am and how I am geting (sic) along. My dear Ma and Pa, I have such good news to write you. Our army has been blessed again with a great victory at the same place they caught it the 20th of July 1861 on Bull Run and we are now at Leesburg, but I do not know how long we will stay here for we have four days rations cooked and are expecting marching orders at any moment and I expect we will go into Maryland. I heard today that Gens. Jackson and Longstreet was already in Maryland. I also heard that General Bragg has given them a whiping (sic) in the South west. I wrote you a letter one month ago today but have not received an answer yet. I am well. All the boys are well from round Newton[1] but Joe Gibbs. He is in Richmond at the hospital. The letters is about to be sent off so I must close for this time. As soon as we get stationed I will write you. Must excuse me for not writing more for time will not allow me. Write soon, direct to Richmond. From your most affectionate son.

                                            S B Gulledge

FOOTNOTES

[1] Newton Township, Jasper Co, MS was his home.

Camp near Brucetown   Oct the 12th 1862

My Dear Mother and Father

    I have an opportunity of writing to you once more. I received your letter of Aug 16th a few days ago. Mr McDaniel brought the cloths you sent to me but he lost the letter and I was Sorry of it for I wanted to hear from you all very much. Our Army is lying still at present for the first time in a good while, but it will not supprise (sic) me at any time to get marching orders. The health of the company is very good now. We muster about sixty four men which is the largest company in the regiment. I am sorry to tell you that we have not drawn any money since I wrote to you about it and we move so much that I do not know when we will (have) the chance of drawing; but when we do I will send you some money. I wrote you a short letter at Leesburg as we was on our way into Maryland but I havent heard from it since. Mother, I will tell you what I did. I sold a pare (sic) of them pants you sent me the other day for seven dollars and as soon as I get the money and opportunity I will send it to you. I heard the other day that you was sick with the measles and I am very uneasy about it for nothing troubles me more than to hear of you being sick. I am sorry I put you to so much trouble to mail the cloths you made for me. You wrote about sending them by express if you could get no other chance but to my opinion there would be five chances to one if I ever got them. There is a young man from our com. now at home on furlough. His name is Bottoms and he lives near Normans. If you could see him he might bring the cloths. I heard that Mr. Gibbs was going to hire as a substitute for Allen Glover. Now Pa, you are older than I am but if a man was to offer you $10,000 to substitute for him, dont go, for I know something of the hardships of Camp life and I know that you can not stand it one year and for all the money in Newton County. I would not have my family to go in the Army for no man. The pleasure of being at home with my people is worth all the wealth a man can have.

Tell Dippy[1] and all the children I think of them often and I want to see them very much. Write as soon as you get this for I an anxious to hear from you. Nothing more. I remain as ever

        Your affectionate son
          S B Gulledge

Direct to Richmond, Va in care of C C K Marshall
Co D 13th Miss Regt.

FOOTNOTES

[1] Zilpha Ann (Gulledge) Wyatt, his sister.

         Fredericksburg, Va
          Dec 21st 1862

My Dear Mother

 As I have a chance of writing this morning I will do so. I received your letter of the 8th last Saturday. I was very glad to here (sic) from you. I did not get my clothing until day before yesterday. They pleased me very much and I am a thousand times oblidged to you for them. I must now tell you something about the bombardment and battle of this place. Our division had that portion of the line to guard just opposite the town and when the enemy undertook to cross the river our Brigade was there on picket duty so we had to open the fight. They undertook to cross early in the morning but our Brigade held there (sic) whole Army in check for ten hours under fire of 140 pieces of their cannon. The loss in our Regt was 8 killed and 64 wounded, and 14 missing. Their loss was about 250 killed. This was the night they first came over. In the whole fight acknoledged a loss of 15,000. Our loss is 1800. Our Company lost 2 killed and 2 wounded. My Capt. had his leg shot in two by a cannon ball. He was lying on my leg at the time so you may know I was in a close place but thanks be to God I came out all right and I hope that I will be spared to return home and enjoy a peaceful life. I am well except cold. Martin, Joe and Jim Gibbs is well. I found a letter in my coat pocket stating that Pa[1] was gone to the Army. I want you to let me know where he is and how long he had to be out. Give my best respects to Riley and Dippy.[2] Tell them I would like to get a letter from them. I have wrote you all the news so far as I know so I will close. Write soon. Direct to Richmond Box pro 1080, I remain your son as ever

            S B Gulledge

FOOTNOTES

[1] David Gulledge.

[2] Riley W. Wyatt and Zepha Ann (Gulledge) Wyatt, his brother-in-law and sister.

Fredericksburg, Va   Jan 29 1863

Dear Mother

It has been a long time since I heard from you and I am very anxious to get a letter from you. Our Brigade is in town on picket duty. The weather is very cold. The snow is five or six inches deep but we are very comfortably situated. We have good warm houses. We are on one bank of the river and the enemy on the other. I hear that the North is going to borrow four hundred millions of dollars to carry on the war ninety days and if in that time they fail to whip the South they will have to give it up as a bad job and come to terms of peace. Everything is quiet now but we will not be surprised to be attacked any time. I hear that General Lee has gone to North Carolina and that General Longstreet has taken command of this Army but I do not know how true it is. There is a talk of some of the Company coming home on furlough. If anyone do come home I would be glad if you could send me one or two pairs of gallows[1] for I can find none to buy and those you sent are two (sic) short.

Jan the 31

As furloughs has come this evening for two of the Company and they are going to start home in the morning I will finish my letter and send it without getting any letter from you yet. I had almost forgot to state that I am well. The Company is now in better health than it has been since it has been in the service. Ma, write to me just your situation as to the prospects of making this years crop. If it is bad perhaps I may get a furlough and come home when the others get back to the Company that has already had them although I could do you no good towards making a crop but I would like to see you all very much but if I do not get a furlough I hope peace will soon be made and then we can come home and live in peace the remainder of our lives. Dear Mother, in my opinion if you thought of me as often as I think of you you would write oftener though I do not doubt your affections toward me as your son. I fear something is the matter at home or you would certainly have written before now. Be sure and write as soon as you get this letter. Nothing more at this time. From your son

                                        S B Gulledge

FOOTNOTES

[1] Suspenders

Fredericksburg, Va Feb the 20th 1863

Dear Mother

    I received your letter a few days ago and was very much pleased to here (sic) from you once more in life. My Dear Ma, my mind is so torn up this morning that I hardly know what to say. I have had the priviledge for several days of attending a Methodist protracted meeting in this place. We are expecting every day to get marching orders. Some of the boys in our Company say they heard a Colonel belonging to our Division say yesterday morning that we were ordered to Vicksburg and some say we are going to Charleston, S C but we do not know where we are going nor will until we get there as is always the case with us poor privates. Mother, Company has had very bad luck for the past few months. Since the fight at this place four of this Company has taken sick and died. Though you are not acquainted with any of them I will give you their names: Botton, Huddleston, Osburn, and James. We are now I believe in good health. If we leave Virginia as soon as we get to our place of destination I will write to you again and let you know where we are. I believe Martin has a good clothing as most of the Company. Tell little Harriet[1] that I would be very glad to come home and see her. Martin, Joe Gibbs and J McDaniel sends their respects and best wishes to all the neighbors and most especially to the ladies. You must excuse this short letter. I will try to do better next time. Write soon and often. From your most affectionate son.

                                              S B Gulledge

FOOTNOTES

[1] Harriet Emma Gulledge (10/27/1860--10/20/1903), his sister.

Culpepper C H   March the 15th (1863)

Dear Parents

As I have a chance of sending a letter by Mr. Williams I will write you a few lines to let you know how I am getting along. I am enjoying as good health as I ever did in my life. Pa, I received a letter from you about two weeks ago and I was very proud when I saw your name to it. You said you had a fine potato crop and would like for me to be at home to help you eat them. Nothing would please me better than to be at home with you. I also received a letter from Mother when Mr. Williams got to the Company. Mother, the box of cloths you sent me is at Gordonsville, twenty five miles from here. You wrote to me about what I was owing A B Stone. I was owing him forty five cts and I want you to be sure and pay it for me. You have never written to me whether Joe Gibbs paid you or not. Write and tell me if he did and what kind of money he promised to pay. The gold, if he paid gold, be sure to keep it. I will send you fifty dollars by Mr. Williams. I will get him to leave it with Mr. Doolittle so you can get it. I want you to make out what I have already sent home to $125 and the ballance (sic) of the fifty is yours to do with as you please, but if I was in your place and they were not too dear I would buy five or six head of sheep. I was sorry to hear that Riley[1] was wounded. Tell him to write to me so I can write to him for I dont know where to direct letters to him. Tell Dippy[2] I would like to get a letter from her. Tell Albert[3] I want to know how much is his weight and how long it will be before he can plough. I have such a bad place to write that I will come to a close. Write soon and often. From your son

S B Gulledge

(On the back of the preceding letter were the following notes)

Mr. Williams,

    Please send me the money that my son S B Gulledge sent home by you. Send it by James Goodwin, the bearer of this and you will be obliged.

                        E L Gulledge[4]

Mr. Doolittle,

    Blackwell says he has sent fifty dollars to you for me. If Mr. Williams has given it to you, please send it by the bearer. Respectfully

                        E. L. Gulledge

FOOTNOTES

[1] Riley W. Wyatt, Blackwell's brother-in-law.

[2] Zilpha Ann (Gulledge) Wyatt, Blackwell's sister and wife of Riley.

[3] Albert Joseph Gulledge (11/17/1853--12/1/1903), Blackwell's brother.

[4] Eleanor Lauretta Gulledge, Blackwell's mother.

Fredericksburg, Va   March the 20th 63

Dear Mother

    I received your most welcome letter of March 1st a few days ago. I am enjoying very good health at this time. Our Brigade is still in this place but I do not know how long it will be. It is reported here that the enemy attacked our forces at Vicksburg not long since but was defeated in their object as usual. Mother I have good news to write you. There has been a protracted meeting here for thirty-two days and is still going on and upward of one hundred has professed religion and joined the Church since it began. Among them is Martin and J McDaniel. O Mother, would to God I could write and tell you in truth that I was among the number. I know it would be the greatest pleasure to you that I could write... yes, what a pleasure it would be to have a hope that if we never meet on earth we would meet in heaven. I expect we will soon have to begin our Spring campaign for I think we have lay still almost as long as we can so near the enemy. The weather is very unpleasenat today. The snow is on the ground but we are in a good house. Next Friday is the day appointed by the President as Fast Day and I hope every Christian in the South will meet at their churches on that day and offer up prayer to the most High God in behalf of our Country. I am very sorry to hear of Rileys and Dippy[1] having so much sickness. Tell them to write to me and I will return their letter. I want you to write to Uncle William[2] when you get this and tell him to write to me for I would like to hear from him now and then. Our Cavalry had a skirmish some days ago with the enemy. They succeeded in whipping them and driving them across the Rappanannack (sic) River with considerable loss. Our loss in killed and wounded and missing is estimated at about 250.

I would like to see you all very much but I cannot say when that will be. Our dependence must be on (Jesus?) and all will be well with us. Will close for this time. From your affectionate son

                                 S B Gulledge

FOOTNOTES

[1] Riley W. Wyatt and Zilpha Ann Gulledge Wyatt, his brother-in-law and sister.

[2] J. William McBride, Lauretta's half-brother, who was serving in the 12 LA Regiment, CSA.

                   Fredericksburg, Va   April 2nd 1863

Mrs E L Gulledge
My Dear Mother

     I again address to you a few lines. This leaves me in the enjoyment of good health. Hoping you and family may be enjoying the same great Blessing of God for which we should be very thankful. I am scarce of general news at this time. Nothing of any note has taken place of late. Times still remaining quiet on this line. I cannot say how long it will remain so. The opinion seems generally to be that General Lee will soon commence active operations. I do not care how long times remain quiet for we are fairing so well in town. I hear nothing from any other portion of the Army worth relating. Dear Mother general news are so scarce that I will at once give you some of the local news and the meeting that is going on in this place with this Brigade is the best we have to tell.

It has been going on now for 6 weeks evey day and really seems that the Spirit is doing a great work here. Don't get frightened at numbers when I tell you that 170 or 180 have united themselves with the church from this Brigade and now it is not with that same hard heart I hope, but with a light heart that I venture with my pen to tell you that I am one of that number and how it is that I fell to embrace the words of the young convert the other night. Oh! how I love my Saviour and O how often Mother has prayed for me. Yes, I hope I now know how to appreciate the prayers of Christians. Yes Mother, I know you have often prayed for me and do not forget me now for I still feel the need of prayer that I may be kept in duties both that I may have grace sufficient to overcome temptations that may come before me for I know they will be numerous, that I may ever be a faithful Soldier of Christ as well as of my Country. I would love that you could be here to see the good feeling that exist amongst the soldiers at this place. Brother West, Chaplin of the Regt. has written you a letter today in which he has sent you a Certificate of my Baptism. I suppose he has given you the plan upon which the Camp Church is established in this Brigade but it is this. They have established what is called the Camp Church which is nothing, only a Christian Association; also a regular Church for the acception of members to any church the applicant wishes to unite themselves to by bringing forth the proper testimony giving them a certificate of their acceptance to any church the applicant desires. Please write soon. Your son as ever

S B Gulledge

Fredricksburg

Fredericksburg, Va May the 10th 1863

My Dear Parents

It is with heartfelt gratitude and thankfulness to my Maker that I am permitted this beautiful Sabbeth (sic) morning once more to drop you a few lines to let you know that I have been spared through another great struggle for our independence. We have had another great battle around this place and another great victory. It is reported the Yankee force was 200,000 while ours was 60,000. It is supposed their loss was 35,000 and ours 10,000. The fight lasted near a week but General Lee at last succeeded in driving them back across the river. They crossed the river in two places. One division and our Brigade was left to guard this place while the remainder of the Army was sent to fight about eight or ten miles above. The Yankees found out our ford here and attacked and was about to flank our weak force here and we were compelled to pull back but we got reinforcements and the next morning we regained our first position. The loss in our Brigade was very heavy though I cannot tell exactly what it is. Our Company lost 1 killed, R R Adams and two wounded, J T Jones and G W Russell. The rest of the Company is well. Ben David has been at the hospital in Richmond for a long time but we expect him every day.

I received a letter from you dated 1st April some time ago but I have not had the chance of writing. I am very anxious to get a letter from you now for I want to know what has been done with the letter Brother West sent to the Church for me. Mother, I ask you always to remember me in your prayers and I also ask the prayers of the Church for I feel the good of prayer more than I ever did before in my life. Dear Ma, I just received your letter and I was

very glad to hear from you. When you get this
write to me if I was rec'd in full fellowship
with the Church or not. Martin is well and he
would like to get a letter from you. The Gibb
boys is well. I had about forgotten to write
about the clothing Mr Allen started from Newton
with. He says he put them in the box with his
cloths and they were carried from Maridian
(sic) somewhere above Decatur. I am in hopes
you will get them. Give my respects to all of
my acquaintance. I send my love to you all.
Write often. Don't wait to get a letter every
time before you write for you have a chance of
writing oftener that I do and I am always glad
to hear from you.
   I remain your son

              As ever

              S B Gulledge

      Culpepper C H Va June the 11th 1863

My Dear Mother

  I have just received your letters of the
23rd and 31st. I was very glad to hear from
you once more. I have been sick for several
days but I am now about well. Our Army has
been on the march for about a week but we are
now still although we will not be surprised to
have marching orders any moment for it is
thought that Gen Lee's intention is to make an
advance movement in the direction o Manassa.
Ma, you said some thing some time ago about
sending to Richmond for cards. I would have
doen so but I had no one to send by so I could
not get them but whenever I have the chance I
will try to get them. You done the best in

selling the cloths you made for me to get corn. I lately have drawn plenty of clothing to last me till next winter. You wanted to know how many fights the 13th Regt has been in. As near as I can tell it has been in nine fights besides 25 or 30 days at one beat on picket and under fire of the enemys guns around Richmond and in the bombardment of Fredericksburg.

Dear Ma, since I last wrote to you we have organized a prayer meeting in our camp. First one conduct it and then another until we get round but for the last few nights we have had our beloved Chaplin to lead for us. We have a good Chaplin I believe as any Regt in the army. He takes a great delight in instructing the young converts and teaching us the way of righteousness. Tell Pa I say I want very much to see him and talk with him. We know not that we will ever be permitted to meet on earth but I hope if we never see one another in this unhappy world we may be blessed with the Priviledge of meeting in heaven to part no more. I would be very glad for him to send some word in letters to me as paper is scarce and I will also write to him. No, my Pa don't think I have forgot you for I think of you every day. Write often. Don't wait to get a letter everytime before writing for I expect we will be moving very often now. I will not have a chance of writing often. From your son

                                          S B Gulledge

(This letter to his sister Zilpha Ann Gulledge and her husband Riley was written on the same letter)

Mr W R Wyatt

Dear Brother and Sister

    I received a letter from you today. I was very much pleased to hear from you and that you was getting well again. I would be glad to be at home to see you and tell you some things I have seen and heard since we last saw one another. Dippy[1] I still have your likeness. It is in Richmond in Mr Hammonds trunk. If I live to come home I expect to bring it with me. If I never come it will be sent home. Riley,[2] I got a letter from Oakley not long ago. He was in Alabama at home. He was wounded in the battles before Richmond last year in the knee. His leg is stiff and he thinks he will not get over it in a long time. I have written all the news that is of any interest so I will close. Write soon from your Brother

                                        S B Gulledge

FOOTNOTES

[1] Zilpha Ann (Gulledge) McBride, his sister, called Dippy.

[2] Riley W. Wyatt, his brother-in-law.

Culpepper C H Va   Aug 4th 1863

Mrs E L Gulledge[1]

As soon as the dark clouds of War began to spread these dismal shadows over the land, your son (S B Gulledge) volunteered amongst the first of our noble Patriots who came forth under a sense of duty, to offer their live, if need be, a sacrifice in defence (sic) of Southern rights and independence. He nobly redeemed every promise he has made, and all of the hopes of his numerous friends. He was always at his post, and always in front of danger. His gallantry in battle, and his chivalrous daring amidst the stern realities of War, (ever) the theme for praise from all his Comrades, (a) Cooler, more Cheerful and more manly spirit than his did not exist--always ready to do his duty, not only willingly but with alacrity. He passed through the battles of Manasses, Leesburg, around Richmond, Sharpsburg, the two (2) battles of Fredericksburg, unharmed, But at the terrific Battle of Gettysburg, when so many of the precious sons of the South met a partiots death, and found a Patriots grave, he was so mortally wounded (through the head). He was taken from the battlefield to the hospital, where he received Every attention which the skill of physicians could bestow, and when we left he was speechless, senseless and not even a faint hope of his recovery. I feel safe in saying that death soon closed the scene. "The lightening may flash, and the loud thunders rattle, He heeds not, he hears not, he's far from all pain. He sleeps his last sleep. He has fought his last battle. No Sound can awake him to glory (on Earth) again"; He lies in a Patriots grave, with a Patriots scar on his (bosom). His life and his blood are the costly price of his countrys freedom. His memory is Cherished with the warmest affection by his sorrowing Comrades, all of whom morn "his loss as that of a brother, but a light breaks through this gloom, the coffin has grasped but his form; the Spirit has fled away, and is at rest...having escaped from the wintery storm; 'He died in Jesus and is blest'".

His Bible and Hymn books were his daily companions. He was one of the Company prayer leaders. He has now reached the Ocean of Peace, of Rest, of Love. He dreaded not the dividing point between time and eternity. He was on the watch. All is well now. Sweet is the memory of the Patriots son and the Christian Soldier.

Very Respt

Your Obedient

(N?) R Walkins

FOOTNOTES

1   Eleanor Lauretta (McBride) Gulledge, Samuel Blackwell Gulledge's mother.

Camp Barksdales Brigade, Va
Sept 3rd 1863

Mrs Gulledge,

I received your kind note of the (?). I have postponed answering until I could hear something definite from Blackwell and can now say to you that we received a letter from Mr. Thomas Keith who was wounded and Sent to David's Island, N Y. He stated that Black died at Gettysburg Hospital a few days before he was removed. We suppose about the 7th or 8th of

July or at least he is marked dead from the 8th on the Roll Book.

I have enquired (sic) of all his Bussiness (sic) and I cannot hear of any claims either way. James Gibbs requested me to say to you that he carried Black from the field the first knight (sic) in his ambulance and that he was with him untill (sic) we left there and that he was not in his Senses whilst he was with him now would not talk at all. I can easily Simpathise (sic) with you but that there is no use of grieving because he has paid the debt that was required of him and which is required of all of us. He died in a glorious Cause; a true Son to his Country, to his parents and to his Devine (sic) Father and Peace be with him. May he rest with his Heavenly Father untill (sic) all immortal Souls will be called to the Tribunel (sic) Bar of God. I hope you will excuse my Short letter at this time as I go on Drill directly. No news that I know of from the Lines. Hoping to hear from you again Soon. I must close. Give my respects to your family and friends.

      Very Respectfully Your Friend

          Benj. David

BIBLIOGRAPHY

Boddie, William Willis. *History of Williamsburg.* Spartanburg, SC: The Reprint Company, 1992.

Cawthon, John Ardis. *The Inevitable Guest Life and Letters of Jemima Darby.* San Antonio, TX: The Naylor Company, 1965.

Coggeshall, Robert Walden. *Ancestors and Kin.* Spartanburg, SC: The Reprint Company, Publishers, 1988.

Cook, Harvey Toliver. *Rambles in the Pee Dee Basin South Carolina.* Vol. 1. Columbia, SC: The State Company, 1926.

Darlington County Historical Commission, Darlington, SC. Family Surname Files.

Ervin, Eliza Cowan and Horace Fraser Rudisill, eds. *Darlingtoniana A History of People, Places and Events in Darlington County, South Carolina.* Spartanburg, SC: The Reprint Company, 1976.

Family Bible of Samuel Blackwell, III. and Sarah Harrell Blackwell. Hartford: Silas Andrus, 1831.

Family Bible of David Gulledge and Eleanor Lauretta McBride Gulledge. New York: American Bible Society, 1858.

Family Bible of James A. Gulledge. New York: American Bible Society, 1878.

Green, Fletcher M., ed. *The Lides Go South...And West, The Record of a Planter Migration in 1835.* Columbia, SC: University of South Carolina Press, 1952.

Gregg, Alexander. *History of the Old Cheraws.* Columbia, SC: The State Company, 1925., reprinted Greenville, SC: Southern Historical Press, Inc., 1991.

King, G. Wayne. *Rise Up So Early A History of Florence County South Carolina.* Spartanburg, SC: The Reprint Company, 1981.

Orlando Public Library, Orlando, FL. B. B. Commander files.

Pettigrew, George R. *Annals of Ebenezer 1778-1950 A Record of Achievement.* Privately printed.

Rogers, Jr., George C. *The History of Georgetown County, South Carolina.* Spartanburg, SC: The Reprint Company, Publishers, 1990.

Rudisill, Horace Fraser. *Doctors of Darlington County, South Carolina 1760--1912.* Darlinton, SC: Darlington County Historical Society, 1962.

Sellers, W. W. *A History of Marion County, South Carolina From Its Earliest Times to the Present, 1901.* Columbia, SC: The R. L. Bryan Company, 1902.

Thomas, J. A. W. *A History of Marlboro County, With Traditions and Sketches of Numerous Families.* Baltimore: Gateway Press, Inc., 1989.

Townsend, Leah. *South Carolina Baptists 1670-1805.* Baltimore: Genealogical Publishing Co., Inc., 1978.

United States Census Records. 1850, 1860, Darlington Co., SC; Chesterfield Co., SC; Marion Co., SC; Sumter Co., SC; Jasper Co., MS.

Wilson, Jane Lide Coker. *Memories of Society Hill, S.C.* Reprinted John M. Wilson, MD, 1989.

APPENDIX

FAMILY GROUP SHEETS

15-MAY-1993   Family group sheet
==
Husband: John Hamlin BLACKWELL

    Born: 12-DEC-1815   in: Darlington Co., SC   1
Baptized: 1850   in: Ebenezer Baptist Ch., Florence Co., SC 2
    Died: 15-JAN-1891   in: Florence, SC   3
  Buried: in: Ebenezer Churchyd, Florence, SC   4
Religion: Baptist   in: 5
     Ref: Occupation: MD
  Father: Samuel BLACKWELL, II.
  Mother: Mary Ann HAMLIN
              1860, 1880 Darlington Census. Darlington Co. Historical Commission.
              Deacon in Baptist Church, serving many years at Ebenezer. Gregg: p. 603-4.
              Was in legislature 1850-1 & 60-1. Brant & Fuller: Cyclopedia of Eminent Men.
              Letters to Lauretta (6/1/1853 give marriage date). Member State Legislature
              Per Gregg, Dr. John H. Blackwell studied medicine under Dr. Timothy JK Dargan
              of Darlington, grad Charleston Med College, practiced med for 40 yrs in Darl
              & Florence Cos. Died at age 76 in 1891 at home in Florence Co., SC
==
   Wife: Aletha WINDOM
Married: 15-DEC-18??   in: AL   6

    Born: in: AL   7
    Died: in:
  Father:
  Mother:
              Per Dr. WJ Bray, Abilene, TX. Aletha may be dau of Benj. Windom and Sarah
              Nettles, d/o Sarah Daniels & Malichi Nettles, s/o Joseph Nettles of Darl'ton
              SC b. 1735. They moved to Ft. Chadborne, AL.
              Annals of Ebenezer by George Pettigrew.
==
M Child 1 Edward John Burch BLACKWELL
    Born: c. 1839   in: SC   8
Baptized: 1857   in: Ebenezer Baptist Ch., Florence Co., SC 9
    Died: in: 5
Religion: Baptist   in: 10
  Spouse: Fannie H. RANSFORD
Married: 27-AUG-1865   in: 11
              Annals of Ebenezer by George Pettigrew, p64. Served in Confederate Army.
              Member of Ebenezer Church, 1878.

(Family of John Hamlin BLACKWELL - Continued)

F Child 2 Carrie Aletha BLACKWELL
   Born: in: 12
   Baptized: SEP-1857   in: Ebenezer Church, Florence Co., SC   13
   Died: in:
   Religion: Baptist   in: 14
   Ref: Occupation: Teacher
        Dismissed fm Ebenezer Church, 1880. Annals of Ebenezer by George Pettigrew.
        "Caroline" Blackwell.
===
  Wife: Sarah A. S. PETTIGREW
Married: 2-MAR-1853   in: Darlington Co., SC   8

   Born: 1830   in: 15
   Baptized: SEP-1850   in: Ebenezer Bapt. Ch, Florence, SC   16
   Died: 1913   in: 17
   Religion: Baptist   in: 16
   Father: Robert A. PETTIGREW
   Mother: Elizabeth Sparks PEARCE
        Per Gregg, History of the Old Cheraws, her Father was Robert Pettigrew and
        mother of Robert Pettigrew was Elizabeth Dargan, dau. of Rev. Timothy Dargan.
        Darlington Co. Historical Commission files. Note: John Hamlin Blackwell's
        half sister, Elizabeth Blackwell married James Alexander Pettigrew. Sarah was
        cousin of James. DAR records member #121264
        Annals of Ebenezer, p. 64.
===
M Child 1 Robert James BLACKWELL
   Born: 10-DEC-1854   in: Marion Co., SC   18
   Died: 1927   in: Marion, SC   18
   Buried: 1927   in: Rose Hill Cem., Marion, SC.   18
   Religion: Baptist   in:
   Ref: Occupation: Merchant
   Spouse: Celeste Langdon YOUNG
Married: 08-DEC-1881   in: 11
        Lived in Marion, SC. Janette Catalano. Annals of Ebenezer by George
        Pettigrew. Brant & Fuller: Cyclopedia of Eminent & Rep. Men...Vol 1, p 592.
        Clerk in Gen Store. 1874 studied in commercial college, then moved to
        Marion, SC. 1879 in mercantile business with Mr. Young, then Mr. G.A.
        Norwood, of Greenville. President of the Cotton-seed Oil Mill Co.
        By 1892 had 2 sons & two daughters.

(Family of John Hamlin BLACKWELL - Continued)

F Child 2 Elizabeth BLACKWELL
  Born: 04-FEB-1858 in: 11
  Died: 24-JAN-1941 in: Sumter, SC   11
 Spouse: George Washington LEE, Jr.
 Married: in: Mt. Hope, SC   11
                Janette Catalano. Annals of Ebenezer by George Pettigrew, p. 64.
                Second wife.

F Child 3 Anna C. BLACKWELL
  Born: 1877   in: Darlington Co., SC   19
  Died: OCT-1953   in: prob. Marion Co., SC   19
 Buried: in: Rose Hill Cem, Marion Co., SC 18
Religion: Baptist   in:
 Spouse: Louis Mowry PETTIGREW
Married: 19-JUN-1895 in: 19
                Annals of Ebenezer by George Pettigrew, p. 64.
                Cemeteries in Marion Co., SC by The Marion Co. Historical Soc.
===

1 Pettigrew, George R. Annals of Ebenezer 1778-1950, A Record of Achievement Privately printed, 1952 63

2 Pettigrew, George R. Annals of Ebenezer 1778-1950, A Record of Achievement Privately printed, 1952 48

3 Pettigrew, George R. Annals of Ebenezer 1778-1950, A Record of Achievement Privately printed, 1952. 64

4 Leonardo Andrea files, South Caroliniana Library.

5 Pettigrew, George R. Annals of Ebenezer 1778-1950, A Record of Achievement Privately printed, 1952

6 Gregg, Alexander. History of The Old Cheraws. Columbia: The State Co. 1925 (Reprinted, 1991: Southern Historical Press)

7 Pettigrew, George R: Annals of Ebenezer 1778-1950, A Record of Achievement 64

8 W. J. Bray

9 Pettigrew, George R. Annals of Ebenezer 1778-1950, A Record of Achievement Privately printed, 1952 54

(Family of John Hamlin BLACKWELL - Continued)

10 Pettigrew, George R. Annals of Ebenezer 1778-1950, A Record of Achievement Privately printed, 1952 72

11 Janette Catalano

12 Pettigrew, George R. Annals of Ebenezer 1778-1950, A Record of Achievement Privately printed, 1952 64

13 Pettigrew, George R. Annals of Ebenezer 1778-1950, A Record of Achievement Privately printed, 1952 57

14 Pettigrew, George R. Annals of Ebenezer 1778-1950, A Record of Achievement Privately printed, 1952 78

15 DAR 121264

16 Letters to Lauretta; Elizabeth Blackwell Pettigrew 9/30/1850

17 DAR 1212164

18 101 Cemeteries in Marion Co., SC; Marion Co. Historical Society, Marion, SC 1983.

19 Darlington Co. Historical Commission files

15-MAY-1993   Family group sheet
==
Husband: Samuel BLACKWELL, II.

   Born: 21-AUG-1774   in: Georgetown, SC   1
   Died: 14-FEB-1823   in: 13 mi. S.,Florence, Darlington Co., SC   2
   Buried: in: Blackwell Cem, Burch's Csrds, Florence, SC 3
Religion: Baptist   in: 4
   Ref: Occupation: Planter
 Father: Samuel BLACKWELL, I.
 Mother: Elizabeth DOZIER
            Eq. Bill 50 Will dated 10/31/1822, rec'd 4/3/1823 Darlington Co., SC. Mills
            Atlas 1820, Sam Blackwell property in Darlington Co., SC, adjoining Marion Co.
            nr Jeffries Cr. Janie Revill notes--William Brice Archives, Sumter. Settled
            Hadralls Pt., now Mt. Pleasant nr Charleston & Georgetown on Black Creek.
            Will apt A, Pkg 1348 Darl'ton Co.,SC.-S. Blackwell's nephew James Lane, exec'r
            Mem. Ebenezer Church. 7200 acres. Cem. 3mi. below Florence off Pamplico Rd.
            Gregg: p. 603. Moved to Jeffries Creek after marriage to second wife.
==
   Wife: (Miss) COMMANDER
Married: est. 1797   in: Georgetown, SC   1

   Born: c. 1770/5   in: SC   4
   Died: c. 1802   in: SC   4
 Father: James COMMANDER, I.
 Mother: ?-?-?
            Died possibly post partum.
            Gregg: p. 603. "From Georgetown and an heiress for her day."
==
F Child 1 Mary Jane BLACKWELL
   Born: 1798   in: Georgetown, SC   1
   Died: 1831   in: Darlington District, SC   1
Religion: Baptist   in: 4
 Spouse: William McBRIDE
Married: JUN-1818   in: Darlington Co., SC   5
            Was 1st wife of Dr. William McBride.
            Letters to Lauretta fm Elizabeth Blackwell Pettigrew dtd 1/3/1850 mentions
            enjoying Christmas knowing "all of sister's daughters are married."

F Child 2 Elizabeth H. BLACKWELL
    Born: 07-SEP-1802   in: SC   6
Baptized: MAY-1827   in: Ebenezer Church, Florence Co., SC   7
    Died: 09-DEC-1861   in: Darlington Co., SC   3
  Buried: in: Blackwell Cem., Florence, SC   3

(Family of Samuel BLACKWELL, II. - Continued)

Religion: Baptist   in: Ebenezer Church, Florence Co., SC   7
  Spouse: James Alexander PETTIGREW
  Married: 03-JAN-1821   in: Darlington Co., SC   8
            Married James A. Pettigrew, 1/3/1821. Annals of Ebenezer by Geo. Pettigrew.
            Wrote series of Letters to Lauretta McBride Gulledge, her niece, which give
            much information on family during period 1849-1863.
            Ltr dtd 7/1/1853 says she has lost 6 children at that time.
            Birth: Ltrs to Lauretta dtd 9/7/1859 "today I am 57 yrs old, Edward is 18."
            Ltr from Blackwell Gulledge to his mother Lauretta dtd 3/18/1862 says: "Aunt
            E. B. Pettigrew died last Nov."
===
    Wife: Mary Ann HAMLIN
  Married: 30-JUN-1803   in: Georgetown, SC   1

     Born: 08-OCT-1786   in: Prince Frederick Parish, Winyaw, SC   9
  Baptized: in: Prince Frederick Parish, Winyaw, SC   9
     Died: 20-NOV-1869   in: Darlington Village, SC   10
   Buried: in: Blackwell Cem, nr Burch's Crsrds, SC   10
 Religion: Baptist   in: Ebenezer Church, Florence, SC   11
   Father: John HAMLIN
   Mother: Joanna WHITE
            Lived on Jeffries Creek, member of Ebenezer Church, originally from Georgetown
            Granted letter of dismission fm Ebenezer Church in 1839 (Annals of Ebenezer,
            p. 39). Register Book for Prince Frederick Parish, Winyaw, SC. Bapt. by
            Rev. James Twifoot. Gregg: p 603. Movd to Darlington Village after husband's
            death. Died aged 84. Purchased home near Pearl St. c. 1856. Darlingtoniana
            p. 343. Darlington Co., SC Census 1850, p. 379.
            See Marion Co., SC Book W, p.174-6.
===
F Child 1 Joanna White BLACKWELL
     Born: 15-MAY-1804   in: SC   3
 Baptized: AUG-1848   in: Ebenezer Bapt. Ch, Florence, SC   12
     Died: 19-MAY-1884   in: Darlington Co., SC   3
   Buried: in: Ebenezer Churchyd, Florence, SC   3
 Religion: Baptist   in: 13
   Spouse: Edward Sebrey BURCH
  Married: 15-OCT-1823   in: 14
            Member Ebenezer Church. 1850 Darlington Census
            Annals of Ebenezer, p. 45. Gregg: p. 603.

(Family of Samuel BLACKWELL, II. - Continued)

F Child 2 Isabella Ann BLACKWELL
   Born: 21-SEP-1805   in: 1
   Died: fl 1871   in: Darlington Co., SC   15
Religion: Baptist   in: 16
  Spouse: William W. WINGATE
Married: 24-SEP-1823   in: 1
        Member Ebenezer Church. 1850 Darlington Census
        Darlingtoniana by Ervin & Rudisill. p. 475, 477. Gregg: p. 603.
        Annals of Ebenezer by Geo. Pettigrew, Final Mtg of Ebenezer Ch for 1828 welcomed Isabella Ann Wingate into fellowship.
        Sold her home at Pearl & Edwards, Darl, to J J Ward, in 1871.

M Child 3 Samuel BLACKWELL, III.
   Born: 17-MAR-1807   in: Darlington Co, SC   17
   Died: 26-JUL-1847   in: Jeffries Creek, Darlington Co., SC   17
  Spouse: Caroline Matilda HUNTER
Married: 22-JUL-1830   in: SC   17
  Spouse: Sarah Amanda Perkins HARRELL
Married: 07-JAN-1840   in: SC   17
        1850, 1860 Darlington Co. Census
        Family Bible. Also Darlington Co. Historical Commission
        Members Ebenezer Baptist Church.
        Happy Heritage, p. 123.
        Children became wards of Joseph Louis Harrell, Sarah's brother, after Samuel's death. Died intestate. See Roll 101, 10/27/1847; also BK 6, p.162/3
        1/31/1849 Edward S. Burch, John H. Blackwell & Joseph L. Harrell administrators.

F Child 4 Hannah Mara BLACKWELL
   Born: 10-OCT-1807   in: Darlington Co., SC   3
   Died: 15-SEP-1889   in: Darlington Co., SC   3
  Buried: in: Old Cem, Historic Dist, Darlington   3
  Spouse: Edmund GEE (1795-1831), son of John & Judith Gee.
        Attorney; early member of Darlington, SC Bar.
Married: in:
  Spouse: Joseph Burch NETTLES
Married: 1832   in: 18
        Married 1st Edmund Gee; 2nd 1832 Gen. Joseph Nettles (b. 1804)
        1850 Darlington Census, p 344. Gregg: p. 603.
        Commander Family, p. 250/1.

F Child 5 Martha Johnson BLACKWELL
   Born: 13-JUN-1811   in: Darlington Co., SC   19

(Family of Samuel BLACKWELL, II. - Continued)

```
     Died: 16-DEC-1880    in: Camden, Ouachita Co., AR           19
   Buried:                in: Oakland Cem., Ouachita Co., AR     19
 Religion: Baptist         in:                                    20
   Spouse: Eli Hugh LIDE
  Married: 19 JUL 1830    in: SC                                 21
```
             1850 Census Dallas Co., AL (age 39--brthplce SC). Gregg: p. 603.
             1860 Annotated Census, Liberty Town, Ouachita Co., AR p.7. by Bobbie J McLane
             with sons James E. (17) and Sam'l B (13) and dau. Hannah (15).
             The Cemetery Records for Ouachita Co., AR pub by Ouachita Co. Extension Home-
             makers Council. 1870 census Ouachita Co., AR, p. 324
             Mvd to AR in 1857, settld on farm 6 mi. fm Camden. Goodspeed's Historical
             Memoirs of Southern AR, pub 1890.

M Child 6 John Hamlin BLACKWELL
```
     Born: 12-DEC-1815    in: Darlington Co., SC                 22
 Baptized: 1850           in: Ebenezer Baptist Ch., Florence Co., SC  23
     Died: 15-JAN-1891    in: Florence, SC                       24
   Buried:                in: Ebenezer Churchyd, Florence, SC    25
 Religion: Baptist         in:                                    26
      Ref:                      Occupation: MD
   Spouse: Aletha WINDOM
  Married: 15-DEC-18??    in: AL                                  8
   Spouse: Sarah A. S. PETTIGREW
  Married: 2-MAR-1853     in: Darlington Co., SC                  4
```
             1860, 1880 Darlington Census. Darlington Co. Historical Commission.
             Deacon in Baptist Church, serving many years at Ebenezer. Gregg: p. 603-4.
             Was in legislature 1850-1 & 60-1. Brant & Fuller: Cyclopedia of Eminent Men.
             Letters to Lauretta (6/1/1853 give marriage date). Member State Legislature
             Per Gregg, Dr. John H. Blackwell studied medicine under Dr. Timothy JK Dargan
             of Darlington, grad Charleston Med College, practiced med for 40 yrs in Darl
             & Florence Cos. Died at age 76 in 1891 at home in Florence Co., SC
==

1 Janette Catalano

2 Newspaper notice

3 Cemetery Marker

4 W. J. Bray

(Family of Samuel BLACKWELL, II. - Continued)

5 Gregg, Alexander. History of The Old Cheraws. Columbia: The State Co. 1925
(Reprinted, 1991: Southern Historical Press) 603

6 Letters to Lauretta; Elizabeth Blackwell Pettigrew 9/7/1859

7 Pettigrew, George R. Annals of Ebenezer 1778-1950, A Record of Achievement
Privately printed, 1952 25

8 Gregg, Alexander. History of The Old Cheraws. Columbia: The State Co. 1925
(Reprinted, 1991: Southern Historical Press)

9 Register Book for Prince Frederick Parish, Winyaw, SC.

10 Cemetery Marker, Blackwell Cemetery, Burches Crossroads, Florence, SC.
Leonardo Andrea files, SCL.

11 Pettigrew, George R. Annals of Ebenezer 1778-1950, A Record of Achievement
Privately printed, 1952 39

12 Pettigrew, George R. Annals of Ebenezer 1778-1950, A Record of Achievement
Privately printed, 1952 44

13 Pettigrew, George R. Annals of Ebenezer 1778-1950, A Record of Achievement
Privately printed, 1952 45

14 Leonardo Andrea files, SCL

15 Ervin, Eliza Cowan & Rudisill, Horace Fraser. Darlingtoniana A History of
People, Places and Events in Darlington County, South Carolina. Spartanburg,
SC: The Reprint Co. 1976. 475

16 Pettigrew, George R. Annals of Ebenezer 1778-1950, A Record of Achievement
Privately printed, 1952 27

17 Family Bible of Samuel Blackwell, III. & Sarah Harrell Blackwell

18 Ervin, Eliza Cowan & Rudisill, Horace Fraser: Darlingtoniana A History of
People, Places and Events in Darlington County, South Carolina; The Reprint
Co, Spartanburg, SC 1976. Marriage contract signed 10/5/1832.

19 Cemetery Records

(Family of Samuel BLACKWELL, II. - Continued)

20 Centre Ridge Baptist Church Minutes, Dallas Co., AL.

21 Kolb, Avery. Daughter of Johannes Kolb, Sarah Kolb Lide and Her Descendants.

22 Pettigrew, George R. Annals of Ebenezer 1778-1950, A Record of Achievement Privately printed, 1952 63

23 Pettigrew, George R. Annals of Ebenezer 1778-1950, A Record of Achievement Privately printed, 1952 48

24 Pettigrew, George R. Annals of Ebenezer 1778-1950, A Record of Achievement Privately printed, 1952. 64

25 Leonardo Andrea files, South Caroliniana Library.

26 Pettigrew, George R. Annals of Ebenezer 1778-1950, A Record of Achievement Privately printed, 1952

18-MAY-1993   Family group sheet
===
Husband: Samuel BLACKWELL, III.

   Born: 17-MAR-1807   in: Darlington Co, SC   1
   Died: 26-JUL-1847   in: Jeffries Creek, Darlington Co., SC   1
   Father: Samuel BLACKWELL, II.
   Mother: Mary Ann HAMLIN
            1850, 1860 Darlington Co. Census
            Family Bible. Also Darlington Co. Historical Commission
            Members Ebenezer Baptist Church.
            Happy Heritage, p. 123.
            Children became wards of Joseph Louis Harrell, Sarah's brother, after Samuel's
            death. Died intestate. See Roll 101, 10/27/1847; also BK 6, p.162/3 1/31/1849
            Edward S. Burch, John H. Blackwell & Joseph L. Harrell administrators.
===
   Wife: Caroline Matilda HUNTER
Married: 22-JUL-1830   in: SC   1

   Born: AUG 1795   in: prob. SC   2
   Died: 11-APR-1837   in: prob. Georgetown Co., SC   1
   Father: Issac HUNTER
   Mother: Janette GEE
            Grand-daughter of Andrew HUNTER. Brother: Robert, Sisters: Elizabeth & Jane.
            Great grand-daughter of David HUNTER.
            Bible of husband, Samuel Blackwell, III. & 2nd wife Sarah Harrell Blackwell.
            Gregg: p. 603.
===
F Child 1 Martha Aurelia BLACKWELL
   Born: 17-APR-1831   in: prob. SC   1
   Died: 05-JUN-1913   in: 2
   Spouse: William King RYAN (1/27/1827--12/27/1895)
Married: 30-JUL-1851
            Janette Catalano. Gregg: p. 601.
            Martha Aurelia RYAN was member of DAR, joining in 1893, #4352.
            Family Bible of Samuel Blackwell & 2nd wife Sarah A. Blackwell.

F Child 2 Daughter BLACKWELL
   Born: 15-JAN-1833   in: prob. SC   1
   Died: 15-JAN-1833   in: prob. SC   1
            Family Bible of father Samuel Blackwell

M Child 3 Samuel Issac BLACKWELL
   Born: 11-OCT-1834   in: Darlington, SC   1

(Family of Samuel BLACKWELL, III. - Continued)

```
Baptized: 1855          in: Darlington, SC                      3
   Died: 03-SEP-1898    in: Darlington Co., SC                  2
 Buried:                in: Ebenezer Churchyd, Florence, SC     4
    Ref:                   Occupation: Doctor
 Spouse: Anna Colby HAMLIN
Married: 1859           in:                                     2
 Spouse: Hanna STANHACKER
Married:                in:
```
        Gregg: p. 601. Became Doctor, 10/31/1859.
        1880 Darlington Census, Vol 10, ED 33, Ebenezer Township.
        Married 2nd Hannah Starhecker. Cemetery Marker says b. 10/9/1835.
        Member of Ebenezer Red Shirt Club. (Annals of Ebenezer, p. 69)

M Child 4 John Caroline BLACKWELL
```
   Born: 11-APR-1837    in: prob. Georgetown Co., SC.           1
   Died: 22-MAR-1910    in: Darlington, SC                      2
 Spouse: Emma S. BURCH (1842-1904)
Married: 01-OCT-1860    in: SC                                  2
 Spouse: Alice HENDERSON
Married:                in:
```
        1880 Darlington Census, Palmetto TWP. Darlington Co. Historicial
        Commission Blackwell Family Bible of father Samuel Blackwell.
        Ebenezer Church. Cavalry Captain. Annals of Ebenezer, p. 69.
        Gregg: p. 601. Sheriff of Darlington Co.

===

```
   Wife: Sarah Amanda Perkins HARRELL
Married: 07-JAN-1840    in: SC                                  1
```

```
    Born: 11-Feb-1822   in: prob. Darlington Co., SC            1
Baptized: OCT-1847      in: Ebenezer Ch., Florence, SC          5
    Died: 05-NOV-1863   in: Timmonsville, Darlington Co., SC    1
Religion: Baptist       in:                                     5
  Father: James H. HARRELL
  Mother: Mary Hollingsworth BURCH
```
        Darlington Co., SC 1850 Census, p 284. Living next to J. L. Harrell.
        Mentioned in letter from Sister-in-law Elizabeth Blackwell Pettigrew 4/13/1849
        & 8/8/1854. Ltr 1/29/1853 says married in Dec., 1852, second husband, James
        Owens, a widower with 5 children. 1860 SC Census.
        Family Bible of Sarah Harrell Blackwell & 1st husband, Samuel Blackwell.

===

(Family of Samuel BLACKWELL, III. - Continued)

F Child 1 Mary Annah BLACKWELL
   Born: 29-MAY-1841   in: Darlington Co., SC   1
   Died: 25-JUN-1877   in: Darlington Co., SC   2
   Buried: in: Swamp Creek Bapt. Cem   2
   Spouse: Cephas COLE
Married: 1859   in: 2
   Spouse: Samuel Kinchen ATKINSON (b.11/25/1836; d. 10/20/1878)
Married: 13-AUG-1865   in: Timmonsville, Darlington Co., SC   2
               Had rheumatism. See letter from aunt Elizabeth Blackwell Pettigrew 8/8/1854.
               See also Letters to Lauretta dtd 9/1/1859.

F Child 2 Elizabeth Isabella BLACKWELL
   Born: 11-NOV-1842   in: Darlington Co., SC   6
   Died: 1923   in: 2
   Spouse: James Tazwell BRISTOW
Married: 13-MAR-1865   in: 2
               Janette Catalano. Mentioned in Letter to Lauretta fm aunt Elizabeth Blackwell
               Pettigrew 8/8/1854. Son Louis J. Bristow m. Caroline Winkler, had dau Gwen.
               Letters to Lauretta dtd 6/27/1861 state has 1 son and 1 daughter.

M Child 3 James Harrell BLACKWELL
   Born: 08-JAN-1844   in: Darlington Co., SC   1
   Died: 13-MAY-1928   in: Lake City, Florence Co., SC   2
   Buried: in: Lake City Cemetery   7
   Ref: Occupation: Capt. Co. A
   Spouse: Martha Isadora TIMMONS
Married: 01-MAR-1865   in: Timmonsville, Darlington Co., SC   1
               Bible of Father & Mother Samuel & Sarah A. Blackwell.
               Youngest son. Adopted Mary Annah's children 1877. Survey Florence Co. Cem.
               Lake City once called Grahms Crossroads. During the Am Rev, Gen Francis
               Marion camped in the town. James H. Blackwell was Capt. in Civil War.
               Served 2 terms in State Legislature under Gov. Tilman and was Mayor of Lake
               City many years. When his sister Mary Annah Blackwell Atkinson was dying she
               gave her 2 youngest children to James and his wife to raise. 1880 Darlington
               census.

M Child 4 Joseph Sebrey BLACKWELL
   Born: 29-AUG-1845   in: SC   1
   Died: 30-JUN-1846   in: SC   (age 10 months)   1
==

(Family of Samuel Blackwell, III. - Continued)

1 Family Bible of Samuel Blackwell, III. & Sarah Harrell Blackwell

2 Janette Catalano

3 Letters to Lauretta; Elizabeth Blackwell Pettigrew 11/24/1855

4 Cemetery Marker

5 Pettigrew, George R: Annals of Ebenezer 1778-1950, A Record of Achievement 43

6 Bible

7 Cemetery Records

18-MAY-1993   Family group sheet
==
Husband: Edward Sebrey BURCH

    Born: 30-DEC-1806   in: SC   1
Baptized: AUG-1848   in: Ebenezer Bapt. Ch, Florence, SC   2
    Died: 06-SEP-1864   in: Darlington Co., SC   1
  Buried: in: Ebenezer Baptist Church, Florence, SC 1
Religion: Baptist   in: 2
     Ref: Occupation: Farmer
              Ordained as deacon, 1850, Ebenezer Baptist Church, Annals of Ebenezer, p. 48.
              1850 Darlington Co. census. Annals of Ebenezer, p.43. Buried Ebenezer Chyd
==
    Wife: Joanna White BLACKWELL
 Married: 15-OCT-1823   in: 3

    Born: 15-MAY-1804   in: SC   1
Baptized: AUG-1848   in: Ebenezer Bapt. Ch, Florence, SC   2
    Died: 19-MAY-1884   in: Darlington Co., SC   1
  Buried: in: Ebenezer Churchyd, Florence, SC   1
Religion: Baptist   in: 4
  Father: Samuel BLACKWELL, II.
  Mother: Mary Ann HAMLIN
              Member Ebenezer Church. 1850 Darlington Census
              Annals of Ebenezer, p. 45. Gregg: p. 603.
==
F Child 1 Mary Ann BURCH
    Born: 1825   in: 5
Baptized: 1850   in: Ebenezer Church, Florence Co., SC   6
    Died: in:
Religion: Baptist   in: 6
              Married a Moore (see Ltrs to Lauretta dtd 6/27/1861)
              No children as of 6/27/1861.

M Child 2 James E. BURCH
    Born: 11-FEB-1826   in: SC   1
Baptized: 1850   in: Ebenezer Baptist Ch., Florence Co., SC 6
    Died: 11-APR-1882   in: Darlington, SC   1
  Buried: in: Blackwell Cem, Burches Csrd, Florence 1
Religion: Baptist   in: 4
  Spouse: Mary J. SINCLAIR
 Married: bef. 8/7/1850 in: SC   7

227

(Family of Edward Sebrey BURCH - Continued)

                    Letters to Lauretta dtd 9/30/1850.
                    Marriage noted in Letters to Lauretta dtd 3/28/1850.
                    Survey of Cemeteries of Lower Florence Co., SC, Vol III. Blackwell Cem.
                    located app. 500 yds behind Greenwood Bapt. Ch, Claussen Rd, Florence, SC
                    1850 SC Census, Darlington Co., p.288.
                    Per Letters to Lauretta dtd 6/27/1861, had a girl and a boy. (Children of a
                    second marriage?)

M Child 3 Joseph Samuel BURCH
    Born: 13-JUL-1828   in: SC   8
    Died: 15-APR-1889   in: SC   8
    Buried: in: Ebenezer Bapt. Chyd., Florence, SC   8
    Religion: Baptist   in: Ebenezer Baptist Ch, Florence, SC   9
    Spouse: Eugenia SINCLAIR
    Married: c. 1852   in: SC
                    Died of Burns. Clerk of Ebenezer Church, 1866.
                    Ltrs to Lauretta dtd 6/27/1861. Had 3 boys and 2 girls, but 1 girl died of
                    burns. She was the oldest.

F Child 4 Joanna Louisa BURCH
    Born: 09-MAR-1832   in: Darlington, SC   8
    Baptized: JAN-1850   in: Ebenezer Ch, Florence, SC   10
    Died: 03-NOV-1902   in: SC   8
    Buried: in: Ebenezer Churchyd, Florence, SC   8
    Ref: Occupation: teacher   11
    Spouse: Samuel Blackwell McBRIDE
    Married: FEB 1854   in: Darlington Co., SC   12
                    She married the son of Mary Jane Blackwell McBride, who was the half-sister
                    of Joanna White Blackwell.
                    1850 SC Census, Darlington Co, p288

F Child 5 Elizabeth T. BURCH
    Born: 1834   in: 13
    Baptized: 1850   in: Ebenezer Church, Florence Co., SC   6
    Died: in:
    Religion: Baptist   in: 6
                    Letters to Lauretta, dtd 4/15/1849. "Betty"
                    Letters to Lauretta dtd 6/27/1861, had 1 boy and 2 girls.

(Family of Edward Sebrey BURCH - Continued)

F Child 6 Martha Isabella BURCH
   Born: 31-OCT-1835   in: SC   14
   Died: 11-AUG-1842   in: Darlington Co.,SC   14
   Buried: in: Blackwell Cemetery, Florence, SC   14
           Letters to Lauretta dtd 9/30/1850, say "James Burch was converted at his
           sister Martha's grave."

F Child 7 Hannah M. BURCH
   Born: 1836   in: SC   13
   Baptized: 1850   in: Ebenezer Church, Florence Co., SC   6
   Died: in:
           Letters to Lauretta dtd 9/30/1850.
           Boarded at Mary Ann Hamlin Blackwell's home in 1849. Letters to Lauretta
           dtd 4/13/1849.
           Married Jack Branson (Ltrs to Lauretta dtd 6/27/1861).
           Ltrs to Lauretta dtd 6/27/1861, had 1 little girl at that time.

M Child 8 John Blackwell BURCH
   Born: 11-MAY-1837   in: Darlington Co., SC   1
   Baptized: AUG-1874   in: Gee's Mill, Florence Co., SC   15
   Died: 12-MAR-1913   in: Darlington Co., SC   1
   Buried: in: Ebenezer Chyd, Florence   1
   Spouse: Mary A. --?--
   Married: in: prob. Darlington Co., SC

M Child 9 Sebrey BURCH
   Born: 1839   in: SC   16
   Died: in:
           Name in 1850 Census, Celery, and female.
           Could name possibly be Sebrey (for father)
           Letters to Lauretta dtd 6/27/1861 mention Sebry Burch, volunteering for 3
           years or war's duration.

FChild 10 Emma S. BURCH
   Born: 30-OCT-1842   in: SC   16
   Baptized: 1858   in: Ebenezer Church, Florence Co., SC   17
   Died: 24-SEP-1904   in: 16
   Spouse: John Caroline BLACKWELL
   Married: 01-OCT-1860 in: SC   16
           1850 SC Census, Darlington Co, p288 listed as Susan.

(Family of Edward Sebrey BURCH - Continued)

FChild 11 Susan BURCH
   Born: 1843   in: 16
   Died: in:

FChild 12 Ada BURCH
   Born: 23-JUL-1850   in: Darlington Co., SC   18
   Died: in:
                Letters to Lauretta (Elizabeth Blackwell Pettigrew to niece Lauretta McBride Gulledge) dtd 8/30/1850. In 1861, only child single at that time. (Letters to Lauretta, dtd 8/30/1850.)
==

1 Cemetery Marker

2 Pettigrew, George R. Annals of Ebenezer 1778-1950, A Record of Achievement Privately printed, 1952 44

3 Leonardo Andrea files, SCL

4 Pettigrew, George R. Annals of Ebenezer 1778-1950, A Record of Achievement Privately printed, 1952 45

5 1850 SC Census, Darlington Co 288

6 Pettigrew, George R. Annals of Ebenezer 1778-1950, A Record of Achievement Privately printed, 1952 48

7 1850 SC Census, Darlington Co. dtd 8/7/1850
Letters to Lauretta; Elizabeth Blackwell Pettigrew 3/28/1850

8 Cemetery Marker as listed in Leonardo Andrea files, South Caroliniana Library

9 Pettigrew, George R. Annals of Ebenezer 1778-1950, A Record of Achievement Privately printed, 1952 59

10 Letters to Lauretta; Elizabeth Blackwell Pettigrew 1/3/1850

11 Letters to Lauretta; J. William McBride 6/1/1878

12 Letters to Lauretta; Elizabeth Blackwell Pettigrew 8/8/1854

13 1850 SC Census, Darlington Co. 288

(Family of Edward Sebrey BURCH - Continued)
---

14 Cemetery Marker, Blackwell Cemetery, Burches Crossroads, Florence, SC.
Leonardo Andrea files, SCL.

15 Pettigrew, George R. Annals of Ebenezer 1778-1950, A Record of Achievement
Privately printed, 1952 72

16 Janette Catalano

17 Pettigrew, George R. Annals of Ebenezer 1778-1950, A Record of Achievement
Privately printed, 1952 55

18 Letters to Lauretta; Elizabeth Blackwell Pettigrew 8/30/1850.

18-MAY-1993   Family group sheet
==
Husband: James COMMANDER, I.

   Born: c. 1727   in: Winyah or Sumter, SC   1
   Died: in: prob. Georgetown area, SC   1
   Ref: Occupation: Planter
 Father: Samuel COMMANDER, II.
 Mother: possibly Sarah ?
            Dr. W. J. Bray, Abilene, TX. 1790 SC Georgetown, Prince Fred Par.
            1759-60 pvt. Capt Dan Davidson, Col. Rich Richardson, SC Militia.
            1790 SC Census, Georgetown, Prince Fred. Par. 1s>16, 4s<16, 2fem.
==
   Wife: ?-?-?
Married: est. 1759   in:
==
F Child 1 Elizabeth COMMANDER
   Born: 1769   in: 2
   Died: 1797   in: 2
 Spouse: Joseph HOULE
            Son Jas. Commander Houle m. Eliz. Stanley (1799-1887).
            Also spelled Hoole.

F Child 2 Miss COMMANDER
   Born: c. 1770/5   in: SC   3
   Died: c. 1802   in: SC   3
 Spouse: Samuel BLACKWELL, II.
Married: est. 1797   in: Georgetown, SC   4
            Died possibly post partum.
            Gregg: p. 603. "From Georgetown and an heiress for her day."

F Child 3 Margaret COMMANDER
   Born: bef. 1755   in: SC   5
 Spouse: John WALKER
            Daughter Margaret (Walker) Withers mentioned in Elizabeth Blackwell
            Pettigrew's Ltrs to Lauretta as her mother's sister's daughter.

M Child 4 Samuel COMMANDER
   Born: 1755-74   in: Georgetown District, SC   1
   Died: in:
 Spouse: Elizabeth ALLSTON
Married: 7-MAY-1812   in: Georgetown District, SC   3
 Spouse: Jane ?-?--

(Family of James COMMANDER, I. - Continued)

M Child 5 John COMMANDER
    Born: 1774-90   in: 1

M Child 6 Son1 COMMANDER
    Born: 1774-90   in: 1

M Child 7 Son2 COMMANDER
    Born: 1774-90   in: 1

M Child 8 Son3 COMMANDER
    Born: 1774-90   in: 1

M Child 9 James COMMANDER, II.
    Born: bef. 1774   in: prob. Georgetown, SC   1
            1790 Census, Georgetown, Prince Fred. Par. M. bef. 1790. (father of 1 son
            under 16 in 1790 Census)
==

1 Commander, Beatrice Brown. "Commander" A Colonial Family of South Carolina
Manuscript compiled 1965. Orlando Public Library, Orlando, FL.

2 Lineage Chart, Gertrude McLaurin Shaw, 8 Hasall St, Sumter, SC 29150 4/1976.

3 W. J. Bray

4 Janette Catalano

5 Letters to Lauretta; Elizabeth Blackwell Pettigrew 1/15/1852

18-MAY-1993   Family group sheet
==
Husband: James M. COMMANDER

   Born: 1818   in: SC   1
   Died: in: prob. Ocala, Marion Co., FL
   Ref: Occupation: planter
 Father: Samuel COMMANDER
 Mother: Elizabeth ALLSTON
           History of Georgetown states. "Commander's was the last of the rice plantation
           on the N. Santee. The Commander family, one of the oldest in the district,
           was represented in 1850 by James M. Commander, sheriff and brigadier general
           of the militia. He grew 180,000 lbs of rice w/36 slaves." Ltrs to Lauretta:
           Fine looking man, portly, weighs same as Mr. Pettigrew, has blue eyes and lght
           auburn hair. Has 3 children, 2 sons & 1 dau. Lost 2 eldest sons. Moved to
           FL 3/3/1853. 1860/70 census Marion Co, FL. 1855 in Orange Lake, FL.
==
   Wife: Eliza HOWLE
Married: in:

   Born: 1822   in: SC   1
   Died: in: prob. Marion Co., FL
 Father:
 Mother:
           Letters to Lauretta; Elizabeth Blackwell Pettigrew 2/23/1851 mentions Eliza's
           mother, Mrs. Hull (or Howle) and her sister Mrs. Vernon.
           1860/70 Census Marion Co., FL
==
M Child 1 Male1 COMMANDER
   Born: bef 1845   in: Georgetown, SC   2
   Died: bef 1/15/1852 in: Georgetown, SC   2
           Letters to Lauretta dtd 1/15/1852 speaking of James M. Commander, "He has
           lost two sons, the two eldest children."

M Child 2 Male2 COMMANDER
   Born: bef 1846   in: Georgetown, SC   2
   Died: bef 1/15/1852 in: Georgetown, SC   2
           Letters to Lauretta 1/15/1852 speaking of James M. Commander. "He has lost
           two sons, the two eldest children."

F Child 3 Blanche COMMANDER
   Born: 1846   in: SC   3
   Died: in:
           1860/70 Census Marion Co., FL

(Family of James M. COMMANDER - Continued)

M Child 4 R. COMMANDER
   Born: 1847   in: SC   1
   Died: in:
              1860 Census Marion Co., FL. Possibly Eugene R.
              Note: Not in 1870 Census for Marion Co., FL. Did he die during War?

M Child 5 James M. COMMANDER, Jr.
   Born: 1850   in: SC   1
   Died: in:
              1860/70 Census Marion Co., FL

M Child 6 O. B. COMMANDER
   Born: 1852   in: SC   1
   Died: in:
              1860 Census Marion Co., FL
              Prob. left home or died by 1870, not in 1870 Census.

M Child 7 Reginald H. COMMANDER
   Born: 1859   in: FL   4
   Died: in:
              1870 Census Marion Co., FL

M Child 8 Francis M. COMMANDER
   Born: 1862   in: FL   4
   Died: in:
              1870 Census Marion Co., FL

===

1 FL Census, 1860, Marion Co, p. 332.

2 Letters to Lauretta; Elizabeth Blackwell Pettigrew 1/15/1852

3 FL Census, 1860, Marion Co., p. 332

4 FL Census, 1870, Marion Co.

18-MAY-1993   Family group sheet
===
Husband: J. O. B. DARGAN

     Born: 9-AUG-1813   in: SC   1
 Baptized: OCT-1831   in: Ebenezer Church, Florence Co., SC   2
     Died: 1882   in: SC   3
 Religion: Baptist   in: Ebenezer Church   4
      Ref: Occupation: Baptist Clergyman
   Father: Timothy DARGAN, III.
   Mother: Lydia KEITH
              John Orr Beasley Dargan. Licensed 1833, attnd Furman Theological Inst. Ordaind
              Pastor Cheraw. Ancestral Key to the PEEDEE. Member Ebenezer Church, Jan 1823.
              Pastor of Black Creek Church for 43 yrs, commencing on 2/3/1838. Supply pastor
              Ebenezer Ch, 1853. Had home in Springville, SC, called Harmony Hall.
              Brothers were Chancellor George W. Dargan and Dr. W. Edwin Dargan (father
              of Congressman George W. Dargan). Annals of Ebenezer, p76.
===
    Wife: Margaret Jane LIDE
 Married: 13-JUN-1837   in: Springfield, Darlington Co., SC   5
   Other: in: by Rev. R. W. Bailey

     Born: 10-NOV-1815   in: SC   6
     Died: 1886   in: SC   7
   Father: Hugh LIDE
   Mother: Elizabeth PUGH
              Marriage and death Notices from the Southern Christian Herald, 6/23/1837,
              held by Emory University, Atlanta, GA   Also SCHM Vol 6, p. 153.
              Called "auntie" by relatives. Cawthon: The Inevitable Guest, p. 159.
              Cook: Rambles in the PeeDee Basin
===
M Child 1 James Furman DARGAN
     Born: 01-APR-1838   in: 6
     Died: 06-JUN-1907   in: 6
   Spouse: Mary Atmar SMITH
  Married: 13-JUL-1870   in: Charleston, SC   6
              Father of Ralph and Margaret Dargan of Darlington.
              Kolb Family Chart. Chi Psi Fraternity. Formerly professor in Converse
              College. Cawthon: The Inevitable Guest, p. 157, 362.
              Named for Dr. James C. Furman friend of Dargans and instructor of the sons.

M Child 2 Timothy George DARGAN
     Born: 1840   in: 6
     Died: 1881   in: 6

236

(Family of J. O. B. DARGAN - Continued)

   Spouse: Clara Louise DARGAN
Married: 15-NOV-1866 in: 6
        Cawthon: The Inevitable Guest, p. 155, 220.
        Graduated fm The Citadel in 1861, married his cousin Louise Dargan and enlstd
        in Hampton's Legion, Bonhams's Rgmt in the cavalry at Manassas, VA.

F Child 3 Elizabeth Pugh DARGAN
   Born: 03-MAY-1842 in: 6
   Died: 1883   in: Selma, AL   6
   Buried: in: Dargan Lot, Baptist Ch, Darlington, SC   6
   Spouse: Eldred J. FORRESTER
Married: 15-MAY-1878 in: 6
        Kolb Family Chart. Cawthon: The Inevitable Guest p. 90, 157, 351, 362, 364.
        Graduated fm Limestone Academy, Spring, 1860.
        Moved with her husband to Fort Deposit, Lowndes Co. AL.

F Child 4 Margaret Lydia Keith DARGAN
   Born: 16-SEP-1844 in: SC   6
   Died: 29-APR-1911 in: SC   6
   Spouse: Eldred J. FORRESTER
Married: 06-JAN-1855 in: 6
        Cawthon: The Inevitable Guest p. 90, 362

M Child 5 Preston DARGAN
   Born: in: 8
   Died: in:
        Prof. Romance languages at Univ. North Carolina and Univ. of Chicago.

M Child 6 Robert Lide DARGAN
   Born: in: 9
   Died: in:

M Child 7 Edwin Charles DARGAN
   Born: 17-NOV-1852 in: Darlington, SC   6
   Died: 26-OCT-1930 in: 6
   Ref: Occupation: Minister
   Spouse: Lucy GRAVES
Married: 12-JUN-1872 in: 6
        Preacher, lecturer, and writer. Author of Harmony Hall. Member Chi Psi.
        Pastor of the Citadel Square Baptist Ch, Charleston, SC; prof.Southern
        Baptist Theological Seminary, Louisville, KY; president Southern Baptist
        Convention.

(Family of J. O. B. DARGAN - Continued)

                Cawthon: The Inevitable Guest, p. 221, 322, 362.
                Married Lucy Graves, 6/12/1872.
                Served several small churches in VA, then became pastor of Baptist Ch in
                Dixon, CA.
===

1 Cawthon. The Inevitable Guest, p. 227.

2 Pettigrew, George R. Annals of Ebenezer 1778-1950, A Record of Achievement Privately printed, 1952 32,76

3 Ervin, Eliza Cowan & Rudisill, Horace Fraser: Darlingtoniana A History of People, Places and Events in Darlington County, South Carolina; The Reprint Co, Spartanburg, SC 1976

4 Pettigrew, George R. Annals of Ebenezer 1778-1950, A Record of Achievement Privately printed, 1952 20,53,76

5 Pettigrew, George R. Annals of Ebenezer 1778-1950, A Record of Achievement Privately printed, 1952 77

6 Cawthon. The Inevitable Guest.

7 Cook. Rambles in the Pee Dee Basin.

8 Ervin & Rudisill. Darlingtoniana.

9 Kolb Family Chart.

18-MAY-1993   Family group sheet
==
Husband: Julius Alfred DARGAN

    Born: c. 1816   in: SC   1
 Baptized: OCT-1831   in: Ebenezer Church, Florence Co., SC   2
    Died: MAR-1861   in: 3
 Religion: Baptist   in: Ebenezer Church   4
     Ref: Occupation: attorney
  Father: Timothy DARGAN, III.
  Mother: Lydia KEITH
          Member of the Secession Convention and a signer of the Ordinance of Secession
          (Cawthon, p. 122)
          Estate Pro. 1230, Jan 2, 1869, James A. Pettigrew, Appraiser.
          Member Ebenezer Baptist Ch, Jan. 1823.
==
  Wife: Martha J. WOODS

    Born: c. 1820   in: 5
 Baptized: OCT-1831   in: Ebenezer Church, Florence Co., SC   2
 Religion: Baptist   in: Ebenezer Church   6
  Father: Joseph WOODS
  Mother: Hepzibah DARGAN
          Member of Ebenezer Church Jan 1823. Her sister, Elizabeth Woods, m. John
                    Morrison.
==

1 W. J. Bray

2 Pettigrew, George R. Annals of Ebenezer 1778-1950, A Record of Achievement
Privately printed, 1952 32

3 Cawthon, John Ardis: The Inevitable Guest Life and Letters of Jemima Darby
copyright 1965, The Naylor Co., San Antonio, TX, Library of Congress Cat. No.
64-8903. 47,223

4 Pettigrew, George R. Annals of Ebenezer 1778-1950, A Record of Achievement
Privately printed, 1952 32,35

5 Cawthon, John Ardis: The Inevitable Guest Life and Letters of Jemima Darby
copyright 1965, The Naylor Co., San Antonio, TX, Library of Congress Cat. No.
64-8903.

6 Pettigrew, George R. Annals of Ebenezer 1778-1950, A Record of Achievement
Privately printed, 1952 20,35

18-MAY-1993   Family group sheet
==
Husband: Timothy DARGAN, II.

   Born: 1743   in: VA   1
   Died: SEP-1783   in: Jeffries Cr., Darl. Co., SC   1
   Buried: 28-SEP-1783   in: SC   2
   Religion: Baptist   in: 3
   Ref: Occupation: Baptist Minister
   Father: Timothy DARGAN, I.
   Mother: Catherine APPLEBY
               South Carolina Baptists by Townsend p. 107. Was founder of Ebenezer Baptist
               Church, Jeffries Cr., SC. & pastor at death. In French & Indian War fm VA.
               Active in Rev., had to flee SC w/Richard Furman & take refuge in NC w/bro.
               Rev Jeremiah Dargan. 1769 preacher Congaree Ch; 1773 Planter of Craven Co.;
               ordained at High Hills Santee 1777. Purchased lands both sides Jeffries Cr.
               Friend of Rev. Evan Pugh who preached his funeral
==
   Wife: Ann BEASLEY
Married: bef. 1771   in:

   Born: in:
   Died: c. 10/8/1819   in: SC   4
   Father:
   Mother:
               Will BK 5, p.226. Darlington Co. Historical Commission files.
==
F Child 1 Hepzibah DARGAN
   Born: 1781   in: 5
   Died: 22-MAR-1855   in: Darlington Co., SC   6
   Religion: Baptist   in: Ebenezer Church   7
   Spouse: Joseph WOODS
Married: in:
               Member Ebenezer Church, Jan 1823, Jun 1827, Sep 1829.
               Died at the home of Elizabeth and James Pettigrew. Ltrs to Lauretta dtd
               3/27/1855.

M Child 2 Timothy DARGAN, III.
   Born: 1771   in: prob. Darlington, SC   8
   Died: 26-MAY-1839   in: Darlington, SC   8
   Buried: in: Darlington Baptist Chyd, Darlington, SC 8
   Religion: Baptist   in: 9
   Spouse: Lydia KEITH
Married: est. 1802   in: SC   5

(Family of Timothy DARGAN, II. - Continued)

Marr. Ceremony? Y/N: Y   Divorced/Annulled/Separated: End Year:
   Will dtd 1/8/1834, prvd 1/8/1840.
   30 years deacon of Baptist Church, member of SC State General Assembly.
   Only son of Rev. Timothy Dargan. Annals of Ebenezer by Pettigrew, p. 41.

F Child 3 Mary DARGAN
   Born: c. 1784/1790   in: SC   5
   Died: in:
 Spouse: John ORR
Married: in:
   South Carolina Baptists by Townsend p.107n
   Married John ORR of Georgetown Dist, Liberty Co., SC (will BK 2, Darl Co. SC
   28 Jan 1797) Children: John Dargan Orr, William James Orr, Mary Dargan Orr,
   Ann Orr.

F Child 4 Ann DARGAN
   Born: 29-JAN-1769   in: SC   10
   Died: 1824   in: SC   10
 Spouse: Robert Alexander PETTIGREW
Married: in: 10
 Spouse: Samuel ECCLES
Married: c. APR-MAY 1808 in: Darlington Co., SC   11
Marr. Ceremony? Y/N: Y   Divorced/Annulled/Separated: End Year:
   South Carolina Baptists by Townsend, p.107n
   Marriage Bonds, Darlington Co., SC BkB, p. 70. dtd 21 Apr 1808. Marriage to
   occur shortly between Samuel Eccles and Ann Pettigrew of Darlington District,
   widow of Alexander Pettigrew. Timothy Dargan & William Zimmerman trustees.
       (JJH note: 1st husband Robert Alexander Pettigrew, perhaps called Alexander)

F Child 5 Susannah DARGAN
   Born: 11-FEB-1779   in: prob. Darlington Co. SC   12
   Died: 13-SEP-1846   in: prob. Darlington Co. SC   10
 Spouse: William PETTIGREW
Married: 19-DEC-1799   in: SC   12
 Spouse: William CONNELL
Married: 20-NOV-1804   in: SC   12
 Spouse: John GOOD
Married: 06-MAR-1816   in: SC   12
   See Letters to Lauretta dtd 12/5/1849, p.17
   Estate of William Pettigrew divided 10/5/1807 at which time Susannah was
   m. to 2nd husband William Connell. 9/5/1829 1st appeared on rolls of
   Ebenezer Ch. Marriage dates from Bible of Lewis Johnson, father of James A.

(Family of Timothy DARGAN, II. - Continued)

        Pettigrew's second wife, Sarah Elizabeth Johnson Dickson.
        Died as Susannah Good. Named James A. Pettigrew (son) sole Exec. Wills BK10,
        p. 125 (Jan 28, 1843). Equity Roll 475. South Carolina Baptists, p. 107n.

F Child 6 Phoebe DARGAN
  Born: in: 13
  Died: in:
        Annals of Ebenezer, p12. Had no descendants.

===

1 Townsend, Leah: History of South Carolina Baptists 1670-1805

2 Pugh, Rev. Evan: DIARY

3 Pettigrew, George R: Annals of Ebenezer 1778-1950, A Record of Achievement

4 Darlington County Historical Commission files

5 W. J. Bray

6 Letters to Lauretta; Elizabeth Blackwell Pettigrew 3/27/1855

7 Pettigrew, George R. Annals of Ebenezer 1778-1950, A Record of Achievement
Privately printed, 1952 20,25,29,35

8 Cemetery Marker

9 Pettigrew, George R. Annals of Ebenezer 1778-1950, A Record of Achievement
Privately printed, 1952 16,17

10 Darlington County Historical Commission files.

11 BONDS

12 Bible

13 Townsend, Leah: History of South Carolina Baptists 1670-1805 107n

18-MAY-1993   Family group sheet
==
Husband: Timothy DARGAN, III.

    Born: 1771   in: prob. Darlington, SC   1
    Died: 26-MAY-1839   in: Darlington, SC   1
  Buried: in: Darlington Baptist Chyd, Darlington, SC 1
Religion: Baptist   in: 2
  Father: Timothy DARGAN, II.
  Mother: Ann BEASLEY
            Will dtd 1/8/1834, prvd 1/8/1840.
            30 years deacon of Baptist Church, member of SC State General Assembly.
            Only son of Rev. Timothy Dargan. Annals of Ebenezer by Pettigrew, p. 41.
==
   Wife: Lydia KEITH
Married: est. 1802   in: SC   3
Marr. Ceremony? Y/N: Y   Divorced/Annulled/Separated: End Year:

     Born: 13-JUL-1782   in: SC   4
Baptized: OCT-1847   in: Ebenezer Bapt. Ch, Florence, SC   5
    Died: 15-JAN-1849   in: Darlington Co., SC   6
  Buried: 19-JAN-1849   in: Darlington Baptist Ch, Darlington, SC   1
Religion: Baptist   in:
  Father: James KEITH
  Mother: Margaret PERKINS
            Letters to Lauretta; Elizabeth B Pettigrew. 4/13/1849. "aunt D. died in Jan."
            Her sister Harriett m. Sam'l Ervin and moved to GA (dau Harriett m. Burch)
            Father: Col. Keith; Mother: Margaret Perkins whose 1st husband was James
            Dozier of Georgetown. They had dau. Mary who m. Wm F. Zimmerman. Was this
            James Dozier, the bro. of Elizabeth Dozier Blackwell?
            Lived in Doneraile (named for old Irish village), Darlington Co. See
            Darlingtoniana, p.21   Annals of Ebenezer, p. 47, says d. 1/15/1849.
==
M Child 1 George Washington DARGAN
     Born: 03-APR-1802   in: SC   7
     Died: 12-JUN-1859   in: prob. Darlington, SC   7
   Buried: in: Baptist Chyd, Darlington, SC   7
      Ref: Occupation: farmer
   Spouse: Mary Adeline WILSON
  Married: in: 7
   Spouse: Elizabeth M. PLAYER
  Married: 1846   in: 8
Marr. Ceremony? Y/N: Y   Divorced/Annulled/Separated: End Year:
            Darlingtoniana: Chancellor. Uncle of Hon George W. DARGAN

(Family of Timothy DARGAN, III. - Continued)

        VP Darlington District Agricultural Society (1856)
        Great Uncle of George E. and A. S. Dargan

M Child 2 Timothy J. K. DARGAN
  Born: 10-AUG-1804   in: Darlington District, SC nr Ebenezer   9
  Died: 20-JAN-1854   in: Darlington Co., SC   9
  Ref: Occupation: Doctor
  Spouse: Lydia Louisa WILSON
  Married: 02-DEC-1840   in: Darlington Co., SC   10
  Other: double wedding in: w/wife's sister & her husband
        Dr. John H. Blackwell did proctership w/ him. AB SCL 1826, grad SCMedCol 1830. Darlingtoniana by Ervin & Rudisill, Lived on corner of Orange & Sycamore Sts, Darlington, SC. 1849 presented paper at Agricultural Society, Darlington. "Preserving the health of negroes on our plantations." Grandfather of Woods Dargan & Mrs. Alice Dargan Jones. Mayor of Darl, 1852. Lived in home originally owned by Edmund Gee, called Violet Hill.

M Child 3 Jeremiah DARGAN
  Born: c. 1808   in: SC   3
  Died: 1855   in: Darlington, SC   11
  Religion: Baptist   in: Ebenezer Church   12
  Ref: Occupation: teacher
        "Jerry"
        Member of Ebenezer Church August 1832
        Died while in route to church.

M Child 4 J. O. B. DARGAN
  Born: c. 1813   in: SC   3
  Baptized: OCT-1831   in: Ebenezer Church, Florence Co., SC   13
  Died: 1882   in: SC   9
  Religion: Baptist   in: Ebenezer Church   14
  Ref: Occupation: Baptist Clergyman
  Spouse: Margaret Jane LIDE
  Married: 13-JUN-1837   in: Springfield, Darlington Co., SC   15
  Other: in: by Rev. R. W. Bailey
        John Orr Beasley Dargan. Licensed 1833, attnd Furman Theological Inst. Ordaind Pastor Cheraw. Ancestral Key to the PEEDEE. Member Ebenezer Church, Jan 1823. Pastor of Black Creek Church for 43 yrs, commencing on 2/3/1838. Supply pastor Ebenezer Ch, 1853. Had home in Springville, SC, called Harmony Hall. Brothers were Chancellor George W. Dargan and Dr. W. Edwin Dargan (father of Congressman George W. Dargan). Annals of Ebenezer, p76.

(Family of Timothy DARGAN, III. - Continued)

M Child 5 William Edwin DARGAN
    Born: 13-JUL-1811   in: Darlington District, SC nr Ebenezer   16
  Baptized: OCT-1847   in: Ebenezer Bapt. Ch, Florence, SC   17
    Died: 11-DEC-1851   in: Darlington Co., SC   18
  Religion: Baptist   in: Ebenezer Church, Florence Co., SC   19
     Ref: Occupation: Doctor/planter
  Spouse: Sarah Thomas DuBOSE
  Married: Oct-1838   in: Darlington Co., SC   9
        Grad SC Med Col, 1835, Asst. Surgeon 29th Regt SC Militia. Deacon in
        Ebenezer Baptist Ch. Darlingtoniana. Letters to Lauretta p. 34. Doctors of
        Darlington Co. by Rudisill p 17. Bapt. by brother, J.O.B. Dargan, along with
        wife Sarah and Mother, Mrs Lydia Dargan. (Annals of Ebenezer, p. 43, 51.)
        Grandfather of George E. & A. S. Dargan. Organized 1st Bible Study classes
        in area, became Sunday School Superintendent. Chosen to succeed James A.
        Pettigrew as Clerk of Ebenezer Ch. Ordained deacon, 1850.

M Child 6 Julius Alfred DARGAN
    Born: c. 1816   in: SC   3
  Baptized: OCT-1831   in: Ebenezer Church, Florence Co., SC   20
    Died: MAR-1861   in: 21
  Religion: Baptist   in: Ebenezer Church   22
     Ref: Occupation: attorney
  Spouse: Martha J. WOODS
  Married: in: 21
        Married Martha J. Woods (b. c. 1820), per Inevitable Guest by Cawthorn, p.47
        & 223. (Her sister, Elizabeth Woods, m. John Morrison).
        Member of the Secession Convention and a signer of the Ordinance of Secession
        (Cawthorn, p. 122)
        Estate Pro. 1230, Jan 2, 1869, James A. Pettigrew, Appraiser.
        Member Ebenezer Baptist Ch, Jan. 1823.

M Child 7 Sidney R. F. DARGAN
    Born: in: 3
  Baptized: OCT-1831   in: Ebenezer Church, Florence Co., SC   20
    Died: in:
  Religion: Baptist   in: Ebenezer Church, Florence Co., SC   23
        Member of Ebenezer Church, Jan 1823.

M Child 8 Theodore Alonzo DARGAN
    Born: 15-AUG-1822   in: Darlington District, SC nr Ebenezer   24
    Died: 10-SEP-1881   in: 24
     Ref: Occupation: Doctor

(Family of Timothy DARGAN, III. - Continued)

  Spouse: Mary Louisa BACOT
Married: in:
           1860 Census lists as T. A. Dargan, age 37.
           Cawthorn: The Inevitable Guest p. 24, 218
           Doctors of Darlington Co., by Rudisill p. 15.
           Grad. medicine SC Medical College, 1844. Partner with older bro. Timothy J. K. Dargan in medical firm until TJK Dargan's dth 1854. Surgeon on staff of 21st Regmt SCV in War Between States.

M Child 9 Charles A. DARGAN
  Born: c. 1822   in: SC   3
  Died: in:
           In 1840's in Darlington, SC, Member of Cold Water Boys, a temperance group. In 1853, operated after the railroad was constructed, operated an inn on his plantation, managed by J. E. Wingate. (King, History of Florence, p 39).

FChild 10 Harriet M. DARGAN
  Born: in: 3
  Died: in:
  Spouse: James Clement FURMAN
Married: in:
           Married James Furman. Letters to Lauretta, dtd 3/27/1855.

FChild 11 Margaret A. P. DARGAN
  Born: in: 9
  Baptized: OCT-1831   in: Ebenezer Church, Florence Co., SC   20
     Died: 08-JUL-1844 in: 25
  Religion: Baptist   in: Ebenezer Church, Florence Co., SC   26
  Spouse: Alexander Dromgoole SIMS
Married: 28-OCT-1830   in: Darlington Co., SC   27
           Darlingtoniana by Ervin & Rudisill, pp265/6
           Member of Ebenezer Baptist Church, Jan. 1823, given ltr of dismission to unite w/ Darlington Ch in 1838.

FChild 12 Elizabeth DARGAN
  Born: est. 1826   in: 3
  Died: in:

===

1 Cemetery Marker

2 Pettigrew, George R. Annals of Ebenezer 1778-1950, A Record of Achievement

(Family of Timothy DARGAN, III. - Continued)

Privately printed, 1952 16,17

3 W. J. Bray

4 Cemetery Marker

5 Pettigrew, George R. Annals of Ebenezer 1778-1950, A Record of Achievement
Privately printed, 1952 47

6 Pettigrew, George R. Annals of Ebenezer 1778-1950, A Record of Achievement
Privately printed, 1952 46

7 Cawthon, John Ardis: The Inevitable Guest Life and Letters of Jemima Darby
copyright 1965, The Naylor Co., San Antonio, TX, Library of Congress Cat. No.
64-8903. 86,222

8 Cawthon, John Ardis: The Inevitable Guest Life and Letters of Jemima Darby
copyright 1965, The Naylor Co., San Antonio, TX, Library of Congress Cat. No.
64-8903. 86

9 Ervin, Eliza Cowan & Rudisill, Horace Fraser: Darlingtoniana A History of
People, Places and Events in Darlington County, South Carolina; The Reprint
Co, Spartanburg, SC 1976

10 Cheraw Gazette, 12/23/1840

11 Pettigrew, George R. Annals of Ebenezer 1778-1950, A Record of Achievement
Privately printed, 1952. and
Letters to Lauretta; Elizabeth Blackwell Pettigrew. 53; 11/24/1855

12 Pettigrew, George R. Annals of Ebenezer 1778-1950, A Record of Achievement
Privately printed, 1952 35

13 Pettigrew, George R. Annals of Ebenezer 1778-1950, A Record of Achievement
Privately printed, 1952 32,76

14 Pettigrew, George R. Annals of Ebenezer 1778-1950, A Record of Achievement
Privately printed, 1952 20,53,76

15 Pettigrew, George R. Annals of Ebenezer 1778-1950, A Record of Achievement
Privately printed, 1952 77

(Family of Timothy DARGAN, III. - Continued)

16 Rudisill, Horace Fraser: Doctors of Darlington County, South Carolina 1760-1912, Pub. by The Darlington County Historical Society, Darlington, SC 1962 17

17 Pettigrew, George R. Annals of Ebenezer 1778-1950, A Record of Achievement Privately printed, 1952 43,51

18 Rudisill, Horace Fraser: Doctors of Darlington County, South Carolina 1760-1912, Pub. by The Darlington County Historical Society, Darlington, SC 1962

19 Pettigrew, George R. Annals of Ebenezer 1778-1950, A Record of Achievement Privately printed, 1952 43

20 Pettigrew, George R. Annals of Ebenezer 1778-1950, A Record of Achievement Privately printed, 1952 32

21 Cawthon, John Ardis: The Inevitable Guest Life and Letters of Jemima Darby copyright 1965, The Naylor Co., San Antonio, TX, Library of Congress Cat. No. 64-8903. 47,223

22 Pettigrew, George R. Annals of Ebenezer 1778-1950, A Record of Achievement Privately printed, 1952 32,35

23 Pettigrew, George R. Annals of Ebenezer 1778-1950, A Record of Achievement Privately printed, 1952 20

24 Cawthon, John Ardis: The Inevitable Guest Life and Letters of Jemima Darby copyright 1965, The Naylor Co., San Antonio, TX, Library of Congress Cat. No. 64-8903. 24,218

25 Ervin, Eliza Cowan & Rudisill, Horace Fraser: Darlingtoniana A History of People, Places and Events in Darlington County, South Carolina; The Reprint Co, Spartanburg, SC 1976 265,266

26 Pettigrew, George R. Annals of Ebenezer 1778-1950, A Record of Achievement Privately printed, 1952 20,38

27 Brant & Fuller: Cyclopedia of Eminent and Representative Men of the Carolinas Vol I. Madison, WIS, 1892 (Reprinted Spartanburg, SC, The Reprint Co. 1972)

18-MAY-1993   Family group sheet
===
Husband: William Edwin DARGAN

    Born: 13-JUL-1811   in: Darlington District, SC nr Ebenezer   1
    Baptized: OCT-1847   in: Ebenezer Bapt. Ch, Florence, SC   2
    Died: 11-DEC-1851   in: Darlington Co., SC   3
    Religion: Baptist   in: Ebenezer Church, Florence Co., SC   4
    Ref: Occupation: Doctor/planter
    Father: Timothy DARGAN, III.
    Mother: Lydia KEITH
            Grad SC Med Col, 1835, Asst. Surgeon 29th Regt SC Militia. Deacon in Ebenezer
            Baptist Ch. Darlingtoniana. Letters to Lauretta p. 34. Doctors of Darlington
            Co. by Rudisill p 17. Bapt. by brother, J.O.B. Dargan, along with wife Sarah
            and Mother, Mrs Lydia Dargan. (Annals of Ebenezer, p. 43, 51.)
            Grandfather of George E. & A. S. Dargan. Organized 1st Bible Study classes in
            area, became Sunday School Superintendent. Chosen to succeed James A. Petti-
            grew as Clerk of Ebenezer Ch. Ordained deacon, 1850.
===
    Wife: Sarah Thomas DuBOSE
    Married: Oct-1838   in: Darlington Co., SC   5

    Born: in: 6
    Baptized: OCT-1847   in: Ebenezer Bapt. Ch, Florence, SC   7
    Died: c. 1866   in:
    Religion: Baptist   in: Ebenezer Church, Florence Co., SC   7
    Father: Isaiah DuBOSE
    Mother: Gillie Hinton BENTON
            Built 2-story home in Springville, SC and moved into it c. 1856.
            Darlingtoniana p. 282. Baptised by husband's brother, Rev. J.O.B. Dargan
            (Annals of Ebenezer, p.43). Was originally a Methodist.
===
M Child 1 Charles DuBose DARGAN
    Born: 1840   in: SC   8
    Died: c.1865-70   in: 9
            Cawthon: The Inevitable Guest, p.191. Served in Confederate army.
            Died soon after the war from resulting illness.
            Doctors of Darlington Co. by Rudisill p. 17.

M Child 2 George William DARGAN
    Born: 11-MAY-1841   in: Darlington Co., SC   9
    Died: 29-JUN-1898   in: Darlington Co., SC   9
    Ref: Occupation: Attorney/Congressman
    Spouse: Ida Louise HUNTER

(Family of William Edwin DARGAN - Continued)

Married: 1861   in: Darlington Co., SC   6
Congressman from Darlington District for several terms. Solicitor while young man. Member of the 1st company from SC mustered in during the Civil War. 2nd sargeant in Wilds' Co. (Darlingtoniana)
Cawthorn: The Inevitable Guest, p. 121. Annals of Ebenezer, p.51.
Doctors of Darlington Co. by Rudisill, p. 17

M Child 3 William Edwin DARGAN, Jr.
Born: 1845   in: Darlington Co., SC   6
Died: in:
Served in Confederate army.
(JJH note: Mary Hart b. aft. 1843, dau of Dr. R. L. Hart & Eliza A. Flinn m. a W. E. Dargan. Is this the same Dargan?)

F Child 4 Mary Adeline DARGAN
Born: 1847   in: Darlington Co., SC   8
Died: in:
"Addie". Darlingtoniana by Ervin & Rudisill. Doctors of Darlington Co. by Rudisill, p. 17.

M Child 5 John Julius DARGAN
Born: 10-OCT-1848   in: Ebenezer, Florence Co., SC   5
Died: 08-MAR-1925   in: Stateburg, SC   6
Buried: in: Church of Holy Cross, Stateburg, SC   6
Ref: Occupation: atty, educator, historian
Spouse: Theodosia Green WILLIAMSON
Married: 31-OCT-1876   in: Darlington Co, SC   6
Darlingtoniana by Erwin & Rudisill. Served in Confederate War, studied at Furman University. Principal of St. John's Academy, Darlington 1868. Wrote several books, notably a history of SC for school children. Pettigrew,p 51. Admitted to bar in 1874. Practiced law in Sumter, resigned after a few yrs. Became interested in politics, 1876, helped elect Wade Hampton as Governor. Helped end Reconstruction. Became full Colonel on Hampton's staff. Elected to State Legislature 1878. Advocated Free Trade. Opened private school 1896.

F Child 6 Eugenia DARGAN
Born: in: Darlington District, SC   6
Died: at 16   in: 6
Called Gena. Darlingtoniana by Ervin & Rudisill. Doctors of Darlington Co. by Rudisill, p. 17.

(Family of William Edwin DARGAN - Continued)

1 Rudisill, Horace Fraser: Doctors of Darlington County, South Carolina 1760-1912, Pub. by The Darlington County Historical Society, Darlington, SC 1962 17

2 Pettigrew, George R. Annals of Ebenezer 1778-1950, A Record of Achievement Privately printed, 1952 43,51

3 Rudisill, Horace Fraser: Doctors of Darlington County, South Carolina 1760-1912, Pub. by The Darlington County Historical Society, Darlington, SC 1962

4 Pettigrew, George R. Annals of Ebenezer 1778-1950, A Record of Achievement Privately printed, 1952 43

5 Ervin, Eliza Cowan & Rudisill, Horace Fraser: Darlingtoniana A History of People, Places and Events in Darlington County, South Carolina; The Reprint Co, Spartanburg, SC 1976

6 Ervin, Eliza Cowan & Rudisill, Horace Fraser. Darlingtoniana A History of People, Places and Events in Darlington County, South Carolina. Spartanburg, SC: The Reprint Co. 1976.

7 Pettigrew, George R: Annals of Ebenezer 1778-1950, A Record of Achievement 43

8 1850 SC Census, Darlington Co. 284

9 Cawthorn, John Ardis: The Inevitable Guest Life and Letters of Jemima Darby copyright 1965, The Naylor Co., San Antonio, TX, Library of Congress Cat. No. 64-8903.

18-MAY-1993   Family group sheet
==
Husband: David GULLEDGE

  Born: 4-SEP-1813   in: Gulledge Tnshp, Anson Co., NC   1
  Died: 14-SEP-1895   in: Edom, Van Zandt Co., TX   1
  Buried: in: Edom Cem, Edom, TX   2
Religion: Baptist   in:
Father: Joel GULLEDGE
Mother: Zilpha HUNTLEY
        Letters to Lauretta. Living in Jasper Co., MS 1849, Moved to Texas, Fall 1866
        1840 Census, Darlington Co., SC; 1870 Census Van Zandt Co., TX.
        Father: Rev Joel Gulledge s/o William; Mother: Zilpha Huntley d/o Thomas and
        Zilpha (Meadows) Huntley.
        David Gulledge Family Bible & James A. Gulledge Family Bible.
==
  Wife: Eleanor Lauretta McBRIDE
Married: 12-MAR-1839 in: prob. Chesterfield, SC   1

  Born: 01-JAN-1820   in: Darlington Co., SC   1
  Died: 13-JAN-1881   in: Edom, Van Zandt Co., TX   1
  Buried: in: Edom Cem, Van Zandt Co., TX   3
Religion: Baptist   in: 4
Father: William McBRIDE
Mother: Mary Jane BLACKWELL
        Lived Darlington Co., SC 1840; Van Zandt Co., TX 1870 (Census)
        Recipient of Letters to Lauretta from aunt Elizabeth (Blackwell) Pettigrew
        and son Samuel Blackwell Gulledge.
==
M Child 1 Samuel Blackwell GULLEDGE
  Born: 06-FEB-1840   in: Chesterfield Co., SC   1
  Died: 05-JUL-1863   in: Battle of Gettysburg, PA   1
        Called Blackwell. See Letters home to parents while soldier in Confederate
        Army. (In manuscript Letters to Lauretta). Eldest son.
        Died from head wound received during the Battle of Gettysburg.

F Child 2 Mary Eleanor GULLEDGE
  Born: 17-DEC-1841   in: Chesterfield, SC   1
  Died: 1873   in: Van Zandt Co., TX   2
Religion: Baptist   in: 4
        Married Jan. 1872, Wm Pendigrass. Affidavit of James A. Gulledge, her
        brother says had 1 child, Mary Adeline Pendergrass, b. 1873, married Carl
        Jordan, c. 1907. Called "Molly" Pendergrass.
        1870 Census, Van Zandt Co., TX with Father & Mother.

(Family of David GULLEDGE - Continued)

F Child 3 Zilpha Ann GULLEDGE
   Born: 1-MAR-1844   in: Chesterfield Co., SC   1
   Died: 12-SEP-1881 in: Van Zandt Co., TX   2
  Spouse: Riley W. WYATT
Married: in:
        See Letters to Lauretta, written by great aunt Elizabeth Blackwell Pettigrew
        to her mother Lauretta McBride Gulledge. Also Ltrs from brother, Samuel
        Blackwell Gulledge. Called Dippy.
        1870 Census, Van Zandt Co., TX.

F Child 4 Sarah Lauretta GULLEDGE
   Born: 11-DEC-1845 in: SC   5
   Died: 21-MAR-1878 in: Van Zandt Co., TX   2
  Buried: in: Edom, TX   2
  Spouse: Robert W. COKER
Married: 1866   in: prob. Van Zandt Co., TX   2
        Called Sallie Lou. Married Robert W. Coker, 1866
        1870 Census, Van Zandt Co., TX

M Child 5 Thomas Huntley GULLEDGE
   Born: 14-OCT-1847 in: Jasper Co., MS   1
   Died: 15-OCT-1864 in: 1
        Never Married.

F Child 6 Elizabeth Louisa GULLEDGE
   Born: 19-NOV-1849 in: Jasper Co., MS   1
   Died: c. 1881   in: 2
  Spouse: C. C. RAINES
Married: aft 9/22/1870 in: 6
        Letters to Lauretta, ltr to Louisa Woodward dtd 1/3/1850; 12/6/1849.
        1870 Census, Van Zandt Co., TX living with father & mother.
        Also Family group sheet. Married C. C. Raines. Children: Ada 1879; Laura
        1881 Affidavit of James A. Gulledge 8/8/1930 states she had no children.

F Child 7 Martha Adeline GULLEDGE
   Born: 13-OCT-1851 in: MS   1
   Died: 28-JAN-1901 in: Van Zandt Co., TX   3
  Buried: in: Old Liberty Cem, Van Zandt Co., TX   3
  Spouse: Thomas Edward MARRABLE
Married: c. 1888   in: 3
        Called "Addie". Married Thomas E. Marrable
        Information: Lillian Reid Gray, 1702 Cedar Crest Dr, Abilene, TX (1979-80)

(Family of David GULLEDGE - Continued)

                1870, 1880 Census, Van Zandt Co., TX

M Child 8 Albert Joseph GULLEDGE
   Born: 17-NOV-1853   in: MS   1
   Died: 01-DEC-1903   in: Van Zandt Co., TX   2
   Buried: in: Edom Cemetery, Edom, TX   7
   Spouse: Rosa R. ???/??
   Married: bef. 6/19/1880 in: prob. Van Zandt Co., TX.
            Married Maude ?
            David Gulledge Family Bible record says: Joseph Albert Gulledge.
            1900 Census Van Zandt Co., TX ED 186, sheet 16.
            1870 Census Van Zandt Co., TX.

M Child 9 James Alexander GULLEDGE
   Born: 21-JUN-1856   in: Jasper Co., MS   1
   Died: 18-APR-1944   in: Edom, Van Zandt Co., TX   3
   Buried: in: Edom Cemetery, Edom, TX.   8
   Spouse: Laura Amanda Searcy
   Married: 07-DEC-1881 in: prob. Van Zandt Co., TX   9
            Dr. WJ Bray, Abilene, TX 12/1991
            Married c. 1881-2, Laura Amanda Searcy
            1870, 1880 Census, Van Zandt Co., TX

FChild 10 Susan Caroline GULLEDGE
   Born: 27-FEB-1858   in: MS   1
   Died: 09-AUG-1870   in: prob. Van Zandt Co., TX   1
   Buried: in: Edom Cemetery, Edom, Texas   10
            Never married.

FChild 11 Harriett Emma GULLEDGE
   Born: 27-OCT-1860   in: Jasper Co., MS   1
   Died: 20-OCT-1903   in: prob. Van Zandt Co., TX   3
   Spouse: Thomas Edward MARRABLE
   Married: c. 1902   in: 3
            Married as his 3rd wife, her brother-in-law, Thomas E. Marrable (widower of
            her sister Martha Adeline Gullege). No issue.
            Not married on 10/23/1897.
            1870, 1880 Census Van Zandt Co., TX.
==

1 David Gulledge Family Bible

(Family of David GULLEDGE - Continued)

2 Affidavit James A. Gulledge 8/8/1930

3 W. J. Bray

4 Letters to Lauretta; Elizabeth Blackwell Pettigrew 9/1/1859

5 David Gulledge Family Bible
1870 Census, Van Zandt Co., Texas.

6 1870 Census, Van Zandt Co., TX.

7 Cemetery Records

8 Cemetery Record

9 Marriage Certificate

10 Cemetery Marker

18-MAY-1993   Family group sheet
===
Husband: Joseph Louis HARRELL

    Born: 14-NOV-1818   in: SC   1
Baptized: 1857   in: admitted fm Elim Church   2
    Died: 14-NOV-1877   in: Florence, SC   1
Religion: Baptist   in: 1
            1850 SC Census, Darlington Co., p. 284., living next to Sarah A. Blackwell,
            widow of Samuel Blackwell, III., who lived next to her bro-in-law Dr. John
            Hamlin Blackwell. Is he son of James H. Harrell and Mary H. Burch, and bro.
            of Sarah Harrell Blackwell, wid of Samuel Blackwell, III.
            Letters to Lauretta. 1860 SC Census, Darl. p 378. Annals of Ebenezer, p74.
===
    Wife: Mary Ann Eleanor PETTIGREW
 Married: 04-NOV-1840   in: Darlington Co., SC   3

    Born: 08-NOV-1823   in: Darlington Co., SC   4
Baptized: OCT-1847   in: Ebenezer Ch, Florence, SC   5
    Died: 25-AUG-1903   in: 4
Religion: Baptist   in: 5
  Father: James Alexander PETTIGREW
  Mother: Elizabeth H. BLACKWELL
            Darlington Co Historical Commission files. 1850 Census, Darlington Co., p284.
            Annals of Ebenezer, p.43.
===
F Child 1 Elizabeth Susanna HARRELL
    Born: 1842   in: SC   6
            Letters to Lauretta dtd 3/28/1850. "Elizabeth is going to school" in
            Darlington Co., SC. & 9/9/1856 which lists Mary Ann Eleanor Pettigrew Harrell
            children.

F Child 2 Mary Eugenia HARRELL
    Born: 1844   in: SC   7
            Letters to Lauretta dtd 3/28/1850, 9/9/1856.

M Child 3 James Alexander HARRELL
    Born: 1845   in: SC   7
            Letters to Lauretta, dtd 9/9/1856

F Child 4 Sarah Ann HARRELL
    Born: JAN-1846   in: Marion Co., SC   8
    Died: 09-JUN-1849   in: Darlington Co., SC   9
  Buried: in: Blackwell Cem, Burches Csrds, Florence   8

(Family of Joseph Louis HARRELL - Continued)

                Letters to Lauretta dtd 6/20/1849. Says buried at her grandfather's head.
                Survey of Cemeteries in Lower Florence Co., SC Vol III. Blackwell Cem,
                500 yds behind Greenwood Baptist Church, Claussen Rd, Florence, SC.

M Child 5 John Edward HARRELL
   Born: 1848   in: Marion Co., SC   10
                Letters to Lauretta dtd 9/9/1856.
                Living with grandfather James A. Pettigrew in 1860.

M Child 6 Samuel Joseph HARRELL
   Born: JAN-1850   in: Darlington Co., SC   11
   Died: fl 1895   in: 12
                Letters to Lauretta dtd 4/17/1850.
                Member of Florence Red Shirt Club, 1876; Florence Co. Election Commissioner
                1895. King, G. Wayne. Rise Up So Early A History of Florence Co., SC p. 75,
                378, 379. 1850 SC Census, Darlington Co. 8/7/1850

M Child 7 William Lewis HARRELL
   Born: c. 1853   in: SC   13
   Religion: Baptist   in: Ebenezer Baptist Ch, Florence, SC   14
                Letters to Lauretta dtd 9/9/1856
                Member of Ebenezer Church, 1866.
                Florence Co. Auditor 1890-99. King, G. Wayne: Rise Up So Early--A History of
                Florence Co., SC.

M Child 8 Julius Dargan HARRELL
   Born: 30-JUL-1853   in: Darlington Co., SC   15
   Died: Winter, 1854/5 in: Darlington Co., SC   16
                Letters to Lauretta dtd 8/8/1853.
                Death: Ltrs to Lauretta dtd 11/24/1855 "Dear little Julius, the one that
                died last winter."

M Child 9 Thomas Jefferson HARRELL
   Born: APR-1855   in: Darlington Co., SC   17
                Letters to Lauretta dtd 6/13/1855.

MChild 10 George Washington HARRELL
   Born: 29-SEP-1856   in: Darlington Co., SC   18
   Died: in:
                Letters to Lauretta dtd 9/9/1856

(Family of Joseph Louis HARRELL - Continued)

MChild 11 male HARRELL
   Born: c. 1857/8   in: 19
               Letters to Lauretta dtd 6/27/1861.
               His mother was mother to 9 sons and 3 daughters.

MChild 12 male2 HARRELL
   Born: OCT-1859   in: Darlington Co., SC   20
   Died: in:
               Letters to L dtd 9/1/1859: "Eleanor will get down in October. That will be 12 for her, one more than I have had. She is fat and harty."
               Letters to L dtd 6/27/1861: "Eleanor has been the mother of 9 sons and 3 daughters."
===

1 Pettigrew, George R. Annals of Ebenezer 1778-1950, A Record of Achievement Privately printed, 1952 75

2 Pettigrew, George R. Annals of Ebenezer 1778-1950, A Record of Achievement Privately printed, 1952 54

3 **Darlington Co. Historical Commission files**

4 Janette Catalano

5 Pettigrew, George R. Annals of Ebenezer 1778-1950, A Record of Achievement Privately printed, 1952 43

6 1850 SC Census, Darlington Co. (8/7/1850) 284

7 1850 SC Census, Darlington Co. 284

8 **Cemetery Marker, Blackwell Cemetery, Burches Crossroads, Florence, SC.**

9 **Letters to Lauretta; Elizabeth Blackwell Pettigrew 6/20/1849**

10 1850 SC Census, Darlington Co. 9/9/1856

11 **Letters to Lauretta; Elizabeth Blackwell Pettigrew 1/3/1850;4/17/1850**

12 King, G. Wayne: Rise Up So Early A History of Florence County South Carolina The Reprint Co, Pub. 1981. 378

(Family of Joseph Louis HARRELL - Continued)

13 Letters to Lauretta; Elizabeth Blackwell Pettigrew 9/9/1856

14 Pettigrew, George R. Annals of Ebenezer 1778-1950, A Record of Achievement Privately printed, 1952 59

15 Letters to Lauretta; Elizabeth Blackwell Pettigrew 8/8/1853

16 Letters to Lauretta dtd 11/24/1855

17 Letters to Lauretta; Elizabeth Blackwell Pettigrew 6/13/1855

18 W. J. Bray

19 Letters to Lauretta; Elizabeth Blackwell Pettigrew 6/27/1861

20 Letters to Lauretta; Elizabeth Blackwell Pettigrew 9/1/1859

18-MAY-1993   Family group sheet
==
Husband: Robert HEPBURN

    Born: in:
Baptized: OCT-1831   in: Ebenezer Church, Florence Co., SC   1
    Died: 1844   in: Darlington Co., SC   2
Religion: Baptist   in: Ebenezer Church, Florence Co., SC   3
  Father:
  Mother:

            Annals of Ebenezer, p. 42. Member for many years. Listed as member 1823.
            Daughter Elizabeth m. Elihu Muldrow & is buried in Ebenezer Churchyard.
            Deacon at Ebenezer.
            Letters to Lauretta; Elizabeth Blackwell Pettigrew, dtd 4/13/1849; 6/20/1849;
            9/4/1849; 8/30/1850; 9/30/1850; 6/27/1861. SC Census 1850, Darl. p 320; 1860,
            p 423. James A. Pettigrew, surety, Est. Robert Hepburn, 11/15/1844, Pro 402.
==
  Wife: Elizabeth ?STEWART
Married: bef. 1823   in: 3

    Born: 1799   in: SC   4
Baptized: OCT-1831   in: Ebenezer Church, Florence Co., SC   1
    Died: 22-AUG-1859 in: Darlington Co., SC   5
Religion: Baptist   in: Ebenezer Church, Florence Co., SC   6
  Father:
  Mother:

            Letters to Lauretta, dtd 5 Dec 1849 "Mr Stewart is dead and Betsy Hepburn is
            going for her part of the property. She would have got it before but Bateman
            held the division off."
            Listed as Ebenezer Church member, Elizabeth Hepburn, Jan. 1823.
            W. B. Pettigrew, appraiser Estate of Elizabeth S. Hepburn, 1/23/1867, Pro 1454
            Letters to Lauretta, dtd 4/13/1849; 6/20/1849; 8/30/1850; 9/30/1850; 6/27/1861
==
M Child 1 James W. HEPBURN
    Born: c. 1824   in: SC   7
Baptized: SEP-1850   in: Ebenezer Church, Florence, SC   8
    Died: in:
                "W. J." Hepburn

F Child 2 Elizabeth S. HEPBURN
    Born: 17-FEB-1832 in: SC   9
Baptized: 1850   in: Ebenezer Baptist Ch., Florence Co., SC 10
    Died: 17-NOV-1894 in: SC   11
  Buried: in: Ebenezer Chyd, Florence, SC   11

260

(Family of Robert HEPBURN - Continued)

Religion: Baptist   in: 12
  Spouse: Elihu MULDROW
  Married: in:
                       W. J. Bray. "Betty". Married Elihu MULDROW (1831-1907)
                       Listed on membership roll Ebenezer Baptist Church, 1878.
                       Letters to Lauretta; Elizbeth Blackwell Pettigrew, dtd 6/27/1861.

M Child 3 Robert HEPBURN
  Born: 1836   in: SC   7
  Baptized: 1857   in: Ebenezer Church, Florence Co., SC   13
  Died: in:
  Religion: Baptist   in: 13
  Ref: King   Occupation: 14
                       Officer in Pee Dee Light Artillery in Army of Northern VA, c. 1867.
                       1876 1st Vice-President of Florence Mounted Club, a para-military unit,
                       under president W. P. Gee. Became first auditor of Florence Co.

M Child 4 Clement Cogburn HEPBURN
  Born: 22-JUL-1839   in: SC   15
  Died: 09-AUG-1921   in: SC   16
  Buried: in: Ebenezer Churchyd, Florence, SC   16
  Spouse: Sallie BRUNSON
  Married: in:
                       Annals of Ebenezer, p. 67, 69.
                       Member of Ebenezer Red Shirt Club.
==

1 Pettigrew, George R. Annals of Ebenezer 1778-1950, A Record of Achievement
Privately printed, 1952 32

2 Pettigrew, George R. Annals of Ebenezer 1778-1950, A Record of Achievement
Privately printed, 1952 42

3 Pettigrew, George R. Annals of Ebenezer 1778-1950, A Record of Achievement
Privately printed, 1952 20

4 Letters to Lauretta; Elizabeth Blackwell Pettigrew
1850 Census Darlington Co., SC 12/5/1849; 320

5 Letters to Lauretta; Elizabeth Blackwell Pettigrew 9/1/1859

(Family of Robert HEPBURN - Continued)

6 Pettigrew, George R. Annals of Ebenezer 1778-1950, A Record of Achievement
Privately printed, 1952 20,45

7 1850 Census, Darlington Co., SC 320

8 Letters to Lauretta; Elizabeth Blackwell Pettigrew 9/30/1850

9 Cemetery Marker
1850 Census Darlington Co., SC 320

10 Pettigrew, George R. Annals of Ebenezer 1778-1950, A Record of Achievement
Privately printed, 1952 48

11 Cemetery Marker

12 Pettigrew, George R. Annals of Ebenezer 1778-1950, A Record of Achievement
Privately printed, 1952 74

13 Pettigrew, George R. Annals of Ebenezer 1778-1950, A Record of Achievement
Privately printed, 1952 54

14 King, G. Wayne: Rise Up So Early A History of Florence County South Carolina
The Reprint Co, Pub. 1981. 46,74

15 Cemetery marker as recorded in Leonardo Andrea files South Caroliniana Library
1850 Census Darlington Co., SC 320

16 Cemetery marker as recorded in Leonardo Andrea files South Caroliniana Library

18-MAY-1993   Family group sheet
===
Husband: Axalla HOULE

  Born: 1824   in: SC   1
  Died: bef. 1866   in: 2
  Father: James Commander HOULE
  Mother: Elizabeth STANLEY
              Letters to Lauretta 1/3/1850.
              Darlingtoniana, p. 175. Married Miss Betsy Brunson on 3/20/1856 and set out
              for Kansas but returned in about 1 1/2 years. Was Col. in Civil War. (p199)
              8th Regiment. Died during War. (p432)
              1860 Census Darl. Co. shows a L. Cooper (female) age 5 living with him along
              with his mother, brother T.S. (34) and sister E. E. (32).
===
  Wife: Elizabeth G. BRUNSON
  Married: 20-MAR-1856   in: Darlington Co., SC   3

  Born: c. 1834   in: SC   4
  Died: in:
  Father:
  Mother:
              Betsy. Darlingtoniana p175.
===
F Child 1 Ada C. HOULE
  Born: c. 1857   in: prob. Kansas   4
  Died: in:
              Darlingtoniana, p175, 199, 432. Married W. H. Lawrence after 5/1/1880.

M Child 2 W. R. HOULE
  Born: JAN-1860   in: Darlington Co., SC   4
  Died: in:
===

1 SC Census, Darlington Co., 1860, p. 380; 1850 p. 321.

2 Ervin, Eliza Cowan & Rudisill, Horace Fraser. Darlingtoniana A History of
People, Places and Events in Darlington County, South Carolina. Spartanburg,
SC: The Reprint Co. 1976. 432

3 Ervin, Eliza Cowan & Rudisill, Horace Fraser. Darlingtoniana A History of
People, Places and Events in Darlington County, South Carolina. Spartanburg,
SC: The Reprint Co. 1976. 175

4 1860 SC Census, Darlington Co., 6/4/1860. 380

18-MAY-1993   Family group sheet
==
Husband: James Commander HOULE

  Born: in:
  Died: 1826   in: 1
  Father: Joseph HOULE
  Mother: Elizabeth COMMANDER
           SC Census, 1850 Darl. Co, p. 321; 1860 Darl., 380. Letters to Lauretta,
           dtd 1/3/1850.
           SC Census, 1800 Georgetown, p. 373, lists a William Hool.
==
  Wife: Elizabeth STANLEY
Married: 1818   in: 1

  Born: 1799   in: SC   2
  Died: 1887   in: 1
  Father: John STANLEY
  Mother: Elizabeth GARNER
           Letters to Lauretta, dtd 12/5/1849.
           1860 SC Census Darlington, p. 380, living w/ son Axalla & family.
           1850 SC Census Darlington, p. 321.
==
F Child 1 Elizabeth HOULE
  Born: in: 3
  Died: in:
           This person may not be a child but may be confused with daughter, mother, or
           daughter-in-law (wife of Axalla Houle).

F Child 2 Eveline Gertrude HOULE
  Born: 1819   in: Darlington, SC   1
  Died: 1844   in: Sumter, SC   1
  Spouse: John Ervin BROWN
Married: 1842   in: 1
           Letters to Lauretta 1/3/1850. Married John Ervin Brown (1808-98) in 1842.
           SC Census, 1850 Sumter Co., p 424. Children: Dau, E.G. (b. c. 1840)

M Child 3 Axalla HOULE
  Born: 1824   in: SC   4
  Died: bef. 1866 in: 5
  Spouse: Elizabeth G. BRUNSON
Married: 20-MAR-1856 in: Darlington Co., SC   6
           Letters to Lauretta 1/3/1850.
           Darlingtoniana, p. 175. Married Miss Betsy Brunson on 3/20/1856 and set out

(Family of James Commander HOULE - Continued)

       for Kansas but returned in about 1 1/2 years. Was Col. in Civil War. (p199) 8th Regiment. Died during War. (p432)
       1860 Census Darl. Co. shows a L. Cooper (female) age 5 living with him along with his mother, brother T.S. (34) and sister E. E. (32).

M Child 4 Thomas S. HOULE
  Born: 1825   in: SC   4
  Died: in:
               Letters to Lauretta 1/3/1850.
               Wife: E. E. b. c. 1828.

F Child 5 Eufrazer HOULE
  Born: 1827   in: SC   7
  Died: in:
               Letters to Lauretta 1/3/1850.
               Euphagenia in 1850 Census.
               Living with mother and brother, Axalla, 1850, 1860 Darlington Co., SC.

===

1 Lineage Chart, Gertrude McLaurin Shaw, 8 Hasall St, Sumter, SC 29150 4/1976.

2 1860 SC Census, Darlington Co., 6/4/1860.
Lineage Chart, Gertrude McLaurin Shaw (1976)
1850 SC Census, Darlington Co., 10/14/1850 380; - ;321

3 W. J. Bray

4 1860 SC Census, Darlington Co., 6/4/1860.
1850 SC Census, Darlington Co., 10/14/1850 380;321

5 Ervin, Eliza Cowan & Rudisill, Horace Fraser. Darlingtoniana A History of People, Places and Events in Darlington County, South Carolina. Spartanburg, SC: The Reprint Co. 1976. 432

6 Ervin, Eliza Cowan & Rudisill, Horace Fraser. Darlingtoniana A History of People, Places and Events in Darlington County, South Carolina. Spartanburg, SC: The Reprint Co. 1976. 175

7 1860 SC Census, Darlington Co., 6/4/1860.
1850 SC Census, Darlington Co., 10/14/1850. 380;321

18-MAY-1993   Family group sheet
==
Husband: James LANE

   Born: 13-NOV-1760   in: Prince Frederick Parish, SC   1
Baptized: 28-JUN-1761   in: Prince Frederick Parish, SC
   Died: in:
 Father: James LANE, MD (b. 8/19/1719 Prince Frederick Parish, SC) 1
 Mother: Ursula HENNING (b. 3/1737 Prince Frederick Parish, SC)   1
         DAR Lineage Book Vol. 122, p. 85. Gregg's History of the
         Old Cheraws. Prince Frederick Parish Records. Ebenezer Church Records.
         Family History Library, Salt Lake City.
==
   Wife: Rachel BLACKWELL
Married: 1791   in: 2

   Born: 1770   in: Georgetown, SC   3
   Died: 06-MAR-1832   in: Florence, SC   4
Religion: Baptist   in: Ebenezer Church   5
 Father: Samuel BLACKWELL, I.
 Mother: Elizabeth DOZIER
         Member of Ebenezer Church. Darlington Co., SC Will BK 8,
         p. 278. Mentions heirs, Edmund Gee; Jno B. Bruce; son, James Lane; dau,
         Martha Pettigrew, granddau, Martha Ann Lane, Elizabeth Blackwell Lane, grand
         son James Henning Lane, grandsn Samuel Adair Lane, grandau Rachel Louisa Lane
         grandson Thomas Mitchel Lane, grandau Mary Ellinor Lane, grandau Rachel Louisa
         Pettigrew, granddau Cornelia Manning Pettigrew. Will dtd 5/12/1830, prob
         3/8/1832. Codicil mentions 800 ac on Black Cr in Marion Co. DAR #103100
==
M Child 1 James LANE, Jr.
    Born: 24-NOV-1790   in: SC   6
    Died: 20-AUG-1844   in: SC   6
     Ref: Occupation: Doctor
  Spouse: Martha Eleanor ADAIR
 Married: 02-SEP-1813   in: SC   6
          Doctor in Marlboro. Gregg: p. 603.
          Mentioned in Mother's will, Darl Co. BK 8, p 278.
          1850 Census Darlington Co., SC p 284
          Letters to Lauretta dtd4/13/1849, 8/30/1850; 5/19/1852.

F Child 2 Martha L. LANE
    Born: 1798   in: SC   7
    Died: 17-OCT-1851   in: Darlington Co., SC   8
Religion: Baptist   in: 9
  Spouse: Timothy Dargan PETTIGREW

(Family of James LANE - Continued)

Married: c. 1835 in: 10
    Mentioned in Mother's Will Darl Co. BK 8, p 278. Gregg: p. 603.
    DAR #103100. 1850 Darl Census, p. 284.
    Darlington Co. Historical Commission files. Annals of Ebenezer, p. 41, 49.
    Equity Roll 442, widow of Timothy Dargan Pettigrew.
    Rec'd by ltr fm Darlington Ch to Ebenezer Bapt. Ch in early 1840's.
==

1 The Register Book for the Parish Prince Frederick Winyaw

2 Leonardo Andrea files, South Caroliniana Library

3 DAR #103100

4 Pettigrew, George R. Annals of Ebenezer 1778-1950, A Record of Achievement
Privately printed, 1952 34

5 Pettigrew, George R. Annals of Ebenezer 1778-1950, A Record of Achievement
Privately printed, 1952 15

6 From Old burned Bible from Mrs. Riley of Florence, see Leonardo Andrea file, SCL

7 1850 SC Census, Darlington Co. (8/7/1850) 284

8 Pettigrew, George R. Annals of Ebenezer 1778-1950, A Record of Achievement
Privately printed, 1952 49

9 Pettigrew, George R. Annals of Ebenezer 1778-1950, A Record of Achievement
Privately printed, 1952 41,45

10 Janette Catalano

18-MAY-1993   Family group sheet
==

Husband: James LANE, Jr.

    Born: 24-NOV-1790   in: SC   1
    Died: 20-AUG-1844   in: SC   1
    Ref: Occupation: Doctor
  Father: James LANE
  Mother: Rachel BLACKWELL
            Doctor in Marlboro. Gregg: p. 603. Mentioned in Mother's will, Darl Co.
            BK 8, p 278. 1850 Census Darlington Co., SC p 284
            Letters to Lauretta dtd 4/13/1849, 8/30/1850; 5/19/1852.
==

  Wife: Martha Eleanor ADAIR
Married: 02-SEP-1813   in: SC   1

    Born: 01-NOV-1794   in: 1
    Died: in:
  Father:
  Mother:
==

F Child 1 Martha Ann LANE
    Born: 14-AUG-1814   in: Darlington District, SC   2
    Died: 21-APR-1860   in: Marion, AL   2
   Buried: in: Marion Cemetery, Marion, AL   3
  Religion: Baptist   in: Mispah Baptist Ch, Darl.   4
  Spouse: Jesse Holloway LIDE
  Married: 26-DEC-1833   in: prob. Darlington Co., SC   1
            Southern Baptist issue of May 12, 1860 "Died in Marion, Ala on the 21st
            April, Mrs. Martha Ann Lide, wife of J. H. Lide, and daughter of the late Jas
            Lide, of Darlington District, SC..born Aug 14, 1814." (Actually dau-in-law)
            DAR record of Anna Suse Chapman Thompson.
            Mentioned in will of grandmother, Rachel Blackwell Lane, Darl. Co., SC BK 8,
            p. 278. Flora England--AL Cemetery Records, Perry Co. Eldest dau James &
            Martha E. Lane. Were living Marion Co., SC 3 mi fm Darl. Mem Mispah Bapt Ch
----
F Child 2 Elizabeth Blackwell LANE
    Born: 08-MAR-1817   in: SC   1
    Died: 15-AUG-1858   in: SC   1
  Spouse: Rev. Robert Napier, Pastor Mispah Baptist Church   5
            Mentioned in grandmother, Rachel Blackwell Lane's will, Darl Co., SC BK 8,
            p.278. Married Rev. Robert Napier as his 2nd wife.

(Family of James LANE, Jr. - Continued)

M Child 3 James Henning LANE
   Born: 12-JUN-1819   in: SC   1
   Died: in:
   Ref: Occupation: MD
 Spouse: Maria T. B. GAUSE
Married: 30-JAN-1849   in: Clio, SC.   1
                 Mentioned in will of grandmother, Rachel Blackwell Lane, Darl Co., BK 8,
                 p. 278 Marlboro Co., SC 1850 census, p. 126.

M Child 4 Samuel Adair LANE
   Born: 23-JUL-1823   in: 1
   Died: in:
                 Mentioned in will of grandmother, Rachel Blackwell Lane, Darl. Co. BK 8,
                 p 278 Married Laura Pierce, c. 1850, see Letters to Lauretta, dtd 8/30/1850.

F Child 5 Rachael Louise LANE
   Born: 20-JUL-1825   in: 1
   Died: in:
                 Named in will of grndmthr, Rachel Blackwell Lane, Darl. Co., BK 8, p 278.

M Child 6 Thomas Mitchell LANE
   Born: in: 1
   Died: in:
                 Mentioned in will of grandmother, Rachel Blackwell Lane, Darl Co. BK 8, p.278
                 Married dau. of George James, 1849. Letters to Lauretta, dtd 4/13/1849.

F Child 7 Mary Eleanor LANE
   Born: in: 5
   Died: in:
                 Mentioned in will of grandmother, Rachel Blackwell Lane, Darl. Co, BK 8, p278
==

1 From Old burned Bible from Mrs. Riley of Florence, see Leonardo Andrea file, South Caroliniana Library.

2 Southern Baptist issue 5/12/1860.

3 England, Flora: Alabama Cemetery Records, Perry Co.

4 DAR Record

5 Cawthon, John Ardis: The Inevitable Guest, Life and Letters of Jemima Darby copyright 1965, The Naylor Co., San Antonio, TX

18-MAY-1993   Family group sheet
==
  Husband: Eli Hugh LIDE

    Born: 15 April 1796   in: Darlington Co.,SC   1
  Baptized: in: Mechanicsville, SC   2
    Died: 18 May 1854   in: Woodville, Tyler Co.,TX   1
  Buried: in: Woodville, TX
  Religion: Baptist   in:
    Ref: Occupation: Planter
  Father: James LIDE (5/14/1770--11/9/1855)
  Mother: Jane HOLLOWAY (11/21/1778--7/3/1862)
          Birth, death, marriage information see Daughter of Johannes Kolb--Sarah Kolb
          Lide & Her Descendants by Avery Kolb. Also Ancestral Key to the PeeDee; The
          Lides Go South and West...the Story of a Planter Migration.
          Note ltr fm Eli Lide to parents on 15 Apr 1854 states "This day I am 58 years
          old" (See Lides Go Forth). Grad SC college, AB 1818.
          Dallas Co., AL Deed Bk Q101 3/17/1854 mention marriage to Mary Ann Mandeville
          & their children.
==
  Wife: Mary Ann MANDEVILLE
  Married: 14 Feb 1821   in: Darlington Co., SC   3

    Born: in: 4
    Died: 1826   in: Darlington Co.,SC   5
  Father: Cornelius MANDEVILLE
  Mother: Frances ?
          HSL=Henry Stewart Lide notes in possession of daughter-in-law Zula Clark Lide
          Selma, AL 10/29/89. Also Deed BK Q,p.101,Dallas Co.,AL.
          DAR Lineage Book #115866 (Julia E. Lide), p. 270.
==
  F Child 1 Frances Jane LIDE
      Born: c 1822   in: Darlington Co.,SC   6
      Died: in:
    Religion: Baptist   in:
    Spouse: William Maxwell RUMPH
    Married: 04-APR-1839 in: Dallas Co., AL   7

  M Child 2 Cornelius Mandeville LIDE
      Born: 2 JUN 1825   in: Darlington Co., SC   3
      Baptized: 10-JUN-1843 in: Centre Ridge Baptist Ch, Dallas Co., AL 8
      Died: 05-MAY-1907   in: Talledega, AL   9
      Ref: Occupation: Farmer
    Spouse: Mary Huger DAWSON

(Family of Eli Hugh LIDE - Continued)

Married: 07-JAN-1850   in: Dallas Co., AL   7
             Henry S. Lide notes. Priv. under Gen. Bragg, CSA. Mar Rec. Dallas Co., AL
             (1845-1865). (AL Recs Vol 220 p82 by Ganrud). Reg. Students U. AL. by T.W.
             Palmer 1901; class of 1844 lists Cornelius Manderville Lide, enrlld 1844,
             Richmond, (AL-Dallas Co.) 1870 Dallas Co. (Richmond Twnshp) Cen., p581,
             age 46 Mar. Rec Montg Co. AL (1838-50) C. M. Lide to Elizabeth A. Burch
             9/16/1847 by H. Talbird MG. DAR lineage book, p. 270 (Miss Julia E. Lide,
             #115866 & Mary Dawson Lide #115867). Obit Montgomery Adv. 5/5/1907,p. 116,
             col 3.
==
   Wife: Dorcas Jane ALEXANDER
Married: 4 DEC 1827   in: Mecklenburg Co., NC   10
  Other: in: by Rev. R. H. Morrison

    Born: 1802   in: 10
    Died: 10 JAN 1829   in: Darlington, Co.,SC   10
Religion: Presbyterian   in: 10
  Father:
  Mother:
             Birth, death, mariage: Abstracts of Vital Records from Raleigh, NC Newspapers
             1820-1829 Vol II--Reprint Publishers 1983.
             Survivors: husband, mother (Mrs. Jane Alexander), only sister, & 2 brothers.
==
   Wife: Martha Johnson BLACKWELL
Married: 19 JUL 1830   in: SC   1

    Born: 13-JUN-1811   in: Darlington Co., SC   11
    Died: 16-DEC-1880   in: Camden, Ouachita Co., AR   11
  Buried: in: Oakland Cem., Ouachita Co., AR   11
Religion: Baptist   in: 12
  Father: Samuel BLACKWELL, II.
  Mother: Mary Ann HAMLIN
             1850 Census Dallas Co., AL (age 39--brthplce SC). Gregg: p. 603.
             1860 Annotated Census, Liberty Town, Ouachita Co., AR p.7. by Bobbie J McLane
             with sons James E. (17) and Sam'l B (13) and dau. Hannah (15).
             The Cemetery Records for Ouachita Co., AR pub by Ouachita Co. Extension Home-
             makers Council. 1870 census Ouachita Co., AR, p. 324
             Mvd to AR in 1857, settld on farm 6 mi. fm Camden. Goodspeed's Historical
             Memoirs of Southern AR, pub 1890.
==
F Child 1 Mary Ann LIDE
    Born: 10-NOV-1831   in: Darlington, Co.SC   13

(Family of Eli Hugh LIDE - Continued)

Baptized: Nov 1846   in: Centre Ridge Baptist Ch, Dallas Co., AL   8
   Died: 25-JUN-1879   in: Slighville, Lake Co.,FL   3
Religion: Baptist   in:
  Spouse: William Rumph ETHERIDGE
Married: 02-APR-1856   in: Carlowville, Dallas Co., AL   7
            1850 Dallas Co., AL census. HSL=Henry Stewart Lide notes. AL Marriage Rec.
            D. at country home, 3 mi. E. of Lady Lake, Slighville, FL. formerly Sumpter
            Co Dismissed fm Centre Ridge Baptist Ch, May 1856. Staying in AK w/sister
            Carrie per ltr fm aunt Elizabeth Blackwell Pettigrew (9/9/1854). Previously
            engaged to be married, Dec 1849, to Edgar Charles son, fm SC who had gone
            west. He returned to SC a month before wedding and changed his mind. (E.
            Pettigrew ltr 3/28/1850).

F Child 2 Caroline E. LIDE
    Born: 20-JAN-1833   in: Darlington Co., SC   11
    Died: 11-SEP-1884   in: Ouachita Co., AR   11
  Buried: in: Oakland Cem, Ouachita Co., AR   11
Religion: Baptist   in:
  Spouse: Lawrence Edwin DAWSON, Jr.
Married: JAN-1853   in: Dallas Co., AL   11
            The Cemetery Records of Ouachita, Co., AR pub by The Ouachita Co. Extension
            Homemakers Council as noted in The 1860 Annotated Census of Ouachita Co., AR
            by Bobbie McLane.
            Did not go to TX in 1854 (see ltr fm Elizabeth Blackwell Pettigrew 9/9/1854)
            Goodspeed's Historical Memoirs of Southern AR. Had 9 children.
            Ltr fm Elizabeth B Pettigrew 5/19/1852, Darlington Co., SC "Caroline Lide was
            here last night...She is very much like her mother."

F Child 3 Emma Cornelia LIDE
    Born: 30-JAN-1836   in: Dallas Co., AL   3
Baptized: JUL 1852   in: Centre Ridge Baptist Ch, Dallas Co., AL   8
    Died: 21-JUL-1919   in: 3
Religion: Baptist   in:
  Spouse: P. Lynch LEE
Married: 15-SEP-1859   in: 3
            Married P. Lynch Lee 9/15/1859
            Dismissed from Centre Ridge Baptist Church Jan. 1857.
            Born 1 month after mother arrived in AL when family moved from SC.

M Child 4 James Hartwell LIDE
    Born: OCT 1837   in: Dallas Co., AL   14
    Died: APR 1839   in: Dallas Co., AL   14

(Family of Eli Hugh LIDE - Continued)

Buried: in: Carlowville Baptist Cem, Dallas Co., AL   14
                     Lide-Coker Letters--Also Carlowville Baptist Cemetery, Dallas Co., AL
                     inscription: "James Hartwell Lide b. Oct 1837 d. Apr 1839"
                     Ltr fm Eli Hugh Lide to Hannah Coker 3/1/1838. "Our little Alabama boy is no
                     chick I assure you...He is pert and lively and can sit alone and is by far
                     the most robust of any of our children. Has strong lungs and every appear-
                     ance of a fine constitution."

F Child 5 Margaret Hartwell LIDE
   Born: 17-APR-1839   in: Carlowville, Dallas Co., AL   15
   Baptized: 5-JUN-1852   in: Carlowville Baptist Church   8
   Died: 25-FEB-1919   in: Montgomery, AL   11
   Buried: in: Oakwood Cem, Montgomery   16
   Religion: Baptist   in:
   Spouse: Joseph White HALE
   Married: 29-DEC-1859   in: ?   15
          Graduated East Alabama Female College July 8, 1858. Diploma
          Dismissed fm Centre Ridge Bapt. Ch. 10/2/1858. Ch Minutes

---

F Child 6 Sara E. LIDE
   Born: 1840   in: Carlowville, Dallas Co., AL   3
   Died: c. JUL-1859   in: Ouachita Co., AK   17
   Religion: Baptist   in:

M Child 7 James Eli LIDE
   Born: 1842   in: Dallas Co., AL   11
   Died: 1913   in: Camden, Ouachita Co., AR   11
   Buried: in: Oakland Cem, Ouachita Co, AR   11
   Spouse: Lou R. GREENING
   Married: bet 1860-70   in: Ouachita Co., AR   18
   Spouse: Hellen P. McMAHON
   Married: in:
          Married 1st Lou R. Greening; 2nd Hellen P. McMahon per HSL notes.
          The Cemetery Records for Ouachita Co., AR pub by Ouachita Co. Extension Home-
          makers Council. 1860 Ouachita Co Annotated Census by Bobbie Jones McLane,
          p.7 shows L. J. Greening (fmr) 38 m. b. AL., Amanda, 33, f. b. AL, and
          Louisa, 18, b. AL. Two Bayou Cem. records show a Lucius John Greening
          11/14/1821-5/6/1890. 1870 Census Ouachita Co., AR, living with wife & mother
          & sister; shows Greening family as neighbors. 1870 Ouachita Co., AR Census
          p. 324

(Family of Eli Hugh LIDE - Continued)

F Child 8 Hannah Mariah LIDE
   Born: 25-NOV-1844   in: Dallas Co., AL   11
   Died: 16-JUL-1873   in: Camden, Ouachita Co., AR   11
   Buried: in: Oakland Cem, Ouachita Co, AR   11
        In Ouachita Co.(Liberty town), AR in 1860 Census, age 15 with Mother, Martha
        Johnson Blackwell Lide and brothers James E. (17) and Sam'l B. (13).
        The Cemetery Records of Ouachita Co., AR pub. by Ouachita Co. Homemakers Ext
        Council. 1870 Census, living with Mother & brother and his wife.

M Child 9 Samuel Blackwell LIDE
   Born: 28-JAN-1847   in: Carlowville, Dallas Co., AL   3
   Died: 22-NOV-1922   in: Camden, AR   3
   Buried: in: Oakland Cem, Ouachita Co., AR   11
Religion: Baptist   in:
   Ref: Occupation: Treasurer, Ouachita Co.
   Spouse: Sue Washington GRAHAM
Married: 16-FEB-1876   in: Little Bay, Calhoun Co., AR   3
   Spouse: Kittie Thompson SCOTT
Married: 12-JAN-1888   in: Lisbon, Union Co., AR   3
        HSL: Married 1st 2/16/1876 Sue Graham; 2nd 1/12/1888 Kittie Scott.
        Note: Annotated 1860 Census Records of Ouachita Co., by Bobbie McLane
        indicate died 1882, citing Cemetery Records.
        See Goodspeed's Historical Memoirs of Southern Arkansas pub 1890, p. 678.
        Came to AR in 1857, ran off & joined army in 1864 serving until the
        surrender. Entered mercantile business with Dr. J. W. Brown.
===

1 Kolb, Avery E.: Daughter of Johannes Kolb, Sarah Kolb Lide And Her Descendants
(Manuscript in South Caroliniana Library, Columbia, SC P 10673)

2 Green, Fletcher M. ed. The Lides Go South...And West. Columbia: University
of South Carolina Press, 1952.

3 Lide, Henry Stewart family notes.

4 Lide, Henry Stewart family notes.

5 DAR

6 1860 Census, Dallas Co., AL

7 Marriage Records, Dallas Co., AL

(Family of Eli Hugh LIDE - Continued)

8 Minutes of the Centre Ridge Baptist Church, Dallas Co., AL.

9 obituary

10 Abstracts of Vital Records from Raleigh, NC Newspapers 1820-1829, Vol II. Spartanburg, SC: Reprint Co. Publishers, 1983.

11 Cemetery Records

12 Centre Ridge Baptist Church Minutes.

13 1850 Census, Dallas Co., AL

14 Cemetery Marker, Carlowville Baptist Cemetery.

15 Bible

16 Cemetery Marker

17 Arkansas Gazette, 7/9/1859, p 3, col 1., obituaries.

18 1870 Census, Ouachita Co., AR.

18-MAY-1993   Family group sheet
===
Husband: William Rufus KING

   Born: 1830   in: SC   1
   Died: in:
   Father:
   Mother:
             In CSA, Civil War. Mvd to Yell Co., ARK, 1860. In San Saba, Co., TX by 1868.
             Census, TX, 1870 Red River Co.; 1880 San Saba Co. Vol 28, ED 116, sheet 5,
             line 34. His cousin, Wm Rufus King was VP candidate in 1800.
===
   Wife: Ellen McBRIDE
Married: 17-OCT-1850   in: Chesterfield Co., SC   2

   Born: 17-JUN-1830   in: Darlington Co., SC   2
   Died: 12-SEP-1910   in: Abilene, Taylor Co., TX   2
   Father: William McBRIDE
   Mother: Mary Jane BLACKWELL
             Died while on visit to her daughter in Abilene.
===
M Child 1 William Edward KING
   Born: 1852   in: SC   1
   Died: in:
             "Ned". Mvd to Carlsbad, NM. Married 1st Margaret Tallulah Calie; 2nd Donna
             Smith Parr. Settled in Carlsbad, NM.

M Child 2 Henry James KING
   Born: 1854/1857   in: SC   1
   Died: in:

F Child 3 Louisa Henrietta KING
   Born: 1856   in: SC   1
   Died: in:
             Married 1st John V. Winfrey; 2nd E. W. Ridgway.

M Child 4 George Rufus KING
   Born: c. 1859   in: SC   1
   Died: in:
   Ref: Occupation: Peace Officer   2
             Married Molly Wilson. Moved to Arizona.

(Family of William Rufus KING - Continued)

F Child 5 Sarah Ellen KING
   Born: c. 1861   in: Arkansas   1
   Died: in:
       Married 1st B. R. Wilson; 2nd J. S. Avants.

F Child 6 Laura Eliza KING
   Born: c. 1867   in: Arkansas   1
   Died: in:
       Married 1st Red Neal; 2nd Mr. Hughes.

M Child 7 John Thomas KING
   Born: c. 1871   in: Red River Co., TX   3
   Died: 03-APR-1839   in: Abilene, TX   2
   Ref: Occupation: Peace Officer/blacksmith
       Married Frances Isabel Gaston (d. 4/16/1965) 3/9/1892 Coryell Co., TX.

F Child 8 Mary Ann Frances KING
   Born: c. 1873   in: TX   3
   Died: in:
       Married Shelby J. Estes. "Annie".

===

1 1870 Census, Red River Co., TX
1880 Census, San Saba Co., TX, ED 116, St 5, line 34

2 W. J. Bray

3 1880 Census, San Saba Co., TX ED 116, St 5, line 34.

16-MAY-1993   Family group sheet
==
Husband: Thomas Edward MARRABLE

   Born: 16-JUN-1847   in: Talladega, AL   1
   Died: 20-APR-1937   in: Martin's Mill, Van Zandt Co., TX   1
   Buried: in: Old Liberty Cemetery, Van Zandt Co., TX   2
   Father: Thomas Champion MARRABLE
   Mother: Senah Miller McCURDY
==
   Wife: Temple Long SIMS
Married: in:
==
M Child 1 Jonas Alexander MARRABLE
   Born: 09-SEP-1874   in: prob Van Zandt Co., TX   2

F Child 2 Mary MARRABLE
   Born: 01-JAN-1877   in: prob Van Zandt Co., TX   2

M Child 3 John F. MARRABLE
   Born: 05-FEB-1879   in: prob Van Zandt Co., TX   2

F Child 4 Sena Leona MARRABLE
   Born: 11-AUG-1881   in: prob Van Zandt Co., TX   2
   Died: 15-AUG-1881   in: prob Van Zandt Co., TX   2

M Child 5 Archie MARRABLE
   Born: 25-JAN-1887   in: prob Van Zandt Co., TX   2
   Died: JUL-1889   in: prob Van Zandt Co., TX   2

M Child 6 Russell MARRABLE
   Born: 18-MAR-1884   in: prob Van Zandt Co., TX   2
   Died: 1888   in: prob Van Zandt Co., TX   2
==
   Wife: Martha Adeline GULLEDGE
Married: c. 1888   in: 3

   Born: 13-OCT-1851   in: MS   4
   Died: 28-JAN-1901   in: Van Zandt Co., TX   1
   Buried: in: Old Liberty Cem, Van Zandt Co., TX   3
   Father: David GULLEDGE
   Mother: Eleanor Lauretta McBRIDE
             Called "Addie". Married Thomas E. Marrable
             Information: Lillian Reid Gray, 1702 Cedar Crest Dr, Abilene, TX (1979-80)
             1870, 1880 Census, Van Zandt Co., TX

(Family of Thomas Edward MARRABLE - Continued)
==

F Child 1 Verlie Theole MARRABLE
   Born: 07-FEB-1889   in: Ben Wheeler, Van Zandt, TX   5
   Died: 23-JAN-1982   in: Odessa, TX   5
        Married Verner Hutson Littleton Cole 7/13/1913, Martins Mill, Van Zandt Co,
        TX. Children: Verner H., Jr; Alphatique; Willie Ruth; Edward Nile.

F Child 2 Rosemond Gertrude MARRABLE
   Born: 29-JUN-1890   in: 2
        Married Malcolm McKeachern of Canton.
==

   Wife: Harriett Emma GULLEDGE
Married: c. 1902   in: 3

   Born: 27-OCT-1860   in: Jasper Co., MS   4
   Died: 20-OCT-1903   in: prob. Van Zandt Co., TX   3
   Buried: in: Old Liberty Cemetery, Van Zandt Co., TX   1
   Father: David GULLEDGE
   Mother: Eleanor Lauretta McBRIDE
        Married as his 3rd wife, her brother-in-law, Thomas E. Marrable (widower of
        her sister Martha Adeline Gullege). No issue.
        Not married on 10/23/1897.
        1870, 1880 Census Van Zandt Co., TX.
==

   Wife: Paralee McWILLIAMS
Married: in:

   Died: 20-APR-1937   in: Martin's Mill, Van Zandt Co., TX   2
   Buried: in: Old Liberty Cemetery, Van Zandt Co., TX   1
        No Issue
==

1 Van Zandt County History Book Committee, The History of Van Zandt County Texas 1984 194

2 Van Zandt County History Book Committee, The History of Van Zandt County Texas 1984 338

3 W. J. Bray

4 David Gulledge Family Bible

5 Van Zandt County History Book Committee, The History of Van Zandt County Texas 1984 193

18-MAY-1993   Family group sheet
===
Husband: Edward H. McBRIDE

   Born: 20-AUG-1849   in: Chesterfield Co., SC   1
   Ref: Occupation: Doctor   2
   Father: William McBRIDE
   Mother: Harriet BRYAN
           Grad. Louisville Med. College 2/28/1873. Lived Chesterfield Co., SC until
           1878; Abbeville, SC until 1882 when moved to Jackson, TN. and was in the drug
           business. Letters to Lauretta, dtd 4/13/1849. "Harriet has a son."
           Moved to Springfield, MO 1884. Letters to Lauretta; J. Wm McBride 6/1/1878
           1850 Census (dtd 12/30/1850) lists age as 9mos.
===
   Wife: Lizzie CHAPMAN
Married: 22-JAN-1874   in: Chesterfield, SC   3

   Born: in: Chesterfield, SC
   Died: 09-JUL-1876   in: 3
   Father: John C. Chapman
   Mother: Sally Robeson.
===
M Child 1 Edward McBRIDE, Jr.
   Born: 1874/6   in: Chesterfield Co., SC
===
   Wife: Lizzie W. COPE
Married: 11-OCT-1885   in: Springfield, MO   3

Religion: Presbyterian in: 3
   Father: J. P. Cope, MD. (b. KY)
   Mother: Rebecca Gant, Hopkinsville, KY
===
M Child 1 William McBRIDE
   Born: aft 1885   in: Springfield, MO   2

F Child 2 Cornelia McBRIDE
   Born: aft. 1885   in: Springfield, MO   2
===

1 Green Co., MO. Biography.

2 W. J. Bray

3 Green Co., MO Biography of Edward McBride, MD

18-MAY-1993   Family group sheet
==
Husband: John William McBRIDE

   Born: 1840   in: Chesterfield Co., SC   1
   Father: William McBRIDE
   Mother: Harriet BRYAN
            Capt. CSA 12th LA Reg't Battles: Belmont, Shiloh, Corinth, Chicamauga,
            Franklin, Porter Creek, Peachtree Creek. Wounded in arm at Franklin.
            Children: Flora, Emma, Cora, Sallie, Jim Burch.
            Letters to Lauretta; J. Wm McBride 8/27/1879, 6/1/1878.
==
   Wife: Eliza --?--?--

   Born: in: 2
==
F Child 1 Flora McBRIDE
   Born: in: 3
            Oldest daughter.

F Child 2 Emma McBRIDE
   Born: in: 3

F Child 3 Cora McBRIDE
   Born: in: 3

F Child 4 Sallie McBRIDE
   Born: in: 3

M Child 5 Jim Burch McBRIDE
   Born: c. NOV-1877 in: 3
            Only son in 1878.
==

1 Green Co., MO Biography of Edward McBride, MD
1850 Census, Chesterfield Co., SC 297;174

2 Letters to Lauretta; J. Wm McBride 6/1/1878

3 Letters to Lauretta; J. William McBride 6/1/1878

18-MAY-1993   Family group sheet
==
Husband: Samuel Blackwell McBRIDE

    Born: 1821   in: Darlington Co., SC   1
 Baptized: SEP-1850   in: Ebenezer Baptist Ch., Florence Co., SC   2
    Died: DEC-1877   in: Darlington Co., SC   3
Religion: Baptist   in: 4
  Father: William McBRIDE
  Mother: Mary Jane BLACKWELL
          Ltr fm Elizabeth Blackwell Pettigrew to neice, Lauretta (McBride) Gulledge
          8/8/1854. Was overseer for Mr. Witherspoon. Living with Edward S. Burch
                    Family in 1850 census, Darlington Co. Had heart disease for
                    15 yrs prior to death. Purchased 300 acres of land after
                    Civil War.
==
   Wife: Joanna Louisa BURCH
Married: FEB 1854   in: Darlington Co., SC   5

    Born: 09-MAR-1832   in: Darlington, SC   6
 Baptized: JAN-1850   in: Ebenezer Ch, Florence, SC   7
    Died: 03-NOV-1902   in: SC   6
   Buried: in: Ebenezer Churchyd, Florence, SC   6
     Ref: Occupation: teacher   3
  Father: Edward Sebrey BURCH
  Mother: Joanna White BLACKWELL
          She married the son of Mary Jane Blackwell McBride, who was the half-sister
          of Joanna White Blackwell. 1850 SC Census, Darlington Co., p. 288.
==
M Child 1 James Burch McBRIDE
    Born: 24-NOV-1854   in: Darlington Co., SC   8
 Baptized: 1882   in: Ebenezer Bapt. Ch, Florence, SC   8
    Died: 29-JUL-1924   in: Florence, SC   8
   Buried: in: Ebenezer Cem, Florence, SC   8
Religion: Baptist   in: 8
  Spouse: Angie NAPIER (1858-1937)
 Married: 30-DEC-1888   in: Darlington, SC   8
          Annals of Ebenezer, p. 69,104.
          Moved to Florence and served the First Baptist Ch, there.
          Children: Mrs. D. T. Riley of Florence, SC & James N. McBride of Savannah,
          GA Member of Palmetto Red Shirt Club.
          Cemetery marker in Ebenezer Baptist Church, Florence, SC.

M Child 2 Male McBRIDE
    Born: 1855   See Letters to Lauretta 6/13/1855.   9

(Family of Samuel Blackwell McBRIDE - Continued)

M Child 3 Samuel E. McBRIDE
    Born: 05-OCT-1862   in: Florence, SC   6
    Died: 22-JUN-1915   in: Florence, SC   6
    Buried: in: Ebenezer Churchyd, Florence, SC   6

F Child 4 Hanna Marie McBRIDE
    Born: 25-MAY-1860   in: SC   6
    Died: 30-SEP-1915   in: SC   6
    Buried: in: Ebenezer Bapt. Chyd., Florence, SC 6
    Spouse: Joseph H. BURCH

M Child 5 John Blackwell McBRIDE
    Born: 06-JAN-1867   in: Darlington Co., SC   10
    Died: 18-AUG-1903   in: Darlington Co., SC   10
    Buried: in: Ebenezer Churchyd, Florence, SC   10
             W J Bray notes. Ebenezer Churchyard, Florence, SC.

===

1 1850 SC Census, Darlington Co. 288

2 Pettigrew, George R. Annals of Ebenezer 1778-1950, A Record of Achievement Privately printed, 1952. Letters to Lauretta; Elizabeth Blackwell Pettigrew. 48, 9/30/1850

3 Letters to Lauretta; J. William McBride 6/1/1878

4 Pettigrew, George R. Annals of Ebenezer 1778-1950, A Record of Achievement Privately printed, 1952 45

5 W. J. Bray

6 Cemetery Marker as listed in Leonardo Andrea files, South Caroliniana Library

7 Letters to Lauretta; Elizabeth Blackwell Pettigrew 1/3/1850

8 Pettigrew, George R. Annals of Ebenezer 1778-1950, A Record of Achievement Privately printed, 1952

9 W. J. Bray

10 Cemetery Marker

18-MAY-1993   Family group sheet
==
Husband: Thomas J. McBRIDE

   Born: 1845   in: Chesterfield Co., SC   1
   Died: in:
   Father: William McBRIDE
   Mother: Harriet BRYAN
            In Red River Co., TX in 1873. Texas Census, Red River Co., 1880, Vol 27,
            ED 105, sheet 46, line 37. CSA Kelly's Battery, SC Artillery. Married L. C. ?
            Letters to Lauretta; J. Wm McBride 8/27/1879.
            Enlisted before age 16, served as corporal.
==
   Wife: L. C. ??--??
Married: in:

   Born: c. 1846   in: AL   2
   Died: in:

M Child 1 Theodore McBRIDE
   Born: c. 1873   in: Red River Co., TX   3

F Child 2 Theodora McBRIDE
   Born: c. 1876   in: Red River Co., TX   3

F Child 3 Cayte E. McBRIDE
   Born: c. 1878   in: Red River Co., TX   3
==

1 1850 Census, Chesterfield Co., SC 174

2 W. J. Bray

3 Texas Census, Red River Co., 1880, Vol. 27, ED 105, sheet 46, line 37

18-MAY-1993   Family group sheet

Husband: William McBRIDE

```
    Born: 27-JUN-1784    in: PA or NC                              1
 Baptized:                in: or nr Morven/McFarland, Anson Co., NC
    Died: 02-AUG-1861    in: Chesterfield Co., SC                  1
     Ref: Pettigrew        Occupation: Doctor                      2
  Father: John McBRIDE
  Mother: Ellena RYAN
```

Gregg, p. 603: "Of Darlington Co., SC"
May 1821, Am. Journal of Med Sc. article on May Apple.
Annals of Ebenezer by Geo. Pettigrew mention Scipio & Sarah (husband & wife) former slaves Samuel Blackwell, now owned by William McBride of Chesterfield in 1826. 1850 Census, Chesterfield Co., SC shows born NC.
Biography: Lt. in War of 1812, rec'd land grant.
Moved to Chesterfield Co fm Darlington c. 1816.

Wife: Mary Jane BLACKWELL

```
 Married: JUN-1818       in: Darlington Co., SC                    3

    Born: 1798           in: Georgetown, SC                        4
    Died: 1831           in: Darlington District, SC               4
Religion: Baptist        in:                                       5
  Father: Samuel BLACKWELL, II.
  Mother: Sarah? COMMANDER
```

Was 1st wife of Dr. William McBride.
Letters to Lauretta fm Elizabeth Blackwell Pettigrew dtd 1/3/1850 mentions enjoying Christmas knowing "all of sister's daughters are married."

F Child 1 Eleanor Lauretta McBRIDE

```
    Born: 01-JAN-1820    in: Darlington Co., SC                    6
    Died: 13-JAN-1881    in: Edom, Van Zandt Co., TX               6
  Buried:                in: Edom Cem, Van Zandt Co., TX           5
Religion: Baptist        in:                                       7
  Spouse: David GULLEDGE
 Married: 12-MAR-1839    in: prob. Chesterfield, SC                6
```

Lived Darlington Co., SC 1840; Van Zandt Co., TX 1870 (Census)
Recipient of Letters to Lauretta from aunt Elizabeth (Blackwell) Pettigrew and son Samuel Blackwell Gulledge.

M Child 2 Samuel Blackwell McBRIDE

```
    Born: 1821           in: Darlington Co., SC                    8
Baptized: SEP-1850       in: Ebenezer Baptist Ch., Florence Co., SC 9
```

(Family of William McBRIDE - Continued)

```
    Died: DEC-1877       in: Darlington Co., SC              10
Religion: Baptist        in:                                 11
  Spouse: Joanna Louisa BURCH
 Married: FEB 1854       in: Darlington Co., SC               5
```
            Ltr fm Elizabeth Blackwell Pettigrew to neice, Lauretta (McBride) Gulledge
            8/8/1854. Married Lou Burch, Feb. 1854. Was overseer for Mr. Witherspoon.
            Living with Edward S. Burch family in 1850 census, Darlington Co.
            Had heart disease for 15 yrs prior to death. Purchased 300 acres of land
            after Civil War.

F Child 3 Mary Caroline McBRIDE
```
    Born:                in:                                 12
    Died: c. 01-JAN-1859 in: Chesterfield Co., SC             7
  Buried:                in: Chesterfield Co., SC             7
Religion: Baptist        in:                                  7
  Spouse: William P. BAKER
 Married: c. 11/20/1849  in: SC                              13
```
            WJ Bray notations on Letters to Lauretta dtd 12/5/1849; 1/3/1850. Married
            William P. Baker (NC 1850 Union 054) in Nov-Dec 1849, son of a brother to the
            Baker that m. Turner Briants dau. Mother was a Russian (Rushing), not
            related to Russians of Chesterfield.
            Death: Ltrs to Lauretta dtd 1/1/1859. Postpartum. Left infant son few
            weeks old and 2 others, a son & a daughter. Ltrs to L. dtd 9/1/1859 left
            infant & 3 others. Ltrs to L. 6/20/1849 (2); 12/5/1849; 1/3/1850; 1/1/1859.

F Child 4 Eliza Louisa McBRIDE
```
    Born: 22-MAY-1823    in: Chesterfield Co., SC             5
    Died:                in:
  Spouse: Thomas WOODWARD
 Married:                in:
```
            Letters to Lauretta, dtd 6/20/1849. Living 1866 Jackson Par., LA

F Child 1 Ellen McBRIDE
```
    Born: 17-JUN-1830    in: Darlington Co., SC               5
    Died: 12-SEP-1915    in: Abilene, Taylor Co., TX          5
  Spouse: William Rufus KING
 Married: 17-OCT-1850    in: Chesterfield Co., SC             5
```
                        Died while on visit to Abilene. Married 10/17/1850 Wm Rufus
                        KING. Moved to Yell Co., Arkansas before 1860.

===

```
    Wife: Harriet BRYAN
 Married: 10-AUG-1831    in: Darlington Co., SC               1
```

(Family of William MCBRIDE - Continued)

```
    Born: 1810         in: SC                                    14
    Died: c. 1877/8    in: Chesterfield Co., SC                  10
    Father: S. Bryan
    Mother: Margaret Coleman
```
           Daughter of S. Bryan (d. Chesterfield Co., SC) & Margaret Coleman (d. MS, age
           80) of Eastern, NC. Brothers and sisters were: Henry (killed in the Seminole
           War), Mary, and Robert.

M Child 2 Evander Calhoun McBRIDE
```
    Born: 1837         in: Chesterfield Co., SC                   5
    Died: 1861         in:                                        15
```

F Child 3 Henrietta McBRIDE
```
    Born: 1838         in: Chesterfield Co., SC                  16
    Died:              in:
    Spouse: David J. GREEN
    Married:           in:
```
           In Collin Co., TX 1880. Married David Green
           "Hennie". Letters to Lauretta; J. Wm McBride 8/21/1879.

M Child 4 John William McBRIDE
```
    Born: 1840         in: Chesterfield Co., SC                  16
    Died:              in:
    Spouse: Eliza --?--?--
    Married:           in:
```
           Capt. CSA 12th LA Reg't Battles: Belmont, Shiloh, Corinth, Chicamauga,
           Franklin, Porter Creek, Peachtree Creek. Wounded in arm at Franklin.
           Children: Flora, Emma, Cora, Sallie, Jim Burch.
           Letters to Lauretta; J. Wm McBride 8/27/1879, 6/1/1878.

M Child 5 Thomas J. McBRIDE
```
    Born: 1845         in: Chesterfield Co., SC                  14
    Died:              in:
    Spouse: L. C. ??--??
    Married:           in:
```
           In Red River Co., TX in 1873. Texas Census, Red River Co., 1880, Vol 27,
           ED 105, sheet 46, line 37. CSA Kelly's Battery, SC Artillery.
           Married L. C. ? Letters to Lauretta; J. Wm McBride 8/27/1879.
           Enlisted before age 16, served as corporal.

(Family of William McBRIDE - Continued)

M Child 6 Benjamin Franklin McBRIDE
   Born: 1848   in: Chesterfield Co., SC   14
   Died: 1863   in: KIA   17
        In Civil War at age 14, 8th (Cash's) SC Reg't. Died in CSA age 15.

M Child 7 Edward H. McBRIDE
   Born: 20-AUG-1849   in: Chesterfield Co., SC   18
   Died: in:
   Ref: Occupation: Doctor   5
   Spouse: Lizzie CHAPMAN
   Married: 22-JAN-1874   in: Chesterfield, SC   15
   Spouse: Lizzie W. COPE
   Married: 11-OCT-1885   in: Springfield, MO   15
        Grad. Louisville Med. College 2/28/1873. Lived Chesterfield Co., SC until 1878; Abbeville, SC until 1882 when moved to Jackson, TN. and was in the drug business. Letters to Lauretta, dtd 4/13/1849. "Harriet has a son." Moved to Springfield, MO 1884. Letters to Lauretta; J. Wm McBride 6/1/1878 1850 Census (dtd 12/30/1850) lists age as 9mos.

M Child 8 ? McBRIDE
   Born: in: 5
   Died: in:

F Child 9 Sarah McBRIDE
   Born: c. 1854   in: SC   19
   Died: in:
        Living with David J. Green family (of sister Henrietta),Collin Co. TX in 1880. "Sallie". Per Green Co., MO Bio. is said to have married and had family. Letters to Lauretta; J. Wm McBride 8/21/1879.

===

1 Green Co., MO Biography of son, Dr. Edward McBride.

2 Pettigrew, George R. Annals of Ebenezer 1778-1950, A Record of Achievement
Privately printed, 1952 24

3 Gregg, Alexander. History of The Old Cheraws. Columbia: The State Co. 1925 (Reprinted, 1991: Southern Historical Press) 603

4 Janette Catalano

5 W. J. Bray

(Family of William MCBRIDE - Continued)

6 David Gulledge Family Bible

7 Letters to Lauretta; Elizabeth Blackwell Pettigrew 9/1/1859

8 1850 SC Census, Darlington Co. 288

9 Pettigrew, George R. Annals of Ebenezer 1778-1950, A Record of Achievement Privately printed, 1952. Letters to Lauretta; Elizabeth Blackwell Pettigrew. 48, 9/30/1850

10 Letters to Lauretta; J. William McBride 6/1/1878

11 Pettigrew, George R. Annals of Ebenezer 1778-1950, A Record of Achievement Privately printed, 1952 45

12 Letters to Lauretta

13 Letters to Lauretta 12/5/1849;1/3/1850

14 1850 Census, Chesterfield Co., SC 174

15 Green Co., MO Biography of Edward McBride, MD

16 Green Co., MO Biography of Edward McBride, MD
1850 Census, Chesterfield Co., SC 297;174

17 Green Co., MO Biography of Edward McBride, MD 297

18 Green Co., MO. Biography.

19 Texas Census, Collin, Co., 1880. Vol. 7, ED 23, sheet 1, line 17.

18-MAY-1993   Family group sheet
==
Husband: James McCOWN

    Born: 1803   in: SC   1
    Died: in:
    Father: John McCOWAN
    Mother: Sarah -??--?
            Per Dr. W. J. Bray, James McCowan 1847 wit. will Dr. Wm. McBride.
            James McCowan, Vice Pres. Darlington District Agricultural Society, Darling-
            toniana, p178
==
    Wife: Hannah ?/?/?
Married: in:

    Born: 1810   in: SC   1
    Died: in:
    Father:
    Mother:
==
F Child 1 Frances McCOWN
    Born: 1834   in: SC   1
    Died: in:

M Child 2 Joseph John McCOWN
    Born: 1831   in: SC   1
    Died: in:
    Spouse: Emma NETTLES
Married: JUN-1861   in: Darlington District, SC   2
            Married Emma Nettles (dau of Gen Joseph Nettles and Hannah Blackwell Nettles)
            June, 1861. Ltrs to Lauretta dtd 6/27/1861 say son of James McCown.
            Member of the Darlington District Agricultural Society in 1856.
Darlingtoniana
            p178; Commissioner of Roads 1856, p.182.

F Child 3 Martha J. McMCON
    Born: 1836   in: SC   1
    Died: in:

F Child 4 Helen M. McCOWN
    Born: 1838   in: SC   1
    Died: in:

F Child 5 Margaret McCOWN

(Family of James McCOWN - Continued)

```
    Born: 1840          in: SC                                    1
    Died:               in:
```

```
F Child 6 H. M. J. McCOWN
    Born: 1842          in: SC                                    1
    Died:               in:
```

```
F Child 7 Emma M. McCOWN
    Born: 1844          in: SC                                    1
    Died:               in:
```

```
F Child 8 Rebecca McCOWN
    Born: 1847          in: SC                                    1
    Died:               in:
```
===

1 1850 SC Census, Darlington Co 288

2 Letters to Lauretta; Elizabeth Blackwell Pettigrew 6/27/1861

18-MAY-1993   Family group sheet
===
Husband: Joseph Burch NETTLES

    Born: 04-SEP-1804   in: Florence Co., SC   1
    Died: 05-MAR-1886   in: plantation nr Hartsville, SC   1
    Buried: in: Old Cem, Historic Dist, Darlington, SC 1
    Ref: Occupation: General SC Militia
    Father: James NETTLES
    Mother: ------------??
            Darlingtoniana...by Erwin and Rudisill. Born on Lower Fork of Jefferies Cr.,
            (Middle Swamp). Son of James and Mary Burch Nettles. Moved to village, 1823,
            Elected Col of 29th Regt. SCM, succeeding Col. Evans in 1826. In 1847 elected
            Col, 2nd Regt. Cavalry, SCM, in 1849 elected Brigadier Gen. of 4th Brigade of
            Cavalry, SCM. Held position for 8 years. Members of Ebenezer Church.
            Built home in Springville, SC c. 1856. 1850 Census, SC p 344; 1860 p 377, 389.
===
    Wife: Hannah Mara BLACKWELL
Married: 1832   in: 2

    Born: 10-OCT-1807   in: Darlington Co., SC   1
    Died: 15-SEP-1889   in: Darlington Co., SC   1
    Buried: in: Old Cem, Historic Dist, Darlington   1
    Father: Samuel BLACKWELL, II.
    Mother: Mary Ann HAMLIN
            Married 1st Edmund Gee; 2nd 1832 Gen. Joseph Nettles (b. 1804)
            1850 Darlington Census, p 344. Gregg: p. 603.
            Commander Family, p. 250/1.
===
F Child 1 Louisa H. NETTLES
    Born: 1833   in: SC   3
    Died: bef. 1861   in: 4
    Spouse: Benjamin Catesby NORMENT
Married: 07-MAY-1857   in: prob Darlington Co., SC   5
            Darlingtoniana...by Erwin & Rudisill. "Lou".
            The Inevitable Guest by Cawthorn, p. 26, 121.
            Doctors of Darlington, p58.
            1850 Census, Darlington Co., SC p. 344
            Ltrs to Lauretta dtd 6/27/1861. Had 3 sons at that time.

M Child 2 Robert B. NETTLES
    Born: 1835   in: SC   6
    Died: in:

(Family of Joseph Burch NETTLES - Continued)

Spouse: Eugenia Mochelle McCALL
Married: in:
            Darlingtoniana...by Erwin & Rudisill. Confederate Soldier.
            Children: J. B. (dau), b. 1859; 1 dau b. 1861.
            Ltrs to Lauretta dtd 6/27/1861 has 1 son and 1 daughter.

M Child 3 Joseph Edward NETTLES
    Born: 24-AUG-1836   in: Darlington Co., SC   7
    Died: 21-JUN-1899   in: Darlington Co., SC   8
    Buried: in: Darlington Baptist Chyd, Darlington, SC   1
    Ref: democrat   Occupation: lawyer/planter
    Spouse: Gertrude Lydia SIMS
    Married: 07-FEB-1861 in: SC   9
            Ambassador to Trieste, Austria.
            Mentioned in Letters to Lauretta dtd 6/27/1861. "Jose E." Called Edward.
            Admtd bar 1874. 1892 Sen. Member in firm of Nettles & Nettles.
            Cawthorn: The Inevitable Guest, p 121.
            Brant & Fuller: Cyclopedia of Eminent and Representative Men, Vol 1, p. 266
            Studied at Mt Zion Collegiate Institute, Winnsboro, SC. Entered SC College
            1856, grad 1859. Studied law under Julius A. Dargan. Officer in Darlington
            Gds.

F Child 4 Mary A. NETTLES
    Born: 1838   in: SC   10
    Baptized: early 1840's in: Darlington Co., SC   11
    Religion: Baptist   in: 11
            Married ? Moore.

M Child 5 Martha E. NETTLES
    Born: 1840   in: SC   6

F Child 6 Annie NETTLES
    Born: in: 3
    Spouse: John W. HARRINGTON
    Married: in:

M Child 7 Doc NETTLES
    Born: in: 12
            May be same person as Theodore W. Nettles.
            Confederate Soldier.
            Never Married.

(Family of Joseph Burch NETTLES - Continued)

M Child 8 Theodore W. NETTLES
  Born: c. 1845   in: SC   4
  Died: in:
          Is this the same son as Doc Nettles?

F Child 9 Emma NETTLES
  Born: in: 13
  Died: in:
 Spouse: Joseph John McCOWN
 Married: JUN-1861   in: Darlington District, SC   13

F Child 10 Alice A. NETTLES
  Born: 1847   in: SC   3
  Died: in: 14
 Spouse: L. H. COVINGTON
 Married: in:
          1850 SC Census, Darlington Co., p 344.

===

1 Cemetery Marker

2 Ervin, Eliza Cowan & Rudisill, Horace Fraser: Darlingtoniana A History of People, Places and Events in Darlington County, South Carolina; The Reprint Co, Spartanburg, SC 1976. Marriage contract signed 10/5/1832.

3 Ervin, Eliza Cowan & Rudisill, Horace Fraser: Darlingtoniana A History of People, Places and Events in Darlington County, South Carolina; The Reprint Co, Spartanburg, SC 1976 90

4 W. J. Bray

5 Rudisill, Horace Fraser: Doctors of Darlington County, South Carolina 1760-1912, Pub. by The Darlington County Historical Society, Darlington, SC 1962 58

6 1850 SC Census, Darlington Co. 344

(Family of Joseph Burch NETTLES - Continued)

7 Brant & Fuller: Cyclopedia of Eminent and Representative Men of the Carolinas Vol I. Madison, Wisconsin, 1892 (Reprinted 1972, Spartanburg, The Reprint Co.) 266

(Family of Joseph Burch NETTLES - Continued)

8 Cawthorn, John Ardis: The Inevitable Guest Life and Letters of Jemima Darby copyright 1965, The Naylor Co., San Antonio, TX, Library of Congress Cat. No. 64-8903.

9 Brant & Fuller: Cyclopedia of Eminent and Representative Men of the Carolinas Vol I. Madison, WIS, 1892 (Reprinted Spartanburg, SC, The Reprint Co. 1972) 267

10 1850 SC Census, Darlington Co 344

11 Pettigrew, George R. Annals of Ebenezer 1778-1950, A Record of Achievement Privately printed, 1952 41

12 Ervin, Eliza Cowan & Rudisill, Horace Fraser: Darlingtoniana A History of People, Places and Events in Darlington County, South Carolina; The Reprint Co, Spartanburg, SC 1976

13 Letters to Lauretta; Elizabeth Blackwell Pettigrew 6/27/1861

14 Cawthorn, John Ardis: The Inevitable Guest Life and Letters of Jemima Darby copyright 1965, The Naylor Co., San Antonio, TX, Library of Congress Cat. No. 64-8903. 26

18-MAY-1993   Family group sheet
==
Husband: John ORR

   Born: in: 1
   Died: 1820   in: 1
   Father:
   Mother:
              Equity action 45
              Darlington Co. Historical Commission files.
              Per Dr. W. J. Bray. Of Georgetown District, Liberty Co., SC
              1/28/1797 Will written. Bk 2 Darlington Co., SC Exec: Timothy Dargan,
              Alexander Pettigrew.
==
   Wife: Mary DARGAN
Married: in:

   Born: c. 1784/1790   in: SC   2
   Died: in:
   Father: Timothy DARGAN, II.
   Mother: Ann BEASLEY
              South Carolina Baptists by Townsend p.107n
              Married John ORR of Georgetown Dist, Liberty Co., SC (will BK 2, Darl Co. SC
              28 Jan 1797) Children: John Dargan Orr, William James Orr, Mary Dargan Orr,
              Ann Orr.
==
M Child 1 John Dargan ORR
   Born: in: 2
   Died: in:

M Child 2 William James ORR
   Born: in: 2
   Died: in:

F Child 3 Ann ORR
   Born: in: 1
   Died: 16-JUL-1853 in: Florence Co., SC   3
              Cousin Nancy. Letters to Lauretta.

F Child 4 Susannah ORR
   Born: in: 1
   Died: in:
   Religion: Baptist in: Ebenezer Church, Florence Co., SC 4
              Annals of Ebenezer p. 38 indicate Susannah W. Orr given ltr of dismission to

(Family of John ORR - Continued)

            unite w/ Darlington Ch in 1838.

F Child 5 Mary ORR   1
  Born: in:
  Died: in:
            married Andrew B. Woods.

===

1 Darlington Co. Historical Commission files

2 W. J. Bray

3 Letters to Lauretta; Elizabeth Blackwell Pettigrew 7/1/1853

4 Pettigrew, George R: Annals of Ebenezer 1778-1950, A Record of Achievement 38

18-MAY-1993   Family group sheet
==
Husband: James Alexander PETTIGREW

   Born: 04-NOV-1800   in: Darlington Co., SC   1
   Baptized: OCT-1831   in: Ebenezer Church, Florence Co., SC   2
   Died: 14-OCT-1879   in: Darlington Co., SC   1
   Buried: in: Ebenezer Churchyd, Florence, SC   1
   Religion: Baptist   in: Ebenezer Church, Florence Co., SC   3
   Ref: Occupation: Planter
   Father: William PETTIGREW
   Mother: Susannah DARGAN
             Gregg: History of the Old Cheraws, p 603.
             Darlington Co. Historical Comm. files & 1850 Darlington Census.
             26,700 acres. Letters to Lauretta. Built home in 1852 on Cherokee Rd,
             Florence, still standing 10/92. Death: Darlington News 10/16/1879.
             Witnessed will James Nettles, Sr. 5/29/1820 Will Bk 6, p.234
             Member of Ebenezer Church, Jan 1823, Church Clerk 1835. Church Deacon, 1838.
==
   Wife: Elizabeth H. BLACKWELL
   Married: 03-JAN-1821   in: Darlington Co., SC   4

   Born: 07-SEP-1802   in: SC   5
   Baptized: MAY-1827   in: Ebenezer Church, Florence Co., SC   6
   Died: 09-DEC-1861   in: Darlington Co., SC   1
   Buried: in: Blackwell Cem., Florence, SC   1
   Religion: Baptist   in: Ebenezer Church, Florence Co., SC   6
   Father: Samuel BLACKWELL, II.
   Mother: Sarah? COMMANDER
             Married James A. Pettigrew, 1/3/1821. Annals of Ebenezer by Geo. Pettigrew.
             Wrote series of Letters to Lauretta McBride Gulledge, her niece, which give
             much information on family during period 1849-1863.
             Ltr dtd 7/1/1853 says she has lost 6 children at that time.
             Birth: Ltrs to Lauretta dtd 9/7/1859 "today I am 57 yrs old, Edward is 18."
             Ltr from Blackwell Gulledge to his mother Lauretta dtd 3/18/1862 says: "Aunt
             E. B. Pettigrew died last Nov."
==
M Child 1 William A. PETTIGREW
   Born: 24-MAY-1822   in: Darlington Co., SC   1
   Died: 23-SEP-1823   in: Darlington Co., SC   1
   Buried: in: Blackwell Cem., Florence, SC   1
             Jeanette Catalano.
             Horace Rudisill, Darlington Co. Historical Commission files based on survey
             of cemetery late 1970's.

(Family of James Alexander PETTIGREW - Continued)

F Child 2 Mary Ann Eleanor PETTIGREW
   Born: 08-NOV-1823   in: Darlington Co., SC   7
   Baptized: OCT-1847   in: Ebenezer Ch, Florence, SC   8
   Died: 25-AUG-1903   in: SC   7
   Religion: Baptist   in: 8
   Spouse: Joseph Louis HARRELL
   Married: 04-NOV-1840   in: Darlington Co., SC   9
            Darlington Co Historical Commission files. 1850 Census, Darlington Co., p284.
            Annals of Ebenezer, p.43.

M Child 3 John Alonzo PETTIGREW
   Born: 06-DEC-1825   in: Darlington Co., SC   1
   Died: 11-OCT-1827   in: Darlington Co., SC   1
   Buried: in: Blackwell Cem, Burches Crsrds, Florence   1
            Darlington Co. Historical Commission files (Horace Rudisill)
            Cemetery Marker, Survey of Cemeteries in Lower Florence Co., Vol III. Black-
            well Burch Cemetery located app. 500 yds behind Greenwood Bapt Ch. on
            Claussen Rd, Florence, SC.

M Child 4 James Robert Michael PETTIGREW
   Born: 10-NOV-1828   in: Darlington Co., SC   1
   Died: 30-AUG-1831   in: Darlington Co., SC   1
   Buried: in: Blackwell Cem, Burches Csrds, Florence   1
            Darlington Co. Historical Commission files
            Survey of Lower Florence Co. Cemeteries, Vol III. Blackwell-Burch Cemetery
            located app 500 yds behind Greenwood Bapt. Ch, Claussen Rd, Florence, SC.

M Child 5 Samuel B. PETTIGREW
   Born: 15-JUN-1830   in: Darlington Co., SC   1
   Died: 31-AUG-1831   in: Darlington Co., SC   1
   Buried: in: Blackwell Cem, Burches Csrds, Florence   1
            Darlington Co. Historical Commission files
            Blackwell-Burch Cemetery located app 500 yds behind Greenwood Baptist Ch, on
            Claussen Rd, Florence, SC. Survey of Cemeteries of Lower Florence Co. Vol.
            III

F Child 6 Isabella Susannah PETTIGREW
   Born: 27-MAR-1832   in: Darlington Co., SC   9
   Died: 17-JUL-1832   in: Darlington Co., SC   9
   Buried: in: Blackwell Cem, Burches Csrds, Florence   1
            Darlington Co Historical Commission files.
            Survey of Lower Florence Co. Cems, Vol. III. Blackwell-Burch Cem, located

(Family of James Alexander PETTIGREW - Continued)

                on Clausen Road 500 yds behind Greenwood Baptist Ch, Florence, SC

F Child 7 Olivia Albertina PETTIGREW
    Born: 23-JUL-1833   in: Darlington Co., SC   9
 Baptized: 1849   in: Ebenezer Bapt. Ch, Florence, SC   10
    Died: 04-AUG-1852 in: Darlington Co, SC   11
  Buried: in: Blackwell Cem, Burches Csrd, Florence 1
 Religion: Baptist   in: 12
                See mother, Elizabeth Blackwell Pettigrew's ltr. 1/29/1853; 8/8/1854.
                (Letters to Lauretta). Member of Ebenezer Church for 3 yrs.
                Darlington Co. Historical Commission files. Survey of Lower Florence Co.,
                Cems, Vol III. Blackwell-Burch Cemetery behind Greenwood Baptist Church,
                Claussen Road, Florence, SC.
                Annals of Ebenezer, p.47.

F Child 8 Anna Eugenia PETTIGREW
    Born: SEP-1835   in: Darlington Co., SC   9
    Died: APR-1892   in: Florence, SC   13
  Buried: in: Mt. Hope Cemetery, Florence, SC.   13
  Spouse: Joseph Edward WINGATE
 Married: 26-OCT-1856 in: Darlington, SC   14
   Other: in: by Rev. J.O.B. Dargan
                See Darlingtoniana by Ervin & Rudisill. **Darlington Co. Historical Commission**
                Letters to Lauretta say wedding to take place 11/19/1856
                Mother says in ltr 6/27/1861: "Jenny is pale and lean she is her mother in
                constitution." Father built her a home down the street as a wedding present.
                Married 1st cousin, son of William Wingate and Isabella Blackwell (sister of
                her mother, Elizabeth). Darlington Co. Marriage Bond BK R, p. 630 dtd
                11/22/1856 mentions prop. rec'd fm est. late Mrs. Susannah Good (her
                grdmthr).

M Child 9 Thomas Jefferson PETTIGREW
    Born: 01-JUL-1837 in: Darlington Co., SC   1
    Died: 17-MAR-1855 in: Greenville, SC   15
  Buried: 21-MAR-1855 in: Blackwell Cem, Florence, SC   16
 Religion: **Baptist**   in: Ebenezer Baptist Church   17
                Letter fm Mother Elizabeth Blackwell Pettigrew, 1/29/1853; 9/9/1854 indicates
                he was attending Furman University in Greenville, SC at that time.
                Ltr from Elizabeth Blackwell Pettigrew dtd 3/27/1855. Interred next to
                sister Olivia. Cemetery located behind Greenwood Baptist Ch, Clausen Rd,
                Florence, SC.

(Family of James Alexander PETTIGREW - Continued)

MChild 10 George W. PETTIGREW
  Born: 29-SEP-1838   in: Darlington Co., SC   9
  Died: 21-MAY-1910   in: Darlington Co., SC   1
  Buried: in: Ebenezer Chyd, Florence, SC   1
  Spouse: Alice BOSTICK
  Married: in:
          Letter fm Mother, Elizabeth Blackwell Pettigrew 9/9/1954 indicates he was to
          enroll at Furman University, Greenville, SC in Jan. 1955, accompanying his
          brother Jefferson, already a student there. Letter fm Mother, 6/27/1861
          says he was in The Darlington Guards and on the island when The Star of the
          West was fired into and when Ft. Sumter was taken.
          Jeanette Catalano. Darlington Co. Historical Commission files say d. 1910.

MChild 11 Joseph Edward PETTIGREW
  Born: 07-SEP-1841   in: prob. Darlington Co., SC   5
  Died: 28-MAY-1909   in: Darlington Co., SC   1
  Buried: in: Ebenezer Churchyd, Florence, SC   1
  Religion: Baptist   in: 12
    Ref: King   Occupation: 18
  Spouse: Fannie TILLMAN
  Married: 27-DEC-1865 in: Wadesboro, NC   9
          WJ Bray; Letters to Lauretta McBride Gulledge from Elizabeth Blackwell
          Pettigrew dtd 1/29/1853 Edward to accompany bros. Thomas, George to Furman
          U. in Jan, 1854, Edward being too small to go this year. Eugenia will be
          only child left at home. Ltrs. to Lauretta 9/7/1859: "today I am 57 yrs old,
          Edward is 18". Joined Confederate Army at 20, in 1861, served 4 yrs. Deacon
          in Ebenezer Church. Married Fannie Tillman (4/22/1847--9/25/1903). "Ned"?
          Annals of Ebenezer. Member Pee Dee Light Artillery 1863 & Ebenezer Mtd Club

===

  Wife: Sarah Elizabeth JOHNSON
  Married: 18-FEB-1864 in: Sumter, SC   9
  Other: in: by Rev. Jn Culpepper   9

  Born: 25-DEC-1824   in: Sumterville, SC   19
  Died: 24-JAN-1900   in: Florence, SC   19
  Buried: in: Mt. Hope Cem, Florence Co., SC   1
  Father: Lewis JOHNSON
  Mother: Martha CROSSWELL
          Darlington Co. Historical Commission files. Widow Dickson.
          Daughter of Louis and Martha Crosswell Johnson.
          Bible of Lewis Johnson (typewritten copy in DCHC files)
          1877 Rec'd into Ebenezer Ch fm Darlington Ch. Annals of Ebenezer, p. 74.

(Family of James Alexander PETTIGREW - Continued)
==
F Child 1 Lela E. PETTIGREW
   Born: 10-AUG-1867   in: Darlington Co., SC   19
   Died: 1970   in: 9
   Spouse: Robert Harry FARMER
   Married: 26-JAN-1887 in: Florence Co., SC   9
==

1 Cemetery Marker

2 Pettigrew, George R. Annals of Ebenezer 1778-1950, A Record of Achievement Privately printed, 1952 32

3 Pettigrew, George R. Annals of Ebenezer 1778-1950, A Record of Achievement Privately printed, 1952 20

4 Gregg, Alexander. History of The Old Cheraws. Columbia: The State Co. 1925 (Reprinted, 1991: Southern Historical Press)

5 Letters to Lauretta; Elizabeth Blackwell Pettigrew 9/7/1859

6 Pettigrew, George R. Annals of Ebenezer 1778-1950, A Record of Achievement Privately printed, 1952 25

7 Janette Catalano

8 Pettigrew, George R. Annals of Ebenezer 1778-1950, A Record of Achievement Privately printed, 1952 43

9 Darlington Co. Historical Commission files

10 Pettigrew, George R. Annals of Ebenezer 1778-1950, A Record of Achievement Privately printed, 1952 47

11 Letters to Lauretta; Elizabeth Blackwell Pettigrew 8/8/1854

12 Pettigrew, George R. Annals of Ebenezer 1778-1950, A Record of Achievement Privately printed, 1952

13 Ervin, Eliza Cowan & Rudisill, Horace Fraser: Darlingtoniana A History of People, Places and Events in Darlington County, South Carolina; The Reprint Co, Spartanburg, SC 1976 476

(Family of James Alexander PETTIGREW - Continued)

14 Darlington Flag, Nov. 3, 1856.

15 Cemetery Marker 3/27/1855

16 Letters to Lauretta; Elizabeth Blackwell Pettigrew 3/27/1855

17 Letters to Lauretta; Elizabeth Blackwell Pettigrew

18 King, G. Wayne. Rise Up So Early A History of Florence County South Carolina Spartanburg: 1981, The Reprint Co, 46,74

19 Bible of Lewis Johnson, typewritten copy in Darlington Co. Historical Comm. files.

18-MAY-1993   Family group sheet
===
Husband: Timothy Dargan PETTIGREW

   Born: in: 1
   Died: in: 2
 Religion: Baptist   in: Ebenezer Church   3
 Father: Robert Alexander PETTIGREW
 Mother: Ann DARGAN
           Gregg, History of the Old Cheraws., p 604. Darlingtoniana, p. 17. "In 1825
           T. D. Pettigrew purchased from Col. Bright Williamson his lands on south-west
           of the village (Darlington), and sold off lots starting the improvement of the
           village in that direction." Darlington Co. Historical Commission files.
           Bought slave Will, 6/11/1825 & sold him 8/28/1824. Deed BK J, p. 103 & 150.
           A. T.D. Pettigrew served in FL Seminole War 1837 & died in New Orleans during
           the Mexican War 1846-8. King: Rise Up So Early, p.34.
===
   Wife: Martha L. LANE
 Married: c. 1835   in: 4

   Born: 1798   in: SC   5
   Died: 17-OCT-1851   in: Darlington Co., SC   6
 Religion: Baptist   in: 7
 Father: James LANE
 Mother: Rachel BLACKWELL
           Mentioned in Mother's Will Darl Co. BK 8, p 278. Gregg: p. 603.
           DAR #103100. 1850 Darl Census, p. 284.
           Darlington Co. Historical Commission files. Annals of Ebenezer, p. 41, 49.
           Equity Roll 442, widow of Timothy Dargan Pettigrew.
           Rec'd by ltr fm Darlington Ch to Ebenezer Bapt. Ch in early 1840's.
===
F Child 1 Rachel Louisa PETTIGREW
   Born: in: 8
   Died: aft. 5/12/1830 in: young   9
           Mentioned in grandmother, Rachel Blackwell Lane's will.

F Child 2 Cornelia Manning PETTIGREW
   Born: 1830   in: 10
 Baptized: AUG-1848   in: Ebenezer Bapt. Ch, Florence, SC   11
   Died: in: 8
 Religion: Baptist   in: 11
 Spouse: James A. TILLMAN
 Married: c. 5/27/1856   in: Darlington Co., SC   12
           Mentioned in Grandmother Rachel Blackwell Lane's will.

(Family of Timothy Dargan PETTIGREW - Continued)

    1850 Census, age 20. See notations on Letters to Lauretta by W. J. Bray
    dtd 5/19/1852. Marriage Bond, BK R, p.571 dtd 5/27/1856, Wm B. Pettigrew,
    trustee mentions property fm estate of late Martha L. Pettigrew.
    Annals of Ebenezer, p.45. Ltrs to Lauretta dtd 6/27/1861 state had no child-
    ren at that time.

M Child 3 William Brantley PETTIGREW
    Born: 1832   in: SC   13
  Baptized: AUG-1848   in: Ebenezer Bapt. Ch, Florence, SC   14
     Died: 1884   in: Florence Co., SC   15
   Buried: in: Ebenezer Chyd, Florence, SC   15
 Religion: Baptist   in: Ebenezer Church, Florence Co., SC   16
   Spouse: Mary Ella TILLMAN
  Married: 11-JUL-1865 in: SC   17
    1850 Census. See also notations by W. J. Bray on Letters to Lauretta dtd
    5/19/1852. Gregg, History of Old Cheraws, p. 604.
    Surety Estate of James W. Owens Aug 5, 1864 Pro 1469.
    Annals of Ebenezer, p.45, 53. Elected clerk of Ebenezer Church Jan 1855.
    Returned Ebenezer in 1872. Ltrs to Lauretta dtd 6/27/1861 state still single
    & living with mother.

F Child 4 Amarintha B. PETTIGREW
    Born: 06-NOV-1836   in: 2
  Baptized: 1857   in: Ebenezer Baptist Ch., Florence Co., SC 18
     Died: 23-AUG-1907 in: 9
   Spouse: Joseph E. McKNIGHT
  Married: 1858   in: Hopewell Bapt Ch, Florence, SC   1
                   DAR #103100
    SC Census, 1850 Darlington Co. age 14
    Ltrs to Lauretta dtd 6/27/1861, state has a daughter and son, the son being
    the youngest.

===

1 DAR

2 Darlington County Historical Commission files

3 Pettigrew, George R: Annals of Ebenezer 1778-1950, A Record of Achievement 35

4 Janette Catalano

5 1850 SC Census, Darlington Co. (8/7/1850) 284

(**Family** of Timothy Dargan PETTIGREW - Continued)

6 Pettigrew, George R. Annals of Ebenezer 1778-1950, A Record of Achievement **Privately printed, 1952 49**

7 Pettigrew, George R. Annals of Ebenezer 1778-1950, A Record of Achievement **Privately printed, 1952 41,45**

8 will

9 Darlington Co. Historical Commission files

10 1850 SC Census, Darlington Co (8/7/1850) 284

11 Pettigrew, George R. Annals of Ebenezer 1778-1950, A Record of Achievement **Privately printed, 1952 44**

12 MBond

13 1850 SC Census, Darlington Co. (8/7/1850)

14 Pettigrew, **George R: Annals of Ebenezer 1778-1950, A Record of Achievement 44**

15 **Cemetery Marker**

16 Pettigrew, **George R: Annals of Ebenezer 1778-1950, A Record of Achievement 45**

17 DCHC

18 Pettigrew, George R. Annals of Ebenezer 1778-1950, A Record of Achievement **Privately printed, 1952 54**

18-MAY-1993   Family group sheet
==
Husband: Joseph Edward WINGATE

```
   Born: 1830          in: SC                                      1
   Died: 1888          in: Florence, SC                            2
   Buried:             in: Mt. Hope Cem., Florence, SC             3
Religion: Baptist      in:                                         4
 Father: William W. WINGATE
 Mother: Isabella Ann BLACKWELL
```
        Darlingtoniana by Ervin & Rudisill pp 474-478.
        Lived at corner of Pearl St and Edwards Ave., Darlington, SC in 1854. Home
        was purchased in 1871 from Mrs. Isabella Wingate by J. J. Ward.
        Married his cousin. Rec'd tract of land on father-in-laws plantation.
        Confederate soldier in Inglis Light Artillery. Baptist, member of Darlington
        Church, Ebenezer then Florence Church in 1866. Horticulturalist.
        Wingate College named for family. (A J. E. Wingate, managed a RR inn in 1853)
==
```
   Wife: Anna Eugenia PETTIGREW
Married: 26-OCT-1856   in: Darlington, SC                          5
  Other:               in: by Rev. J.O.B. Dargan
```

```
   Born: SEP-1835      in: Darlington Co., SC                      6
   Died: APR-1892      in: Florence, SC                            7
   Buried:             in: Mt. Hope Cemetery, Florence, SC.        7
 Father: James Alexander PETTIGREW
 Mother: Elizabeth H. BLACKWELL
```
        See Darlingtoniana by Ervin & Rudisill. Darlington Co. Historical Commission
        Letters to Lauretta say wedding to take place 11/19/1856
        Mother says in ltr 6/27/1861: "Jenny is pale and lean she is her mother in
        constitution." Father built her a home down the street as a wedding present.
        Married 1st cousin, son of William Wingate and Isabella Blackwell (sister of
        her mother, Elizabeth). Darlington Co. Marriage Bond BK R, p. 630 dtd
        11/22/1856 mentions prop. rec'd fm est. late Mrs. Susannah Good (her grdmthr).
==
F Child 1 Jenny WINGATE
```
   Born: c. 1857       in: Darlington Co., SC                      8
   Died: prob young    in:                                         7
```
        Letters to Lauretta, June 27, 1861. "Eugenia has been mother of one son
        and two daughters. Both her first were girls."
        Darlingtoniana, p. 476 indicates only 2 children for J E Wingate & Anna.
        They were Joseph E., Jr. and Ellen. Letters to Lauretta, dtd 9/1/1859.
        "Eugenias little girl is a running all about and tries hard to talk. She can
        say a few words. She is sick at this time with a sore mouth and fever."

(Family of Joseph Edward WINGATE - Continued)

F Child 2 Ellen WINGATE
   Born: aft. 9/1/1859 in: Darlington Co., SC   8
                Janette Catalano. Darlingtoniana by Ervin & Rudisill, p. 476. Married Davis
                Brunson. Letters to Lauretta 9/1/1859 mention only her sister.
                Letters to Lauretta dtd 6/27/1861.

M Child 3 William Pettigrew WINGATE
   Born: 03-MAY-1860 in: 9
   Died: prob. young in: 7
                Elizabeth Blackwell Pettigrew. Letters to Lauretta dtd 6/27/1861.
                "will be 10 months old 3 of July". Darlingtoniana, p 476 indicates only 2
                children, Joseph Edward, Jr. and Ellen.

M Child 4 Joseph Edward WINGATE, Jr.
   Born: after 1861 in: 7
                Darlingtoniana by Ervin & Rudisill, p 476.
                Lts to Lauretta, p. 63, dtd 27 June 1861, at that time his mother had only
                1 son and two daughters.
==
1 1850 Census, Darlington Co., SC 349

2 Ervin, Eliza Cowan & Rudisill, Horace Fraser. Darlingtoniana A History of
People, Places and Events in Darlington County, South Carolina. Spartanburg,
SC: The Reprint Co. 1976. 474-478

3 Ervin, Eliza Cowan & Rudisill, Horace Fraser. Darlingtoniana A History of
People, Places and Events in Darlington County, South Carolina. Spartanburg,
SC: The Reprint Co. 1976. 476

4 Pettigrew, George R. Annals of Ebenezer 1778-1950, A Record of Achievement
Privately printed, 1952 60

5 Darlington Flag, Nov. 3, 1856.

6 Darlington Co. Historical Commission files

7 Ervin, Eliza Cowan & Rudisill, Horace Fraser: Darlingtoniana A History of
People, Places and Events in Darlington County, South Carolina; The Reprint
Co, Spartanburg, SC 1976 476

8 Letters to Lauretta; Elizabeth Blackwell Pettigrew 9/1/1859

9 Letters to Lauretta; Elizabeth Blackwell Pettigrew 6/27/1861

18-MAY-1993   Family group sheet

==

Husband: William W. WINGATE

  Born: 06-SEP-1793   in: 1
  Died: 07-JUN-1845   in: Darlington Co., SC   2
Religion: Baptist   in: Ebenezer Church, Florence Co., SC   3
  Ref: Occupation: Merchant
 Father:
 Mother:

      Will recd. Darl. Co. BK 10, p 86, written 4/25/1844; prvd 6/10/1845.
      1850 Darl. Co. SC census, p 349. #DWL 1268.
      Darlington Co. Historical Commission. Member Ebenezer Church 1823.
      Father was Manley WINGATE.
      Darlingtoniana by Ervin & Rudisill, p. 477. Veteran of War of 1812 under Capt
      Bright Williamson. Darlington District Sheriff 2 terms. Rep. to State
      Legislature 1838-40. Merchant with Wingate & Lide, Darl. 10/23/1839.

==

  Wife: Isabella Ann BLACKWELL
Married: 24-SEP-1823   in: 1

  Born: 21-SEP-1805   in: 1
  Died: fl 1871   in: Darlington Co., SC   4
Religion: Baptist   in: 5
 Father: Samuel BLACKWELL, II.
 Mother: Mary Ann HAMLIN

      Member Ebenezer Church. 1850 Darlington Census
      Darlingtoniana by Ervin & Rudisill. p. 475, 477. Gregg: p. 603.
      Annals of Ebenezer by Geo. Pettigrew, Final Mtg of Ebenezer Ch for 1828 wel-
      comed Isabella Ann Wingate into fellowship.
      Sold her home at Pearl & Edwards, Darl, to J J Ward, in 1871.

==

? Child 1 Isabella Olivia WINGATE
  Born: 22-MAR-1825   in: 1
Baptized: SEP-1850   in: Ebenezer Bapt. Ch, Florence, SC   6
  Died: in:
      Darlingtoniana by Ervin & Rudisill p. 477, Unmarried and living at home on
      6/26/1854.

M Child 2 Washington Manley WINGATE
  Born: 28-JUL-1828   in: SC   1
  Died: 27-FEB-1879   in: SC   1
Religion: Baptist   in: 7
  Ref: Occupation: Baptist Minister   7

(Family of William W. WINGATE - Continued)

  Spouse: Mary Elizabeth WEBB
  Married: c. 1850   in: 8
                    Darlingtoniana by Ervin & Rudisill. p. 476. President of Wake Forest College
                    Daughter became wife of Dr. E. W. Sikes, a former president of Clemson
                    College. Letters to Lauretta dtd 1/3/1850 (to Louisa Woodward), "Manly is
                    engaged to be married to a girl at Wake Forest...Mary Elizabeth Webb."
                    Gregg: p. 603. Cawthorn: The Inevitable Guest, p. 219. Minister Ebenezer
                    Baptist Ch, 1852. Letters to Lauretta dtd 6/20/1849.

M Child 3 Joseph Edward WINGATE
    Born: 1830   in: 1
    Died: 1888   in: Florence, SC   9
    Buried: in: Mt. Hope Cem., Florence, SC   10
  Religion: Baptist   in: 11
  Spouse: Anna Eugenia PETTIGREW
  Married: 26-OCT-1856   in: Darlington, SC   12
    Other: in: by Rev. J.O.B. Dargan
                    Darlingtoniana by Ervin & Rudisill pp 474-478.
                    Lived at corner of Pearl St and Edwards Ave., Darlington, SC in 1854. Home
                    was purchased in 1871 from Mrs. Isabella Wingate by J. J. Ward.
                    Married his cousin. Rec'd tract of land on father-in-laws plantation.
                    Confederate soldier in Inglis Light Artillery. Baptist, member of Darlington
                    Church, Ebenezer then Florence Church in 1866. Horticulturalist.
                    Wingate College named for family. (A J. E. Wingate, managed a RR inn in
                    1853)
===

1 Janette Catalano

2 Ervin, Eliza Cowan & Rudisill, Horace Fraser. Darlingtoniana A History of
People, Places and Events in Darlington County, South Carolina. Spartanburg,
SC: The Reprint Co. 1976 477

3 Pettigrew, George R. Annals of Ebenezer 1778-1950, A Record of Achievement
Privately printed, 1952 20

4 Ervin, Eliza Cowan & Rudisill, Horace Fraser. Darlingtoniana A History of
People, Places and Events in Darlington County, South Carolina. Spartanburg,
SC: The Reprint Co. 1976. 475

5 Pettigrew, George R. Annals of Ebenezer 1778-1950, A Record of Achievement
Privately printed, 1952 27

(Family of William W. WINGATE - Continued)

6 Letters to Lauretta; Elizabeth Blackwell Pettigrew 9/30/1850

7 Pettigrew, George R. Annals of Ebenezer 1778-1950, A Record of Achievement Privately printed, 1952 51

8 Letters to Lauretta; Elizabeth Blackwell Pettigrew 1/3/1850

9 Ervin, Eliza Cowan & Rudisill, Horace Fraser. Darlingtoniana A History of People, Places and Events in Darlington County, South Carolina. Spartanburg, SC: The Reprint Co. 1976. 474-478

10 Ervin, Eliza Cowan & Rudisill, Horace Fraser. Darlingtoniana A History of People, Places and Events in Darlington County, South Carolina. Spartanburg, SC: The Reprint Co. 1976. 476

11 Pettigrew, George R. Annals of Ebenezer 1778-1950, A Record of Achievement Privately printed, 1952 60

12 Darlington Flag, Nov. 3, 1856.

18-MAY-1993   Family group sheet
==
Husband: Joseph WOODS

   Born: in: 1
   Died: in:
Religion: Baptist   in: Ebenezer Church, Florence Co., SC   2
   Father:
   Mother:
            Clerk of Ebenezer Church 1831. Dismissed 1832 to unite with a neighboring
            church.
==
   Wife: Hepzibah DARGAN
Married: in:

   Born: 1781   in: 3
   Died: 22-MAR-1855   in: Darlington Co., SC   4
Religion: Baptist   in: Ebenezer Church   5
   Father: Timothy DARGAN, II.
   Mother: Ann BEASLEY
            Member Ebenezer Church, Jan 1823, Jun 1827, Sep 1829.
            Died at the home of Elizabeth and James Pettigrew. Ltrs to Lauretta dtd
            3/27/1855.
==
F Child 1 Rosanna E. WOODS
   Born: in: 6
   Died: in:
Religion: Baptist   in: Ebenezer Church, Florence, SC   7
            Member of Ebenezer Church, Jan 1823
            References in the Annals of Ebenezer, p.39 refer to a Mrs. Rosannah Woods,
            who was granted a letter of dismission in 1839.
            Rec'd back into Ebenezer Ch in 1840 from Mispeh Church.
            Operated boarding school in Doneraile section of Darlington in 1848-9.
            See Darlingtoniana, p. 21. Organized temperance society among boys, called
            The Cold Water Boys."

F Child 2 Edith Ann WOODS
   Born: c. 1808   in: 3
Baptized: SEP-1827   in: Ebenezer Church, Florence Co., SC   8
   Died: in:
Religion: Baptist   in: Ebenezer Church, Florence Co., SC   9
   Spouse: John A. BACKHOUSE
Married: bef. 1860   in: 10
            "E.M.A.". "Ann". Edith Ann Backhouse was heiress of Susannah Good Dargan

(Family of Joseph WOODS - Continued)

        e.g. her mother's sister). W. J. Bray. Mrs Edith Woods Bacchus, widow of a Baptist Minister, lived in Springville in 1880s, per Darlingtoniana, p395 quoting Robt. E. Coker. Darlington Co. Historical Commission files.
Member Ebenezer Church Jan 1823, as Edith Ann Woods; member 1860 as Edith Ann Backhouse.

? Child 3 Susannah P. WOODS
  Born: in: 6
  Died: in:
Religion: Baptist   in: 11
        Final Mtg in 1828 of Ebenezer Bapt. Ch. welcomed Susannah Woods into fellowship.

F Child 4 Martha J. WOODS
  Born: c. 1820   in: 12
Baptized: OCT-1831   in: Ebenezer Church, Florence Co., SC   13
  Died: in:
Religion: Baptist   in: Ebenezer Church   14
  Spouse: Julius Alfred DARGAN
Married: in: 15
        Member of Ebenezer Church Jan 1823.

===

1 Darlington County Historical Commission files

2 Pettigrew, George R. Annals of Ebenezer 1778-1950, A Record of Achievement Privately printed, 1952 33

3 W. J. Bray

4 Letters to Lauretta; Elizabeth Blackwell Pettigrew 3/27/1855

5 Pettigrew, George R. Annals of Ebenezer 1778-1950, A Record of Achievement Privately printed, 1952 20,25,29,35

6 Darlington Co. Historical Commission files

7 Pettigrew, George R. Annals of Ebenezer 1778-1950, A Record of Achievement Privately printed, 1952 20,41

8 Pettigrew, George R. Annals of Ebenezer 1778-1950, A Record of Achievement Privately printed, 1952 25

(Family of Joseph WOODS - Continued)

9 Pettigrew, George R. Annals of Ebenezer 1778-1950, A Record of Achievement
Privately printed, 1952 20,29,35,56

10 Pettigrew, George R. Annals of Ebenezer 1778-1950, A Record of Achievement
Privately printed, 1952 56

11 Pettigrew, George R. Annals of Ebenezer 1778-1950, A Record of Achievement
Privately printed, 1952 20

12 Cawthorn, John Ardis: The Inevitable Guest Life and Letters of Jemima Darby
copyright 1965, The Naylor Co., San Antonio, TX, Library of Congress Cat. No.
64-8903.

13 Pettigrew, George R. Annals of Ebenezer 1778-1950, A Record of Achievement
Privately printed, 1952 32

14 Pettigrew, George R. Annals of Ebenezer 1778-1950, A Record of Achievement
Privately printed, 1952 20,35

15 Cawthorn, John Ardis: The Inevitable Guest Life and Letters of Jemima Darby
copyright 1965, The Naylor Co., San Antonio, TX, Library of Congress Cat. No.
64-8903. 47,223

18-MAY-1993   Family group sheet
==
Husband: Thomas WOODWARD

   Born: c. 1822   in: 1
   Died: in:
   Father:
   Mother:
           Of Sumter, SC. Letters to Lauretta, 1/3/1850 (to Louisa McBride Woodward)
           CSA Civil War. Mvd to Jasper Co., MS c. 1846. To TX c. 1872. MS Census
           1850, Jasper Co. p. 55. LA Census, 1860, Jackson Par., p 352. 9/14/1860
           P.O. Vienna, LA. 1866 Co-partner in Steam mill with Mr. Busby, Jackson Par.,
           LA.
==
   Wife: Eliza Louisa McBRIDE
Married: in:

   Born: 22-MAY-1823   in: Chesterfield Co., SC   1
   Died: in:
   Father: William McBRIDE
   Mother: Mary Jane BLACKWELL
           Letters to Lauretta, dtd 6/20/1849. Living 1866 Jackson Par., LA
==
F Child 1 Eleanor Lauretta WOODWARD
   Born: c. 1850   in: MS   1
   Died: in:
           Letters to Lauretta, WJB notations 1/3/1850

M Child 2 William McBride WOODWARD
   Born: c. 1848   in: SC   1
   Died: in:
           CSA Civil War. "Billy"

F Child 3 Anna WOODWARD
   Born: in: 1
   Died: in:

M Child 4 John S. WOODWARD
   Born: c. 1852   in: MS   2
   Died: in:
           Texas Census 1880, Ellis Co. Married Anabelle (b. c. 1858, TX). Children:
           Loula A. (b. 1874); Lizzie P. (b. 1876); Thomas J. (b. 1877).

M Child 5 Thomas C. WOODWARD

315

(Family of Thomas WOODWARD - Continued)

    Born: c. 1854   in: MS   3
    Died: in:
        Married Sarah (b. c. 1858, TX); Children: William (b. 1876), Walter (b. 1879).

M Child 6 Crawford WOODWARD
    Born: in: 1
    Died: in:
        Youngest son. Could be same child as Thomas C. Woodward.

F Child 7 Alice L. E. WOODWARD
    Born: 1857   in: MS   1
    Died: in:

==

1 W. J. Bray

2 Texas Census, Ellis Co., 1880

3 Texas Census, Harris Co., 1880. Vol. 16, **ED 79, Sheet 14, line 23.**

18-MAY-1993   Family group sheet
==
Husband: Riley W. WYATT

  Born: AUG-1836   in: N.C.   1
  Died: 18-SEP-1913   in: Van Zandt Co., TX   2
  Father:
  Mother:
            Served in Civil War; CSA. Mentioned throughout Letters to Lauretta.
            1870 Census Van Zant Co., TX, p 138, #225B, Canton.
            1880 Census, Henderson Co., TX, Vol 17, ED 34, sht 17 or 167, line 32, pct 4.
            1900 Census Van Zant Co, TX, p185A, ED 133, sht 7, pct 5.
            1930 Notarized statement by J. A. Gulledge, brother of Zilpha Ann Gulledge
            Wyatt. Notation: David Gulledge family Bible: Greenberg Wyatt b. 29 Nov. 1852.
            1880 Census next door to RW Wyatt, Y. Wyatt, 27 w/ family (Yancy? Greenberg)
==
  Wife: Zilpha Ann GULLEDGE
Married: c. 1861   in: 1

  Born: 1-MAR-1844   in: Chesterfield Co., SC   3
  Died: 12-SEP-1881   in: Van Zandt Co., TX   2
  Father: David GULLEDGE
  Mother: Eleanor Lauretta McBRIDE
            See Letters to Lauretta, written by great aunt Elizabeth Blackwell Pettigrew
            to her mother Lauretta McBride Gulledge. Also Ltrs from brother, Samuel
            Blackwell Gulledge. Called Dippy.
            1870 Census, Van Zandt Co., TX.
==
M Child 1 John H. WYATT
  Born: APR-1862   in: MS   4
  Died: 04-MAY-1910   in: Henderson or Van Zandt Co., TX
            W. J. Bray. Married c. 1882, Mary E. b. May, 1868, TN.
            Children: Claud H. (June 1883); Lanna L. (Mar 1886); Archie E. (Oct 1887);
            Riley F. (Sep 1889); Lora L. (Jul 1890); Lucy L. (Feb 1896); Elbert (May
1896)
            Letters to Lauretta from Samuel B. Gulledge dtd 6/18/1862.

M Child 2 William B. WYATT
  Born: JUN-1864   in: MS   5
  Died: in:
            W. J. Bray. Married c. 1886, Louella b. FEB-1868, TX., d. bef. 1910.
            Children: Oscar K. (Jun 1887); Carrie A. (Jan 1889); Elmo F. (Aug 1892);
            Roy M. (Sep 1894); Effie E. (Jun 1899)

(Family of Riley W. WYATT - Continued)

M Child 3 Thomas A. WYATT
   Born: NOV-1868   in: MS   6
   Died: in:
                Married R. C. ? (b. c. 1878), Children: Taylor (b. Jul-1881, TX) & Earl
                (b. Jul-1899, TX).

M Child 4 Charles D. WYATT
   Born: 30-JUL-1875   in: TX   7
   Died: 18-SEP-1912   in: Van Zandt Co, TX
                Boarder with M. A. Boykin in 1900 Census.
                Married 1st c. 1861; 2nd c. 1893.

M Child 5 Crawford W. WYATT
   Born: FEB-1879   in: TX   8
   Died: in:
                Married Donnie ? (b. Aug-1883, TX).
==
  Wife: Mary E. ?///?
Married: c. 1892   in: TX

   Born: SEP-1846   in: MS   9
   Died: in:
 Father:
 Mother:
                Mother of 1 child.
==

1 W. J. Bray

2 Affidavit James A. Gulledge 9/8/1930

3 David Gulledge Family Bible

4 1880 Texas Census, Henderson Co.
1900 Texas Census, Henderson Co., Vol. 67, ED 28, Sht 3, line 36, pct 4.

5 1880 Texas Census, Henderson Co.
1900 Texas Census, Henderson Co., Vol 57, ED 58, sht 8, line 113, pct 4.

6 1880 Texas Census, Henderson Co.
1900 Texas Census, Houston Co., Vol 61, ED 13, Sht 21, line 65, pct 1

7 1880 Texas Census, Henderson Co.
Affidavit James A. Gulledge, 8/8/1930
1900 Texas Census, Van Zandt Co., Vol. 106, ED 33, sht 1, line 89, pct 5.

8 1880 Texas Census, Henderson Co.
1900 Texas Census, Van Zandt Co., Vol. 106, ED 133, sht 4, line 65, pct 5.

9 1900 Texas Census, Van Zandt Co., Bol 106, ED 133, Sht 7 line 18, pct 5.

INDEX OF NAMES

Women's names are indexed under their maiden name, when known. Names may appear more than once on any page. Names on the Family Group Sheets in the Appendix are not included in the Index.

Adair, Martha Eleanor, (Mrs. James Lane, Jr.),
    8, 62, 70, 85, 87, 125, 128.
Adams, R. R., 200.
Aggy, (slave), 85.
Alexander, Joe, 174.
Alfred, (slave), 5.
Allen, John, 186.
Allen, (Mr.), 201.
Allston, Elizabeth (Mrs. Samuel Commander),
    80, 122, 129.
Aneky, (slave), 6, 27, 32, 92, 120, 122, 131,
    133.
Angelina, (Lane?) 4, 59, 66, 70.
Backhouse, (Bacheas) Edith Ann (Woods) see
    Woods.
Backhouse, John, 45.
Backhouse, John A., 39, 44, 115, 118.
Bacot, Caroline A., 57.
Baker, Mary Caroline (McBride), see McBride.
Baker, William P., 7, 19, 25, 41, 43, 45, 46,
    48, 49, 50, 52, 55, 57, 60, 63, 74, 137.
Barkdale, (Col.), 184, 187.
Bass, (see Russ, Martha).
Beasley, Ann (Mrs. Timothy Dargan, II), 117.
Bell, James, 5, 10.
Benton, Gillie, 82.
Bill, (slave), 5.
Blackwell (family), iv, 1, 92, 93.
Blackwell, Caroline Aletha, "Carrie", 19, 24,
    101, 127.
Blackwell, Edward John Burch, 101, 139, 142.
Blackwell, Elizabeth, iii, iv, 1, 2, 3, 6, 7,
    8, 9, 10, 11, 13, 14, 15, 20, 21, 22, 23,
    24, 25, 27, 28, 32, 33, 34, 35, 39, 40,
    41, 43, 45, 46, 49, 50, 51, 53, 55, 56,
    57, 58, 61, 62, 63, 64, 67, 68, 69, 70,
    71, 72, 73, 74, 75, 79, 80, 81, 82, 83,

85, 86, 87, 92, 93, 94, 95, 100, 101, 102,
103, 107, 108, 110, 111, 112, 116, 121,
122, 124, 125, 126, 127, 128, 129, 130,
132, 133, 134, 136, 137, 138, 140, 141,
148, 164, 165, 178, 179.
Blackwell, Elizabeth Isabella, 10, 62, 107,
111, 140, 143.
Blackwell, Hannah Mara (Mrs. Joseph Burch
Nettles), 24, 33, 36, 40, 51, 94, 101,
108, 116, 141, 142, 143.
Blackwell, Isabella Ann, (Mrs. William
Wingate), 3, 7, 8, 19, 24, 29, 33, 34, 36,
37, 40, 41, 42, 46, 51, 52, 65, 66, 68,
69, 93, 94, 95, 101, 104, 108, 112, 116,
117, 125, 129, 131, 133.
Blackwell, James Harrell, 10, 62, 140, 143.
Blackwell, Joanna White, (Mrs. Edward S.
Burch), 8, 11, 14, 15, 23, 24, 28, 33, 40,
41, 43, 51, 56, 59, 62, 63, 66, 68, 70,
71, 95, 99, 103, 108, 109, 128, 138, 140,
141, 142, 143, 148.
Blackwell, John Caroline, 11, 113, 117, 140,
143.
Blackwell, John Hamlin, MD, 5, 10, 15, 16, 18,
21, 22, 23, 28, 32, 36, 40, 60, 62, 63,
64, 65, 68, 83, 86, 90, 91, 92, 93, 95,
98, 100, 102, 104, 108, 121, 123, 124,
125, 127, 131, 133, 134, 137, 139, 141,
142.
Blackwell, Joseph Sebrey, 10.
Blackwell, Martha Aurelia, 11, 56, 58.
Blackwell, Martha Johnson (Mrs. Eli Hugh Lide),
26, 57, 71, 86, 105, 109, 112, 115, 117,
118.
Blackwell, Mary Annah, 10, 62, 68, 107, 111,
136, 138, 140, 143.
Blackwell, Mary Ann (Hamlin), see Hamlin.
Blackwell, Mary Jane, iii, 1, 6, 7, 8, 34, 41,
50, 61, 74, 102, 108, 110, 130, 137, 153,
165, 179.
Blackwell, Rachel, (Mrs. James Lane, Sr.), 8,
62, 87, 142.
Blackwell, Robert James, 108.
Blackwell, Samuel I., 22.

Blackwell, Samuel II., 1, 7, 8, 10, 15, 21, 22, 24, 26, 34, 40, 49, 62, 71, 87, 100, 108, 110, 116.
Blackwell, Samuel, III., 5, 7, 10, 22, 23, 33, 41, 51, 56, 58, 62, 68, 79, 86, 94, 101, 111, 117, 129, 138, 140, 141, 143.
Blackwell, Samuel Issac, 11, 125, 129.
Blackwell, Sarah Amanda Perkins (Harrell), see Harrell.
Booth, (slave), 78, 82.
Booth, Marcus, 64, 68.
Botton, 194.
Boykin, Elizabeth (Mrs. John D. Witherspoon), 125, 128.
Branson, Jack, 139, 143.
Branson, Laney, 140.
Briant, Turner, 48.
Briston, James Tazwell, 143.
Brown, Eveline Gertrude (Houle), see Houle.
Brown, Eveline Gertrude, 50.
Brown, Henry, 172.
Brown, John Ervin, 50.
Brown, Mary, 5, 12, 20, 25, 28, 31, 32, 35, 39, 40, 44, 45, 48, 49, 52, 54, 57, 59, 61, 67, 71, 72, 73, 74, 79, 83, 85, 88, 100, 106, 107, 110, 111, 114, 115, 117, 127, 132, 140, 141, 144.
Brown, Mary Margaret, 5, 12.
Brown, Mr., 169.
Brunson, Joe, 115.
Bryan, Harriet, (Mrs. William McBride), 4, 9, 49, 146, 148, 150, 151, 153.
Buccannon, (son of May), 18.
Buccannon, May, 17.
Burch, Ada, 62, 70, 143.
Burch, Edward Sebrey, 5, 8, 11, 12, 14, 17, 23, 24, 28, 33, 34, 36, 40, 41, 43, 46, 51, 54, 56, 59, 62, 63, 66, 68, 70, 71, 81, 95, 100, 101, 103, 104, 108, 109, 110, 128, 138, 141, 142, 148.
Burch, Elizabeth T. "Betty", 13, 14, 15, 19, 24, 37, 38, 41, 43, 46, 51, 64, 68, 140, 143.
Burch, Emma S., 59, 62, 140, 143.

Burch, Hannah M., 3, 8, 19, 24, 37, 41, 64, 65,
    66, 68, 71, 104, 109, 139, 140, 142, 143.
Burch, James E., 18, 23, 29, 33, 54, 56, 64,
    65, 67, 68, 71, 104, 108, 140, 143.
Burch, Joanna White (Blackwell), see Blackwell.
Burch, Joanna Louisa "Lou", 36, 37, 41, 46, 51,
    60, 63, 74, 104, 105, 108, 110, 122, 125,
    128, 139, 140, 148.
Burch, John Blackwell, "Blackwell", 136, 138,
    139, 142.
Burch, Joseph, 60.
Burch, Joseph Jr., 80.
Burch, Joseph Samuel "Sam Joe", 92, 95, 147,
    148.
Burch, Martha Isabella, 67, 71.
Burch, Mary Ann, 19, 24, 139, 140, 142, 143.
Burch, Mary Hollingsworth (Mrs. James H.
    Harrell), 41, 80, 101.
Burch, Mary Jane (Sinclair), see Sinclair.
Burch, Sebrey, 36, 40, 139, 141, 142.
Burch, Samuel Joseph, 140.
Burch, Sarah (Mrs. Streater), 60.
Burris, Benjamin, 64, 68.
Burras, Tabitha, "Betha", 64, 68.
Burrus, Ivy, 4, 5.
Busby, (Mr.), 153.
"C", (Miss), 162, 178.
Calvin, (slave), 60, 63, 78.
Campbell, Bob, 84.
Cannon, Robert, 4, 17, 31, 35.
Carlton, (Capt), 159.
Ceny, (slave), 83.
Chany, (slave), 83.
Charles, (slave), 28, 32.
Charles, Andrew Blackwood, 57.
Charles, Edgar Welles (Col.), 55, 57, 58.
Charles, Hugh Lide, 57.
Childs, C. (Mr.), 163.
Cinder, (slave), 32, 79, 83.
Clarinda, (slave), 5.
Cogdel, Ursula, 135.
Cogshell, Oliver, 125.
Coker, Hannah (Lide), 86.
Coker, Robert W., 168.

Cole, Cephas, 68, 136, 138, 143.
Cole, Elizabeth, (Mrs. Issac), 4, 8, 18, 87.
Cole, Isabella, 84, 87.
Cole, Issac, 4, 8, 87.
Cole, Mary Annah (Blackwell), see Blackwell.
Commander (family), iv.
Commander, Abigail (Mrs. John Smith), 9.
Commander, Eliza (Howle), see Howle.
Commander, Elizabeth (Mrs. Joseph Houle), 42.
Commander, James I., 1, 26, 30, 34, 80, 81, 110, 122, 129.
Commander, James M., 76, 77, 80, 105, 106, 110, 119, 120, 121, 122, 125, 129, 132, 134.
Commander, James Perry, Jr., 20, 26.
Commander, Jesse, 26.
Commander, Margaret, 81, 102, 110, 122, 128, 130.
Commander, (Miss), 1, 26, 122.
Commander, Samuel, 80, 110, 122, 129.
Commander, Samuel II., 9.
Connell, William, 26.
Cooper, Silas, 60.
Crecy, (slave), 91.
Culpepper, John, 47, 51, 64, 66, 69, 70.
Darcas, (slave), 5, 27.
Dargan (family), iv.
Dargan, Ann, 92, 142.
Dargan, Charles A., 82, 129.
Dargan, George Washington, 82, 129.
Dargan, Harriet (Mrs. James Clement Furman), 117, 123.
Dargan, Hepzibah (Mrs. Joseph Woods), 12, 43, 45, 114, 115, 117, 118.
Dargan, Jeremiah, "Jerry", 82, 125, 128, 129.
Dargan, John Orr Beasley, (JOB), 4, 9, 13, 14, 37, 38, 41, 43, 47, 51, 66, 69, 82, 125, 129.
Dargan, Julius Alfred, 38, 43, 82, 125, 128, 129.
Dargan, Lydia (Keith), see Keith.
Dargan, Margaret A. P., 9, 144.
Dargan, Mary (Mrs. John Orr), 13, 25, 43, 102.
Dargan, Sarah Thomas (DuBose), see DuBose.
Dargan, Sidney R. F., 82, 129.

Dargan, Susannah, 1, 12, 13, 14, 26, 43, 102, 117.
Dargan, Theodore Alonzo, 82, 125, 128.
Dargan, Timothy I., 14.
Dargan, Timothy II., 43, 82, 117.
Dargan, Timothy III., 9, 14, 42, 43, 51, 69, 82, 117, 128, 129, 144.
Dargan, Timothy J. K., 82, 129.
Dargan, William Edwin (Dr.), 64, 69, 78, 81, 125, 129.
David, Ben, 200, 206.
Dawson, Caroline (Lide), see Lide.
Dawson, Lawrence Edwin, Jr., 105, 109, 118.
Dawson, Lawrence Edwin, Sr., 109.
Dawson, Mary (Huger), see Huger.
Dice, (slave), 15, 21, 131, 133.
Doby, N. (Mr.), 159.
Doolittle, Calvin H., 174, 178, 181, 184, 185, 186.
Doolittle, (Mr.), 196.
DuBose, Sarah Thomas (Mrs. William Edwin Dargan), 78, 82, 129.
DuBose, Isiah, 82.
Dozier, Elizabeth, 22.
Edmund (Lane?), 59, 62, 66, 70.
Etheridge, William Rumph, 58.
Evans, General, 172.
Evans, George Washington, 4.
Evans, Mary Ann, 4.
Evans, Mrs., (in Darlington), 4, 29.
Evans, Mrs., (in MS), 20, 39.
Furman, Harriet (Dargan) Furman, see Dargan.
Furman, James Clement, 112, 117, 121, 123.
Furman, Richard (Rev.), 11, 117, 123.
Gandy, Abel, 68.
Gandy, Lafayette, 68.
Gardner, Mr., 174.
Gause, Emily, 8.
Gause, Maria, T. B., 4, 8.
Gee, Caroline, 84.
Gee, Edmund, 33, 40, 101.
Gee, Jacquilling, 105, 110.
Gee, James Redden, 64, 68.
Gee, Thomas, 84.
George, (slave), 5.

Gibbs, James "Jim", 155, 157, 163, 171, 172, 181, 184, 186, 191, 200, 206.
Gibbs, Joe, 157, 163, 167, 168, 171, 172, 181, 184, 186, 188, 191, 194, 195, 200.
Gibbs, John, 167.
Gibbs, Mr., 168, 171, 186, 189.
Gilbert, John, 157, 163, 171, 181.
Gilbert, Van, 157, 163, 173.
Ginny, (slave), 4, 5, 78.
Glover, Allen, 189.
Goddard, Mr., 18.
Goddard, Mary (Whitworth), see Whitworth.
Good, John, 26
Goodwin, James, 196.
Graham, D., 186.
Graham, (Mr.), 162.
Green, Addie, 151.
Green, Charles D., 151.
Green, David J., 151.
Green, Francis R., 151.
Green, Hattie B., 151.
Green, Mary A., 151.
Green, Sam, 125.
Gregg, Joseph, 178.
Griffith, General, 172, 186.
Gulledge (family), iv, 13.
Gulledge, Albert Joseph, 111, 146, 148, 195, 196.
Gulledge, David, iii, iv, 1, 5, 6, 12, 20, 25, 26, 30, 31, 34, 37, 39, 40, 43, 44, 48, 52, 56, 59, 60, 61, 63, 67, 71, 72, 73, 74, 85, 88, 92, 94, 100, 103, 106, 107, 110, 116, 119, 120, 122, 126, 127, 130, 132, 136, 141, 146, 147, 148, 151, 155, 166, 167, 179, 191, 202.
Gulledge, Eleanor Lauretta (McBride), see McBride.
Gulledge, Elizabeth Louisa, 23, 34, 111.
Gulledge?, Gracy, 167.
Gulledge, Harriet Emma, 194.
Gulledge, James Alexander, 146, 148.
Gulledge, Joel, 25.
Gulledge, Martha Adeline, 82, 111.

Gulledge, Mary Eleanor, 6, 12, 19, 25, 26, 39,
    44, 85, 88, 107, 111, 115, 118, 135, 136,
    138, 146, 148, 167, 168.
Gulledge, Samuel Blackwell "Blackwell", iv, 6,
    12, 19, 25, 26, 44, 49, 52, 85, 88, 92,
    94, 107, 111, 115, 118, 138, 141, 146,
    148, 155, 156, 157, 158, 159, 161, 162,
    163, 165, 166, 167, 168, 169, 170, 171,
    173, 174, 175, 177, 179, 180, 181, 182,
    183, 185, 186, 187, 188, 190, 193, 194,
    195, 196, 198, 199, 201, 202, 203, 205,
    206.
Gulledge, Sarah Lauretta "Sallie Lou", 26, 30,
    34, 39, 44, 85, 88, 107, 146, 148, 167,
    168.
Gulledge, Thomas Huntley, 26, 111, 146, 148.
Gulledge, Zilpha Ann "Dippy" (Mrs. Riley
    Wyatt), 26, 39, 44, 79, 82, 85, 88, 107,
    111, 146, 148, 157, 159, 160, 161, 162,
    167, 168, 174, 179, 181, 182, 184, 185,
    190, 191, 195, 196, 197, 198, 203.
Gulledge, Zilpha (Huntley), see Huntley.
Hager, (slave), 5.
Hamlin, Joanna (White), see White.
Hamlin, John, 1.
Hamlin, Mary Ann, "Ma", (widow of Samuel
    Blackwell, II.), 1, 3, 7, 10, 14, 15, 18,
    19, 21, 23, 24, 26, 29, 33, 34, 35, 40,
    45, 46, 49, 51, 59, 62, 71, 100, 105, 108,
    109, 138, 141.
Hammond, (Mr.), 203.
Hana, General, 149.
Hana, Mrs., 149.
Hancock, Becky, 149.
Hancock, Joe Pete, 149.
Hancock, Bill, 149.
Harper, Mr., 84.
Harrel, Josiah, 49.
Harrell (family), iv.
Harrell, Elizabeth, "Betty", 55, 57, 125, 127,
    130, 133.
Harrell, Elizabeth Susanna, 128, 130, 132.
Harrell, Eugenia, 75.
Harrell, George Washington, 132, 133.

Harrell, James Alexander, 15, 21, 132.
Harrell, James H. Harrell, 80.
Harrell, John Edward, 15, 21, 22, 28, 33, 132.
Harrell, Joe, 186.
Harrell, Joseph Louis, 3, 7, 14, 15, 16, 17,
    18, 21, 22, 23, 28, 29, 32, 33, 36, 40,
    45, 46, 51, 54, 56, 57, 59, 60, 61, 63,
    64, 65, 66, 68, 69, 71, 73, 74, 75, 78,
    79, 80, 81, 84, 85, 86, 88, 92, 94, 95,
    97, 99, 100, 102, 103, 104, 108, 114,
    121, 122, 124, 127, 128, 130, 131, 133,
    134, 135, 137, 138, 141.
Harrell, Julius Dargan, 100, 103, 117, 124,
    127, 132.
Harrell, Mary Ann Eleanor (Pettigrew), see
    Pettigrew.
Harrell, Mary Eugenia, 13, 14, 16, 22, 55, 57,
    127, 130, 132.
Harrell, Mary Hollingsworth (Burch), see Burch.
Harrell, Samuel Joseph, 56, 132.
Harrell, Sarah Amanda Perkins, (Mrs. Samuel
    Blackwell, III.), (Mrs. James Owens), 3,
    5, 7, 10, 15, 18, 22, 23, 28, 33, 36, 41,
    46, 51, 54, 56, 58, 59, 62, 68, 75, 79,
    80, 84, 86, 91, 94, 96, 101, 107, 111,
    138, 143.
Harrell, Sarah Ann, 16, 22, 28, 29, 33, 132.
Harrell, Thomas Jefferson, 117, 121, 122, 124,
    127, 132.
Harrell, William Lewis, 117, 132.
Hepburn, Clement Cogburn, 139, 142.
Hepburn, Elizabeth S. "Cousin Betsy", 4, 7, 9,
    19, 21, 25, 29, 34, 39, 41, 44, 59, 62,
    66, 68, 71, 87, 135, 136, 137, 142.
Hepburn, Elizabeth "Betty", 37, 38, 39, 41, 44,
    139, 142.
Hepburn, James W., 3, 7, 15, 21, 64, 68, 84,
    87.
Hepburn, Robert, 7, 9, 21, 25, 34, 41, 44, 62,
    68, 71, 87, 137, 142.
Hepburn, Robert Jr., 139, 142.
Hewet, Mrs., 136.
Hill, James, 91,
Hills, 91.

Hollingsworth, Mary, 80.
Holloway, Jane, 58, 109.
Houle, Axalla, 37, 42, 46, 50, 54, 57.
Houle, Elizabeth Stanley "Cousin Betsy", 37,
    42, 46, 50, 57.
Houle, Eufrazer, 37, 42, 46, 50.
Houle, Eveline Gertrude, 50.
Houle, James Commander, 42, 50, 57.
Houle, Joseph, 42.
Howle, Eliza (Mrs. James M. Commander), 77,
    81, 106, 110.
Howle, (Hull) Mrs., 77, 78, 81.
Huddleston, 194.
Huger, Mary (Mrs. Lawrence Edwin Dawson, Sr.),
    109.
Humphrey, Mr., 173.
Hunter, Caroline Matilda, (Mrs. John Hamlin
    Blackwell), 7, 10, 58, 117, 129, 143.
Huntley, Zilpha (Mrs. Joel Gulledge), 25.
Hunter, Isabella Jannett, 10.
Hunter, Martha, 115.
Hutchenson, Evander, 38.
Irene, (slave), 120, 122.
Issac, (slave), 5.
Jackson, Stonewall (Gen.), 187, 188.
Jacob, 4, 5.
James, 194.
James, George, 4.
James, John T., 4, 5, 10, 11.
Jarrot, James Howard (Dr.), 105, 110, 131, 133.
Jarrot, Margaret, (Mrs. James Howard Jarrot),
    105.
Jerry, (slave), 4.
John, (slave), 132.
Johnson, J. R., 169.
Johnson, W., 186.
Johnston, D. (Mr.), 160.
Jones, J. T., 200.
Judy, (slave), 29.
Keith, James, (Col.), 9.
Keith, Lydia, "Aunt Dargan", 4, 9, 14, 41, 43,
    69, 82, 117, 128, 129, 144.
Keith, Thomas, 205.
King, William Rufus, 151.

Koon, (slave), 78, 82.
Laman, Joe, 186.
Lane, Amelia, 125, 128.
Lane, Elizabeth Blackwell, 70.
Lane, James, Sr., 8, 87.
Lane, James, Jr., 8, 62, 70, 84, 87, 128, 142.
Lane, James Henning, 4, 8.
Lane, Martha Eleanor (Adair), see Adair.
Lane, Martha L., 142, 143, 144.
Lane, Rachel (Blackwell), see Blackwell.
Lane, Samuel Adair, 59, 62.
Lane, Thomas Mitchell, 4, 8.
Langston, Martha, 84.
Langston, Mrs., 84.
Lany, (slave), 28.
Law, Thomas C., 86.
Lee, (Gen.), 192, 201.
Liddy, (slave), 19, 67.
Lide (family), 71.
Lide, Caroline E., 84, 86, 105, 109, 118.
Lide, Eli Hugh, 26, 55, 57, 58, 71, 86, 87, 105, 109, 115, 118.
Lide, Hannah Mariah, 109.
Lide, Hugh, 57, 58.
Lide, James, 58, 86, 109.
Lide, James Eli, 109.
Lide, Margaret Jane, 129.
Lide, Martha Johnson Blackwell, see Blackwell.
Lide, Mary Ann, 20, 21, 26, 55, 57, 58, 66, 71, 105, 109.
Lide, Robert (Major), 86.
Lide, Samuel Blackwell, 109.
Lide, Sarah E., 109.
Lide, Sarah Kolb, 57, 58.
Lindy, (slave), 31, 99.
Lizzy, (slave), 5.
Longstreet, (Gen.), 188, 192.
Lyd, (slave), 152.
Martin, 157, 158, 159, 175.
Maria, (slave), 92.
Maria, 115.
Mary, (slave), 120, 122.
McBride (family), iv, 49.
McBride, Calhoun, 49.
McBride, Cora, 147.

McBride, Edward H., 9, 49, 147, 148.
McBride, Eleanor Lauretta, (Mrs. David
    Gulledge), iii, iv, v, 1, 3, 6, 7, 8, 9,
    12, 13, 15, 16, 20, 22, 23, 25, 26, 27,
    30, 34, 35, 37, 40, 41, 42, 43, 44, 47,
    48, 50, 52, 53, 54, 56, 61, 63, 64, 65,
    66, 67, 71, 72, 73, 74, 75, 79, 82, 83,
    84, 87, 88, 89, 90, 92, 94, 95, 96, 97,
    98, 99, 102, 103, 107, 111, 112, 113,
    116, 118, 119, 123, 124, 130, 131, 132,
    134, 138, 141, 145, 146, 148, 149, 150,
    155, 164, 166, 167, 170, 179, 182, 196,
    198, 204, 205.
McBride, Eliza, (Mrs. John William McBride),
    147.
McBride, Elizabeth Louisa, (Mrs. Thomas
    Woodward), 3, 6, 12, 13, 18, 20, 23, 25,
    30, 31, 34, 35, 36, 37, 38, 39, 40, 42,
    44, 45, 47, 50, 52, 53, 56, 58, 60, 63,
    67, 71, 72, 73, 74, 121, 123, 130, 132,
    149, 151, 153.
McBride, Ellen, 49, 149, 151.
McBride, Emma, 147.
McBride, Evander Calhoun, 163, 164.
McBride, Franklin, 49.
McBride, Harriet (Bryan), see Bryan.
McBride, Henrietta, 49, 149, 151.
McBride, James Burch, 122, 128.
McBride, Jim Burch, 147.
McBride, John William "Billy, 49, 146, 148,
    149, 150, 152, 153, 163, 164, 169, 174,
    186, 197, 198.
McBride, Mary Caroline, 3, 7, 17, 19, 22, 25,
    36, 37, 41, 42, 43, 45, 46, 47, 48, 49,
    50, 52, 55, 57, 60, 63, 66, 71, 74, 135,
    136, 137, 138, 145, 146.
McBride, Mary Jane (Blackwell), see Blackwell.
McBride, Sallie, 147.
McBride, Sallie E., 149, 151.
McBride, Samuel Blackwell, 3, 8, 17, 22, 31,
    34, 35, 36, 37, 39, 41, 42, 43, 46, 47,
    50, 52, 54, 56, 58, 61, 65, 69, 70, 72,
    74, 76, 80, 81, 84, 85, 87, 88, 94, 95,
    100, 101, 103, 104, 105, 106, 108, 110,

    120, 122, 125, 126, 127, 128, 130, 131,
    132, 133, 135, 137, 139, 141, 147, 148,
    178, 179.
McBride, Thomas J., 49, 149, 151.
McBride, William (Dr.), iii, 1, 6, 8, 9, 17,
    22, 34, 41, 42, 49, 50, 56, 61, 139, 141,
    145, 146, 148, 150, 151, 153.
McCall, Elizabeth, 11.
McCall, Eugenia Mochelle, 144.
McCall, Will, 5, 11.
McCown, George, 5, 12.
McCown, Hannah, 144.
McCown, James, 12.
McCown, James, 140, 144.
McCown, John, 144.
McCown, Joseph John, 140, 144.
McCown, Mary Ann, 39, 48.
McCown, Mary Margaret (Brown), see Brown.
McCown, (Mrs. Samuel O.), 105.
McCown, Sarah, 144.
McCown, Samuel O., 105, 110.
McDaniel, J., 163, 172, 173, 175, 181, 184,
    186, 194, 197.
McDaniel, (Mr.), 189.
McGee, N., 163.
McGeha, H. H., 184.
McGehee, H., 175.
McGregor, Duncan, 149.
McIlvane, Elizabeth, 128.
McIlvane, H. W. (Mr.), 128.
McIlvane, Harriet, 125, 128.
McIlvane, James L., 128.
McIlvane, Martha E., 128.
McIlvane, Mary, 128.
McIlvane, Sarah, 128.
McKnight, Joseph E., 143.
McLaughlin, Evander, 76, 81.
McLaughlin, Margaret, 81.
McLaughlin, Mary, 81.
McLeneghan, Mrs., 92.
McPherson, Robert, 39, 48.
Meadows, Stephen, 84, 87.
Moore, (Mr.), 139, 143.
Morris, James (Rev.), 38, 43, 47, 51, 66,
    69, 70, 118.

Morrison, Elizabeth, 60.
Mose, (slave), 5.
Muldrow, Alitha, 26.
Muldrow, Elihu, 139, 142.
Muldrow, Hugh, 43.
Muldrow, John, 38, 43.
Muldrow, Mr., 49.
Muldrow, Samuel W., 5, 12, 26, 29, 34, 125, 128.
Muldrow, Ursula, 12, 20, 26, 34, 125, 128.
Nancy, (slave), 54, 92.
Napier (Napare), Robert (Rev), 66, 70.
Nelly, (slave), 5, 31.
Nettles (family), iv.
Nettles, Anna, 104, 109.
Nettles, Emma, 140, 144.
Nettles, Hannah Mara (Blackwell), see Blackwell.
Nettles, James, 62, 70, 101.
Nettles, Joseph Burch, 19, 24, 33, 40, 46, 51, 93, 96, 101, 104, 108, 116, 141, 142, 144.
Nettles, Joseph Edward, 139, 140, 141, 144.
Nettles, Louisa H., 29, 33, 140, 144.
Nettles, Mary Ann, 91, 93.
Nettles, Robert B., 139, 140, 142, 144.
Norice, (slave), 152.
Norman, Mr., 172, 189.
Norman, W. B., 186.
Norment, Benjamin Catesby (Dr.), 144.
Norwood, Joseph, 83.
Orr, John, 13, 25, 43, 102.
Orr, Mary (Dargan), see Dargan.
Orr, Nancy, 6, 13, 20, 25, 26, 38, 43, 49, 52, 99, 102.
Osborn, 194.
Owens, James, 91, 94, 96, 107, 111.
Parker, Mrs., 92.
Pearce, Elizabeth Sparks, (Mrs. Robert A. Pettigrew), 68, 81, 88, 92, 93, 94, 101, 108, 114, 115, 117, 124, 127.
Pendergrass, William, 12, 168.
Peggy, (slave), 92, 100.
Pegon, Martha, 98.

Perkins, Margaret, 9.
Pettigrew (family), iv, 57, 110.
Pettigrew, Amarintha B., 140, 143.
Pettigrew, Anna Eugenia, 8, 12, 14, 15, 16, 19, 21, 22, 24, 25, 35, 44, 50, 52, 61, 63, 64, 68, 69, 73, 74, 76, 77, 81, 85, 88, 91, 93, 98, 100, 102, 103, 106, 107, 110, 112, 114, 115, 116, 117, 121, 122, 127, 130, 132, 133, 134, 135, 137, 138, 141.
Pettigrew, Cornelia Manning, 140, 144.
Pettigrew, Elizabeth (Blackwell), see Blackwell.
Pettigrew, Elizabeth (Pearce), see Pearce.
Pettigrew, George W., 14, 27, 28, 32, 35, 44, 52, 75, 86, 88, 91, 92, 93, 97, 102, 106, 107, 110, 111, 112, 113, 114, 115, 116, 117, 120, 122, 127, 130, 133, 134, 137, 139, 142.
Pettigrew, George R., 67.
Pettigrew, Isabella Susannah, 93.
Pettigrew, James Alexander, 1, 5, 11, 13, 14, 16, 20, 21, 22, 25, 26, 27, 28, 31, 32, 35, 36, 39, 41, 43, 45, 51, 57, 60, 61, 63, 66, 68, 69, 70, 73, 74, 76, 77, 78, 81, 84, 86, 87, 92, 93, 94, 101, 102, 104, 106, 107, 108, 112, 116, 117, 119, 122, 123, 124, 127, 131, 132, 134, 137, 142.
Pettigrew, James Robert, 93.
Pettigrew, John Alonzo, 93.
Pettigrew, Joseph Edward, 14, 19, 25, 44, 52, 66, 70, 75, 85, 88, 91, 92, 93, 97, 102, 107, 111, 125, 127, 128, 130, 133, 134, 135, 137, 138, 139, 142.
Pettigrew, Margaret, 78, 82.
Pettigrew, Mary Ann Eleanor, 7, 14, 16, 17, 18, 20, 21, 22, 23, 25, 29, 30, 32, 33, 34, 35, 36, 40, 46, 51, 56, 57, 58, 59, 61, 63, 68, 69, 73, 74, 78, 79, 86, 92, 94, 95, 99, 100, 101, 102, 103, 108, 114, 117, 121, 122, 124, 127, 128, 130, 132, 133, 135, 137, 138, 141.
Pettigrew, Olivia Albertina, 12, 14, 16, 18, 19, 22, 23, 25, 35, 38, 39, 43, 44, 50, 52, 54, 55, 57, 61, 63, 65, 66, 70, 73,

75, 76, 77, 79, 81, 82, 88, 89, 92, 95,
101, 112, 116, 121, 122, 126, 127, 130.
Pettigrew, Robert A., Jr., 68, 81, 92, 93, 94,
100, 108, 117, 127, 142.
Pettigrew, Robert A., Sr., 92.
Pettigrew, Sarah A. S. (Sally), (Mrs. John
Hamlin Blackwell), 64, 68, 76, 81, 91, 93,
95, 98, 100, 102.
Pettigrew, Samuel B., 93.
Pettigrew, Susannah (Dargan), see Dargan.
Pettigrew, Thomas Jefferson, 14, 28, 32, 35,
44, 52, 75, 86, 88, 91, 93, 97, 102, 106,
110, 112, 113, 116, 120, 121, 122, 123,
124, 126, 127, 130.
Pettigrew, Timothy Dargan, 142, 143, 144.
Pettigrew, William, 1, 12.
Pettigrew, William A., 93.
Pettigrew, William Brantley, 139, 140, 142,
144.
Pettus, Governor, 172.
Pierce, Laura, 59.
Poore, 184.
Pope, (Gen.), 187.
Pugh, Evan (Rev.), 11, 57.
Pugh, Elizabeth, 57.
Railey, Jesse, 186.
Rachel, (slave), 19.
Rose, (slave), 29, 33.
Russ (possibly Bass), Martha, 140.
Russell, G. W., 200.
Russian (Rushing), 48.
Sary, (slave), 120, 122.
Sellers, Hardy, 4.
Sellers, Mary (Sinklah), see Sinklah.
Seny, (slave), 132.
Sims, Alexander Dromgoole, 4, 9, 140, 144.
Sims, Gertrude Lydia, 144.
Sinclair, Mary Jane (Mrs. James E. Burch), 18,
23, 33, 54, 56, 68, 104, 108, 143.
Sinder, (slave), see Cinder.
Sinklah, Mary, (Mrs. Hardy Sellers) 4, 18.
Sinkler, Eugenia, 92, 143.
Sinkler, sister, 92.
Smith, Abigail (Commander), see Commander.

Smith, John, 9.
Smith, (Lt.), 182.
Smith, Mary, 4, 9.
Smith, Thomas (Dr.), 75, 80, 84, 87.
Smoot, Elizabeth "Betty", 64, 68.
Smoot, Sarah Thomas, 68.
Smoot, Thomas W., 68.
Spivey, Laura (Miss), 152.
Stone, A. B., 157, 159, 163, 164, 166, 195.
Stone, Mr., 166.
Streater, 61.
Streater, Sarah (Burch), see Burch.
Stewart, M. L., 178.
Stewart, Mr., 39.
Stought, (Rev.), 135.
Stucky, (slave), 152.
Susan, (slave), 5.
Taylor, Mr., 166.
Terrel, Mrs., 29.
Thomas, Elizabeth, 80.
Thomas, Tristan (Gen.), 80.
Thornell, Mr., 5.
Thurman, Tom, (Capt.), 181, 182.
Tillman, James A., 144.
Tillman, Mary Ella. 144.
Timmons, John Morgan, 38, 43.
Timmons, Martha Isadora, 143.
Tom, (slave), 5.
Vereen, Elizabeth (Allston), see Allston.
Vernon, Mrs., 78.
Walker, Margaret (Mrs. Withers), 77, 81, 98,
    99, 102, 105, 110, 119, 122, 125, 126,
    128, 130, 132, 133.
Walker, John, 81, 102, 110, 122, 128.
Walkins, (Lt.), 173, 205.
Wash, Mr., 167.
Washington, 4.
Watkins?, Martin, 157, 158, 159, 175, 176, 177,
    182, 183, 184, 185, 186, 191, 194, 197,
    201.
Watkins, Mr., 184, 185.
Watts, Battle, 167, 169.
Watts, Tom, 167.
Webb, Mary Elizabeth, 49, 93, 95, 96, 101, 129.
Wells, Ben, 184.

West, Brother, (Chaplain), 199, 200, 202.
White, Joanna, 1.
White, Mrs., 91.
Whitworth, Mary, 18.
Wiggins, Marie Gulledge, iv.
Williams, (Mr.), 195, 196.
Williamson, Mary Ann, 57.
Wilson, Solomon, 78, 136.
Windom, Aletha, 24, 94, 101, 127, 142.
Wingate (family), iv.
Wingate, Ellen, 138, 141.
Wingate, Isabella (Blackwell), see Blackwell.
Wingate, Isabella Olivia, 29, 34, 40, 64, 68, 69, 91, 94, 101.
Wingate, Jenny, 137.
Wingate, Joseph Edward, 3, 8, 19, 29, 33, 40, 65, 66, 69, 95, 101, 132, 133, 137.
Wingate, Washington Manley, 19, 24, 36, 37, 41, 47, 49, 51, 52, 93, 95, 101, 125, 129.
Wingate, William Pettigrew, 138, 141.
Wingate, William W., 7, 8, 24, 29, 33, 34, 40, 41, 51, 52, 68, 69, 94, 101, 108, 129, 133.
Withers, Harriet, 98.
Withers, Margaret (Walker), see Walker.
Withers, Resolve, 98, 105, 110.
Withers, William, 81, 98, 102.
Witherspoon, Gavin, 108.
Witherspoon, John D. (Col.), 104, 108, 125, 128, 135, 137.
Witherspoon, Elizabeth (Boykin)s, see Boykin.
Witherspoon, "Miss Withy", 4, 9, 28, 32, 46, 50, 60, 62.
Woodham, Martha, 173, 174, 177.
Woods, Edith Ann, (Mrs. John A. Backhouse) 38, 40, 43, 115, 118.
Woods, Hepzibah (Dargan), see Dargan.
Woods, Joseph, 12, 43, 117, 118.
Woods, Martha J., (Mrs. Julius Dargan), 43, 129.
Woods, Patty, 60.
Woods, Rosanna E., 5, 12, 115, 118.
Woodward, family, 13.
Woodward, Anna, 152.

Woodward, Crawford, 151.
Woodward, Eleanor Lauretta, 52, 152, 153.
Woodward, Jack (Dr.), 152, 153.
Woodward, Jesse, 154.
Woodward, Louisa (McBride), see McBride.
Woodward, Thomas, 6, 7, 13, 20, 23, 25, 32, 35, 39, 44, 54, 55, 56, 58, 63, 72, 74, 123, 152, 153, 154.
Woodward, William McBride "Billy", 152, 153.
Wyatt, John H., 185.
Wyatt, Lizzie, 159, 160, 162.
Wyatt, Mr., 169.
Wyatt, Riley W., 157, 159, 160, 161, 162, 163, 164, 165, 166, 167, 168, 169, 173, 174, 175, 176, 177, 178, 181, 182, 183, 185, 191, 195, 196, 197, 198, 203.
Zilphy, (slave), 72.
Zimmerman, Henrietta, 48.
Zimmerman, Sidney Gee, 48, 49.

www.ingramcontent.com/pod-product-compliance
Lightning Source LLC
Chambersburg PA
CBHW050332230426
43663CB00010B/1831